The Planting Design Handbook

To Arthur Robinson

The Planting Design Handbook

Nick Robinson

Illustrations by Jia-Hua Wu

Gower

Published by
Gower Publishing Company Limited
Gower House
Croft Road
Aldershot
Hampshire
GU11 3HR
England

Gower Publishing Company Limited
Old Post Road
Brookfield
Vermont 05036
USA

CIP catalogue records for this book are available from the British Library and the US Library of Congress

ISBN 0-566-09008-2

Typeset in 10pt. Plantin by Poole Typesetting (Wessex) Ltd. and printed in Great Britain by The University Press, Cambridge.

Contents

Figures   ix
Plates   xv
Preface   xxxi
Acknowledgements   xxxiii

PART 1: PRINCIPLES

1 **Why Design?**   3
   Planting Design as an Expression of Function   3
   Planting Design as the Management of Natural Vegetation Processes   7
   Planting Design for Aesthetic Pleasure   8
   What is Successful Planting Design?   8

2 **Plants as a Medium for Design**   10
   Plants as Living Materials   10
   Cycles of Plant Growth and Development   12
   The Landscape Designer's View of Plants   13
   Plants as Structural Elements   17
   Plants as Decorative Elements   23
   Plant Selection   24
   Functional and Aesthetic Considerations in Design   25

3 **The Structural Characteristics of Plants**   28
   The Spatial Functions of Plants in the Human Landscape   28
   Ground Level Planting (Carpeting Plants)   30
   Shrubs and Herbs Below Knee Height (Low Planting)   30
   Knee to Eye Level Planting (Medium Height Planting)   33
   Planting Above Eye-Level (Tall Shrub Planting)   33
   Tree Planting   36

4 **Creating Spaces with Plants**   43
   The Experience of Space   43
   The Use of Spaces   44
   The Elements of Spatial Composition   45
   Enclosure   45
      Degree of Enclosure   46
      Permeability of Enclosure   48

Dynamics	50
Shape	50
Vertical Proportion	55
Slope	57
Focus	57
Symmetric Focus	58
Asymmetric Focus	59
Focus on Boundry	61
External Focus	62
5 Composite Space	**64**
Spatial Organisations	64
Linear Organisations	64
Clustered Organisations	65
Contained Organisations	72
Hierarchy of Spaces	72
Hierarchy According to Function	74
Transitions	76
Transitions Between Abutting Spaces	76
Transitions between Interlocking Spaces	77
Transitional Spaces	79
Entrance Zones	80
6 The Visual Properties of Plants	**82**
Subjective and Objective Response to Plants	82
The Ananlysis of Visual Characteristics	84
Form	84
Line and Pattern	92
Texture	96
Colour	100
Visual Energy	103
Combining Plants	103
7 Principles of Visual Composition in Planting Design	**104**
Five Principles of Visual Composition	104
Harmony and Contrast	104
Balance	106
Emphasis	106
Sequence	111
Scale	113
Unity and Variety in Planting Design	116
Design Ideas	116
Inspiration	122
8 Plant Associations	**124**
Plant Communities	124
Designing with Canopy Layers	126
Three Layer Canopy Structures	126
Two Layer Canopy Structures	130
Single Layer Canopy Structures	133
Horticultural Factors in Plant Associations	135
Growth Requirements	136

Relative Competitiveness   136
Mode of Spread   137
   Increase by Seed   137
   Vegetative Increase   137
Habit   139
Longevity and Life Cycles   139
Plant Knowledge   140

PART 2: PROCESS

9   A Method for Planting Design   **145**
Inception   146
   Initial Contact with the Client   146
Analysis   147
   Brief   147
   Survey   147
   The Landscape Assessment   150
Synthesis   153
   Planting Policies   153
   Design Concept   157
   Schematic Planting Design   157
   Master Plan   157
   Sketch Planting Proposals   165
   Detailed Planting Design   171
   Construction Drawings   180
   Specifications   183
Realisation   183
   Planting   185
   Establishment   186
   Management   187
Learning Through the Design Process   188

PART 3: PRACTICE

10   Structure Planting   **191**
Introduction   191
Woodland   191
High Canopy Woodland (High Forest)   195
   Developing a Planting Mix   198
   Constituents of the Mix   198
   Mix Proportions   201
   Spacing and Grouping   202
Subsidiary Mixes   208
Low Canopy Woodland   211
Woodland Scrub   211
Thicket Scrub   212
High Scrub   213
Edges   213
   Tall Edge   215
   Low Edge   215

Perimeter Hedging   217
Outlying Groups   218
Woodland Belts   218
Clumps and Copses   220
Hedges and Hedgerows   221
   Rural Hedges   222
   Species for Rural Hedging   222
   Hedge Mixes   224
   Setting Out and Spacing   224
   Hedgerows   225
Urban and Garden Hedges   226
   Species for Formal Hedging   226
   Species for Informal Hedging   228
   Setting Out and Spacing   229
   Trees in Hedges   229
Avenues   230
   Avenue Species   230
   Setting Out and Spacing   232
Trained Trees   235

11 Ornamental Planting   **237**
Beds and Borders   237
   Layout of Beds and Borders   238
   The Planting of Beds and Borders 241
   Composition and Scale   244
   Accents   245
   Specimen Groups   247
   Planting Patterns   248
   Ecological Ornamental Planting   250
   Plant Spacing   252
   Setting Out   255
Raised Beds and Containers   255
Walls, Pergolas, Trelliage and Living Fences   258
Ornamental Planting for Specialised Habitats   261

12 Conclusion   **263**

References   **265**

Index   **269**

Figures

All drawings are by Jia-Hua Wu, Head of the Environmental Art Department, Zhejiang Academy of Fine Arts, Hangzhou, China, except where otherwise indicated.

2.1	Mature tree form.	12
2.2	Tree form development.	13
2.3	Stages of development of tree, shrub and ground cover planting.	14
2.4	Stages of development of woodland planting.	15
2.5a, b	Tree forms.	16
2.6a	Large scale structure planting of woodland belts creates a framework for various land uses.	18
2.6b	Small scale structure planting of trees, shrubs and hedges creates spaces for various people and uses.	18
2.7	This axonometric vividly illustrates how tree planting will form the green spatial structure to a housing development. (Landscape Design Associates)	22
2.8	Planting can create the floor, walls and ceiling of intimate outdoor rooms.	23
2.9	The function complex (after Papanek, 1971).	26
3.1	Ground level planting (carpeting plants).	29
3.2a	Planting below knee height (low planting).	31
3.2b	Knee to eye-level planting.	32
3.3a, b	Medium shrub planting.	34 – 35
3.4a, b	Tall shrub planting.	37 – 38
3.5a, b, c	Trees.	39 – 41
4.1	Degrees of enclosure.	48
4.2	Permeability of enclosure.	49
4.3	Static spaces and motive spaces.	52
4.4	Static and motive spaces may be combined.	53
4.5	Linear motive spaces.	54
4.6	Height to width ratio of a static space.	56
4.7	Slope can create an inward or an outward orientation.	58
4.8	A focus or landmark.	59
4.9	A symmetric focus.	60
4.10	An asymmetric focus.	60
4.11a	The focus may be located on the boundary.	61
4.11b	The focus may be beyond the space.	61

4.12	The character of any space is a product of its enclosure, dynamics and focus.	62
5.1	Linear progression of spaces. (Drawn by Nick Robinson)	65
5.2	Studley Royal, North Yorkshire. A linear progression of spaces formed by tree avenues and woodland clearings along the valley of the River Skell, culminating in the ruins of Fountains Abbey. (Drawn by Nick Robinson)	66
5.3	Clustered spaces related by proximity.	67
5.4	Circulation in clustered spaces.	68
5.5	Neath Hill, Milton Keynes. Residential, park and garden spaces cluster around a central open space. (Drawn by Nick Robinson)	68
5.6	Hidcote Manor, Gloucestershire. A complex of spaces clustered around the Theatre Lawn and organised about two major axes at right angles. (Drawn by Nick Robinson)	69
5.7	Types of contained spatial organisation.	70
5.8	Dartington Hall, Devon. The Tilt Yard is the focal space contained within enveloping woodland. (Drawn by Nick Robinson)	71
5.9	Contained spaces.	73
5.10	Garden at Newport Rhode Island by Christopher Tunnard, 1949. The lawn, enclosed by clipped hedges, is contained within the boundary wall and tree planting. (Drawn by Nick Robinson)	73
5.11	Spatial hierarchy.	75
5.12	Hierarchy of clustered spaces.	75
5.13	Hierarchy in contained organisations.	75
5.14	Transitions and entries.	77
5.15	Entrances.	78
7.1	Contrast and harmony.	105
7.2	Balances.	108
7.3	Emphasis can be given by prominent form, coarse texture or careful grouping.	109
7.4	Sequence.	111
7.5	Perception of plant groupings depends on viewing distance.	112
7.6	The scale of plant groupings should reflect the speed of movement of the observer.	114
8.1	Three layer canopy structures.	128
8.2	Edge structures.	129
8.3	Two layer canopy structures.	131
8.4	Single layer canopy structures.	134
9.1	A survey plan showing broad categories of existing vegetation and habitats on a site for development as a public park. (Environmental Consultancy, University of Sheffield)	149
9.2	A vegetation survey drawing showing species present and relative abundance. (Prof. A.E. Weddle, Landscape Architect)	150
9.3	Part of a tree survey drawing showing bole position, canopy spread and other information on every individual tree except saplings. Each tree is graded A, B, or C according to its landscape value. (Prof. A.E. Weddle, Landscape Architect)	151
9.4	Part of visual survey drawing showing major views and describing visual character. (Prof. A.E. Weddle, Landscape Architect)	152

9.5   Part of a landscape policy drawing showing site layout and
        a brief statement of policies for vegetation.
        (Prof. A.E. Weddle, Landscape Architect)   154 – 155
9.6   Key elements of the landscape design concept for a new
        settlement, drawn up for presentation. The drawing
        shows woodland structure, fenland country park and
        nature reserve, main open space structure, fields managed in
        accordance with English Heritage requirements, golf course
        and key views. (Landscape Design Associates)   156
9.7   Schematic proposals for structure planting for a new business
        park on a colliery reclamation site. (Robinson Burrows,
        Landscape Architects)   158 – 159
9.8   Schematic planting structure for a new woodland park on a
        landfill site. Likely phasing of planting areas is shown.
        (Environmental Consultancy, University of Sheffield)   160
9.9   Master plan for new woodland park on landfill site.
        (Environmental Consultancy, University of Sheffield)   161
9.10   Master plan for a country park showing existing woodland
        and proposed structure planting which will form a strong
        nature-like structure for recreation and conservation.
        (Landscape Design Associates)   162
9.11   Master plan for an office development showing generous
        woodland belts enclosing the site and car parks, and areas of
        ornamental planting in the building curtilage and courtyards.
        (Prof. A.E. Weddle, Landscape Architect; drawn by Nick
        Robinson)   163
9.12   Master plan for grounds of a Jacobean house to be converted
        into an hotel. Grounds will include car parking and service areas
        in addition to gardeners' and riverside walk. (Prof. A.E. Weddle,
        Landscape Architect; drawn by Nick Robinson)   164
9.13   Part of a planting sketch design for an office building. Graphics
        and notes indicate character and purpose rather than planting
        detail. Species mentioned are illustrative only.
        (Environmental Consultancy, University of Sheffield; drawn by
        Nick Robinson)   166
9.14   Sketch illustrations of planting proposals for an hotel
        development showing the structural role of planting. (Landcare) 167
9.15   Part of a sketch design for a private garden. Good use is made
        of sketch views to show the character of the proposals.
        (Landcare, Landscape Architects)   168
9.16   Sketch proposals plan for layout and planting of courtyard.
        The contrast between geometric and organic form is an
        important element of the design proposals.
        (Landscape Design Associates)   169
9.17   Sketch proposals for a riverside seating area. The character
        and purpose of planting is explained by notes on the plan and
        sketch views. (Landcare)   170
9.18   An example of planting composition studies:
        1. Height categories and locations of key accents in plan.
        2. Abstract height, form and texture study in elevation.
        3. Representative composition study in elevation with possible
           species annotated.
        4. Species areas shown on plan   174 – 175

9.19   Part of a plan showing detailed planting proposals for a business park. Species, stock sizes and planting densities are given but not numbers and locations. (Robinson Burrows, Landscape Architects)   178

9.20   Part of detailed planting proposals for an industrial site illustrated in cross section. (Prof. A.E. Weddle, Landscape Architect)   178

9.21   Detailed planting proposals plan for a private garden showing all species, areas to be occupied by low ground cover and approximate spread of medium and tall shrubs. (Kris Burrows, Landscape Designer)   179

9.22   Construction drawing for ornamental planting in an office courtyard. Species are identified by key letters which would be explained in a schedule on the drawing. Note that the first letters of genus and species are used to aid quick identification. (Appleton Deeley Partnership)   181

9.23   Part of construction drawing for ornamental planting in a garden festival site, including marginal aquatics. The beds shown are keyed into a location plan. Note the rectilinear shape of drifts which assists the calculation of plant numbers and setting out. The angular shapes will be less noticeable on the ground and will soon disappear as plants establish. (Ian White Associates, Landscape Architects)   182

9.24   Construction drawing for outfield planting using species mixes. The schedules indicate numbers, age and stock sizes of each species in each mix. (Richard Sneesby, Landscape Architect)   182

9.25   An example of a repeating unit for woodland planting. The setting out of units would be shown on a separate plan. (Ian White Associates, Landscape Architects)   184

9.26   Construction drawing for urban amenity planting to light industrial units. Note: full name, numbers and spacings are annotated on the plan. Plants are arranged in spot locations, drifts of single species and mixes. (Environmental Consultancy, University of Sheffield)   184

9.27   Part of drawing showing ornamental planting and woodland edge planting linked by a 'semi-ornamental' shrub structure planting mix. The proposals are for a private garden. (Richard Sneesby, Landscape Architect)   185

10.1   Part of a drawing showing woodland planting on a power station pulverised fuel ash reclamation site. Note the use of tables to show plant numbers in each plantation area in an economical way. Species are to be randomly mixed within each mix area. (Prof. A.E. Weddle, Landscape Architect)   204

10.2   Part of a construction drawing for plantations of transplants and standard tree planting. These will form a strong tree planting structure to a new technology park. Notes on the drawing specified that transplants should be planted in single species blocks of 9 in number (3 x 3 metres) and blocks proportionately mixed.   206

10.3   Part of a construction drawing showing nature-like woodland and scrub planting. Note the complex edge to planting areas and the concentration of certain species in selected areas. (Robert Tregay, Landscape Architect, Warrington and Runcorn Development Corporation)   207

10.4   Part of a construction drawing for woodland belt structure planting
to a business park. The table shows number of each species in each
mix area, size of groups of each species and nursery stock size.
Woodland core, woodland edge and perimeter hedge mixes are all
represented. The setting out of mixes areas and plant spacing is
shown in the cross-section in Figure 10.5. (Robinson Burrows,
Landscape Architects)   209

10.5   The use of cross-sections to show the relationship of different
mixes and plant spacings in woodland belts around a business
park. (Robinson Burrows, Landscape Architects)   210

10.6   Part of a detailed planting proposal for a country park. Various
woodland, edge and scrub mixes are proposed to suit
environmental conditions and achieve structural and habitat
diversity. (Martin Popplewell, Landscape Architect)   216

10.7   Part of a drawing showing a repeating unit for hedgerow
planting on a reclamation site. Note close spacing for quick
establishment of a stock proof barrier and standard trees
confined to one row for ease of hedge maintenance. (Redrawn
from Prof. A.E. Weddle, Landscape Architect)   225

11.1   Planting for a public garden showing tall shrub mix enclosing
the site on two sides, ornamental planting and climbers on pergola.
Note the concentration of planting detail near seats and entrances.
(Robinson Burrows, Landscape Architects)   246

11.2   Part of a drawing showing ornamental shrub and tree planting
around a unit in a technology park. (Ian White Associates,
Landscape Architects)   256

11.3   Part of a drawing showing planting for a residential development.
Note the domestic character of the planting which includes
familiar garden species such as lavender, rose, tree mallow
and hosta. (Richard Sneesby, Landscape Architect)   257

Plates

All photographs are by Nick Robinson except where otherwise indicated.

Plates 1 & 2 Planting design makes an essential contribution to an environment fit for living and working (new housing court, Sheffield and Birchwood Boulevard Technology Park, Warrington). 4

Plate 3 Without planting, retaining structures of this scale would be dominating and intrusive. With planting they are well integrated and an asset to the local environment (Munchen Gladbach). (Photo: Owen Manning) 5

Plate 4 Generous tree and shrub planting integrates new buildings and structures of Wuppertal University into the surrounding landscape. (Photo: Owen Manning) 5

Plate 5 Planting helps to create an environment suitable for children's play by providing a comfortable microclimate, the sense of special place, and plenty of robust trees and shrubs for climbing, swinging and imaginative play. 5

Plate 6 Natural processes of colonisation have resulted in the vegetation of this urban nature park with little intervention. 5

Plate 7 No planting or seeding was needed on this cliff face: natural colonisation was sufficient and appropriate. 5

Plate 8 This verge beside a busy trunk road has developed into an attractive species rich meadow. 6

Plate 9 The indigenous dune species marram grass (*Ammophila arenaria*) was appropriate for this coastal fill site, but planting to assist establishment was necessary. (Photo: Prof. A.E.Weddle, Landscape Architect) 6

Plate 10 After 18 months only a few traces of intervention remain visible. The geotextile netting was employed to reduce surface erosion. (Photo: Prof. A.E.Weddle, Landscape Architect) 6

Plate 11   A high degree of control over natural vegetation processes is demonstrated in this highly manicured display of hybridised and selected flowers at Gruga Park, Essen. (Photo: Owen Manning)   6

Plate 12   This successful shelterbelt in North West Scotland combines effective wind speed reduction, ecological diversification and aesthetic harmony with the local landscape.   8

Plate 13   The development of a planting association over its first 10 years: A view one season after planting shows scattered trees and shrubs of a similar size to when they left the nursery.   11

Plate 14   The same view three years after planting shows a well established thicket.   11

Plate 15   After ten years the trees and larger shrubs have attained heights of up to ten meters and have begun to have the visual impact for which they were planted.   11

Plate 16   The favourable microclimate provided by a South facing wall allows the growing of plants which would not survive in the open. *Abutilon* and *Ceanothus* spp. (shown in this photograph), *Fremontodendron californicum* and *Magnolia campbellii* are among the shrubs grown successfully in the walled gardens at Newby Hall in North Yorkshire.   11

Plate 17   The dramatic effects of light can give unpredictable yet memorable qualities to planting.   11

Plate 18   The space beneath the canopy of this single beech (*Fagus sylvatica*) is further delineated and emphasised by a circular hedge and a change of ground level.   18

Plate 19   Hedges of species such as yew (*Taxus baccata*) may be clipped to make green walls of similar form to those built in masonry.   18

Plate 20   The natural growth of belts of trees and shrubs can create informal walls of vegetation.   19

Plate 21   Trained and clipped cypress (*Cupressus* sp.) form a wall with windows giving views in and out of a small urban park in Malaga.   19

Plate 22   Carpets of low ground covering ivy (*Hedera*), blue fescue (*Festuca glauca*) and juniper (*Juniperus*) form an attractive floor to this courtyard. The broad bands between the lines of paving are planted on the roof of a room below. (Photo: Prof. A.E.Weddle, Landscape Architect)   19

Plate 23   *Wisteria* is trained over supports to form a delightful ceiling of foliage above this patio in Majorca.   19

Plate 24   The naturally spreading canopies of these silver maples (*Acer saccharinum*) forms a sheltering and screening ceiling above the car park at Leeds University.   19

Plate 25   Plants such as cypress (*Cupressus* sp.) can be trained to form a
            green gateway of inviting proportions.   20

Plate 26   Natural gateways and windows are formed by gaps in otherwise
            impenetrable vegetation.   20

Plate 27   A single row of small trees forms a green colonnade in this
            residential courtyard in Cologne. (Photo: Owen Manning)   20

Plate 28   A carefully spaced and regularly pruned double row of limes
            (*Tilia* sp.) gives overhead enclosure to form an arcade of trees.
            (Photo: Owen Manning)   20

Plate 29   Regular street tree planting echoes the rhythms of adjacent
            architecture.   21

Plate 30   Analogies in both the structural and decorative aspects of trees
            and built form are employed in the work of Antoni Gaudi in
            Parc Guel, Barcelona.   21

Plate 31   An overgrown beech hedge (*Fagus sylvatica*) creates a sheltering
            canopy and a semi permeable curtain of stems at Formakin,
            Scotland.   21

Plate 32   Sculptural organic form and fluid space are created by the nature
            like planting of clumps of willows (*Salix*) near the water's edge.
            (Photo: Owen Manning)   24

Plate 33   The lavender (*Lavandula*), rose and everlasting (*Anaphalis*) play a
            chiefly decorative role in the spaces created by garden walls and
            buildings.   24

Plate 34   The aesthetic qualities of a planting scheme should be in
            harmony with the character and the function of the site.
            Compare the ground modelling and planting of this entrance
            to an industrial site with the rockery in the next photograph.   26

Plate 35   This rockery and planting at the entrance to an industrial
            compound display aesthetic qualities which disregard the
            character and function of the site.   26

Plate 36   Enclosing boundary tree planting creates a protected, warm,
            sheltered and attractive space for informal games, walking,
            sunbathing and other recreation in Golden Gate Park,
            San Francisco. (Photo: Owen Manning)   46

Plate 37   Tall beech (*Fagus sylvatica*) hedges provide enclosure around the
            entire perimeter of this quiet rondel set within Gruga Botanical
            Gardens. (Photo: Owen Manning)   46

Plate 38   Informal shrub planting provides a semicircle of enclosure behind the seat giving protection and emphasising its outlook beyond this art gallery entrance court in Essen. (Photo: Owen Manning)   47

Plate 39   Planting forms seating enclaves along the edge of an enclosed route in Rudding Park. (Photo: Owen Manning)   47

Plate 40   Full visual and physical enclosure may be desirable around visually intrusive land uses such as this car parking at Broadwater Business Park, Denham and will also provide shelter and a pleasant environment for the people using it. The trees are London planes (*Platanus x hispanica*), the tall shrubs bamboo (*Arundinaria*) and the low shrub edge is composed of *Rubus tricolor*.   49

Plate 41   Full visual and physical enclosure gives shelter and seclusion to a public garden at Birchwood, Warrington.   49

Plate 42   Partial visual and physical enclosure results when windows and doorways remain in a wall of planting. Here they frame views across Willen Lake, Milton Keynes.   49

Plate 43   A stopping and gathering place is most successful if its shape is of largely similar horizontal proportions, such as found in a square or a circle. This example is in museum precincts, Brussels. (Photo: Owen Manning)   51

Plate 44   A pond and clearing provides a natural stopping and gathering place in the woodland at Risley Moss, Warrington.   51

Plate 45   The extended shape of linear spaces express the functions of communication and movement. The photograph shows footpath, cycleway and carriageway firmly defined by trees, shrubs and walls in Leuven.   51

Plate 46   A watercourse creates a natural linear space within dense woodland at Green Park, Aston Clinton, Buckinghamshire.   51

Plate 47   This mature avenue of plane trees (*Platanus*) leading to Castle Arenberg, Belgium is a grand and dynamic element of the landscape structure.   53

Plate 48   If an avenue is very long and has no visual focus it may be daunting for the traveller, especially if they are on foot (Central Milton Keynes).   53

Plate 49   The gate at the end of this *allee* at Hidcote, Gloucestershire provides a focus and also anticipates what may be revealed beyond it.   54

Plate 50   Curving linear spaces create curiosity and anticipation by concealment. The gentle curve and flow of the landform are further enticements to explore (Ashridge, Hertfordshire).   54

Plate 51   This hillside promenade is fully closed along one side but visually open along the other giving an outlook over the distant landscape. The waist height hedge prevents distraction by foreground detail on the slope below the path and emphasises the distinction between here and there. Although the view is at once spectacular, the concealment caused by its curving alignment promises further rewards and draws the observer along its length (Muncaster Castle, Cumbria).   55

Plate 52   The ratio of height to width of a linear space influences its dynamic qualities. A 1:1 ratio gives a strong, purposeful character (Generalife, Granada).   57

Plate 53   A linear space with a height to width ratio of greater than 1:1 can create a pressing sense of urgency and expectation and a consequent desire to move quickly towards its goal (Generalife, Granada).   57

Plate 54   The focus of a space can be provided by a single specimen tree of sufficient stature. In this urban space in Brugge it also makes an informal gathering place.   59

Plate 55   Woodland glades separated by groves of birch (*Betula pendula*) in a Bristol park form a linear progression of spaces explored by a sinuous path. (Photo: Owen Manning)   67

Plate 56   A linear progression of spaces in an urban park in Sheffield. The enclosing structure planting is edged with ornamental shrubs and the path provides both a connecting route and a strong visual element in the composition. (Photo: Owen Manning)   67

Plate 57   The impressive view from the lawn in front of the house at Stowe in Buckinghamshire penetrates a series of three parkland spaces enclosed by belts and clumps of trees and focuses on the Corinthian Arch on the horizon.   67

Plate 58   A gap of a little more than the path width in tall and medium shrub planting creates an informal but concise transition between intensively detailed building curtilage and the more extensive parkland beyond (Hounslow Civic Centre and park, London).   77

Plate 59   A simple narrow gap in an enclosing hedge overhung with the branch of a nearby tree provides a concise transition. The point of entry is precisely defined and a glimpse of what is within is revealed. This public park was once the Bundesgartenschau at Mannheim. (Photo: Owen Manning)   79

Plate 60   An overlapping entrance ensures complete surprise on entering the space (Bodnant, North Wales).   79

Plate 61   A gradual transition is made between two distinct spaces but dynamic tension is created by the sinuous curve of the grass path, by the gap which first narrows and then widens, and by the locations of the clumps of trees being offset either side of the opening (Askham Bryan College, York). 79

Plate 62 This transition is made in stages. As the observer skirts the lake at Stowe, Buckinghamshire new views are opened and the far paddock is revealed in carefully controlled sequence. Finally the focus of the space, the Palladian Bridge, will come into view. 79

Plate 63 Trees and shrubs create a small but well defined transitional space between the precinct in the foreground and the courtyard beyond the arch at Leuven, Belgium. (Photo: Owen Manning) 80

Plate 64 A larger transitional space, enclosed by beech (*Fagus sylvatica*) hedges and pleached lime trees (*Tilia*), forms the entrance zone to a public park in Oakwood, Warrington. 81

Plate 65 The quite prostrate form of this Juniper (*Juniperus*) provides a base to the startling white trunk of Himalayan birch (*Betula jaquemontii*). 86

Plate 66 Prostrate dwarf shrubs such as this *Cotoneaster adpressus* hug the ground and follow the shape of whatever they cover. 86

Plate 67 The hummock and dome forms of herbaceous plants such as *Liriope muscari* and shrubs such as *Hebe rakaiensis* and *Viburnum davidii* anchor this gateway, reflect the curve of its arch and contrast with its rectilinear outline. 86

Plate 68 Many trees in temperate climates ultimately develop a spreading dome-like form if allowed to grow unhindered in an open location and free from a high degree of environmental stress. This photograph shows a group of widely spaced Norway maple (*Acer platanoides*). (Photo: Owen Manning) 86

Plate 69 *Isoplexis canariensis* is a tender shrub with a distinctively erect form, seen here growing out of a low cover of ferns at Tresco Abbey in the Isles of Scilly. 86

Plate 70 New Zealand flax (*Phormium tenax*) has numerous large, linear, erect leaves which make it a dominant element in plant groupings. (Photo: Owen Manning) 87

Plate 71 Shrubs with arching form such as this graceful bamboo (*Arundinaria nitida*) can make fine specimens. 87

Plate 72 The hornbeam cultivar *Carpinus betulus* 'Fastigiata' has, in its early years, an upright oval form. Its restricted spread makes it convenient for planting next to roads which carry high vehicles. Its visual effect here is to punctuate the linear mass of domey and arching shrub planting. 89

Plate 73   The conic form of the two coniferous trees in the foreground is in striking contrast to the long low building at Stirling University.   89

Plate 74   Some conifers such as Italian cypress (*Cupressus sempervirens*), as well as some broadleaved trees, show a narrowly fastigiate or columnar form. In this scene at Bodnant, North Wales, the contrast between the rising, spire like tree form and the solid, stable cube of the old mill is dramatic.   91

Plate 75   The ascending flower raceme of mullein (*Verbascum*) has, on a smaller scale, a similar effect to a fastigiate or columnar tree canopy. (Photo: Owen Manning)   91

Plate 76   Tabulate form is seen in the spreading branches of trees such as this young deodar (*Cedrus deodara*) and Japanese maple (*Acer palmatum*) which give a serene quality to this composition in Sheffield Botanical Gardens.   91

Plate 77   This young specimen of Yoshino cherry (*Prunus x yedoensis*) demonstrates an open irregular habit that is found to a greater or lesser extent in many trees and shrubs.   91

Plate 78   Artificial geometric form is crisply defined in this immaculately maintained yew (*Taxus baccata*) hedge at Bodnant, North Wales. It echoes the built form of the terrace and throws into sharp relief the rising branches of the *Magnolia x veitchii* behind.   91

Plate 79   Trained and clipped form can be treated as sculpture in the landscape. This green wave also has the functional role of a hedge (Castle Arenberg, Belgium). (Photo: Owen Manning)   93

Plate 80   The topiary at Levens Hall, Cumbria, creates an intriguing interplay of form and space.   93

Plate 81   This planting composition depends for much of its impact on the form of the trees and shrubs. The tabulate branches of *Viburnum plicatum* 'Lanarth' are picked out with sprays of brilliant white flower heads and form a striking contrast to the dark fastigiate yew (*Taxus baccata* 'Fastigiata') and the rising branches of the tree in the background. These strongly expressed forms are set within a softly flowing mass of informal foliage which saves the composition from stiffness.   93

Plate 82   Line can be a dominant element in planting composition, especially when we can only see the silhouettes of plants. It is only our ability to interpret perspective that tells us the depth of field in this photograph of an avenue of elm trees (*Ulmus*). (Photo: Owen Manning)   93

Plate 83   The ascending outlines of these fastigiate junipers (*Juniperus* 'Sky Rocket') punctuate and regulate the soft billowing masses of roses and herbs below.   93

Plate 84   Vertical line is also common in the ascending linear leaves of
            monocotyledons such as *Iris* and rushes (*Juncus*), here contrasting
            with the horizontal slab of the stone bridge.   95

Plate 85   Pendulous line is found in the hanging branches of weeping
            willow (*Salix* 'Chrysocoma'). (Photo: Owen Manning)   95

Plate 86   The tabulate branching cedar of Lebanon (*Cedrus libani*) produces
            a strong horizontal component which reflects the lines of the
            brickwork pattern and building eaves.   95

Plate 87   Dynamic diagonals are strongly expressed in the linear leaves
            of New Zealand flax (*Phormium tenax*).   95

Plate 88   Much of the line found in nature is lively and irregular in
            character such as the branches and twigs of this birch (*Betula* sp.).
            (Photo: Owen Manning)   98

Plate 89   Line can be crucial to composition: the crossing of horizontal and
            vertical lines is one of the most dominant aspects of this view.   98

Plate 90   Grass, whether mown or long, and yew hedges both have a fine
            visual texture which add to the feeling of simple spaciousness
            in this orchard at Hardwick Hall, Derbyshire.   98

Plate 91   The bold foliage of *Acanthus* draws attention to the steps and
            balustrade and harmonises with the similar, coarse texture of
            the stone work.   98

Plate 92   A wide range of textures and forms contribute to this composition.
            The fine lawn and domed *Hebe* harmonise with the fine texture
            of the sawn stone. The coarse textured *Drimys winteri* in the
            foreground and *Yucca gloriosa* are well displayed in this subdued
            setting.   99

Plate 93   This plant grouping at Newby Hall, North Yorkshire, relies
            on strong form, dynamic line and textural contrasts for its
            eye-catching effect.   99

Plate 94   Visual harmony can be found amongst natural forms as diverse
            as trees and clouds.   107

Plate 95   Harmony of leaf form and colour supports the strong contrast
            in texture between *Bergenia* and *Saxifraga*.   107

Plate 96   The close relationship between form and texture of *Choisya
            ternata* and *Acer palmatum* 'Dissectum Atropurpureum'
            emphasises the contrast in foliage colour.   107

Plate 97   The decorative characteristics of plants can be delightful when
            related by harmony and contrast to hard landscape materials.
            In this office courtyard the rectilinear geometry of the pool
            and edgings contrast with organic forms of the plants, and the

texture and comparative softness of the pea gravel provides a visual link between 'hard' and 'soft' landscape. (Photo: Landscape Design Associates)   107

Plate 98   On the Victorian Italianate terrace at Tatton Park, Cheshire, the strictly symmetrical layout of grass and floral bedding denotes absolute control of form and articulates the central axis of symmetry. (Photo: Owen Manning)   107

Plate 99   Symmetry is observed in the repetition of trees, shrubs and ground modelling either side of the path. By emphasising the axis of symmetry which arises from the building the planting leads the eye to the entrance to these apartments at Kingston Dock, Glasgow.   110

Plate 100   The drama of a single *Agave* brings a point of emphasis to the remarkable stone work of viaduct and steps at Parc Guel, Barcelona.   110

Plate 101   The steady rhythm of the yew bastions reflects the buttressing of the church at Ashridge, Herts.   110

Plate 102   A regular sequence of spaces is experienced as one moves between the serpentine hedges at Chatsworth, Derbyshire. (Photo: Owen Manning).   110

Plate 103   In this forestry planting the scale of the species drifts is in harmony with the patterns of the vegetation and landform in the surrounding landscape (Snowdonia, Wales).   111

Plate 104   The largest structures in the landscape, such as the Humber Bridge, near Hull, require plantations and tree clumps of generous size to maintain good generic scale relationships.   111

Plate 105   Only variation in tree and shrub species of sufficient scale will be perceived from fast moving vehicles on a trunk road.   114

Plate 106   When vehicles are passing at slower speeds more variation in shape and smaller groups of species can be appreciated.   114

Plate 107   This shrub planting is of suitable scale for stationary or slow moving vehicles and is also in generic scale with the patterns on the buildings' cladding.   114

Plate 108   Planting in a garden, whether public or private, should be of sufficiently small scale to invite prolonged observation and enjoyment. (Photo: Owen Manning)   115

Plate 109   On this business development at Broadwater Park, Denham, a personal style and scale has been introduced into planting of roadside scale and institutional character. Note its location next to the gate lodge.   115

Plate 110   The inspiration for this planting is made explicit. A stream of blue, white and purple pansies (*Viola* hybrids) tumbles down

an artificial hillside at the Stoke National Garden Festival. The
moorland grasses and rushes not only reinforce the suggestion of
an upland stream but their subdued browns and greens provide
a gentle compliment to the brighter colours of the pansies.   119

Plate 111   Use of bold foliaged species can create a jungle-like character
in temperate regions by echoing the macrophyllus plants
characteristic of tropical rain forest.   119

Plate 112   The spring garden is a common seasonal theme. This woodland
walk at Dartington Hall, in Devon, is designed to be at its peak
in spring with carpets of naturalised woodland flowers and
shrubs such as *Camellia* and *Magnolia*.   119

Plate 113   Rose gardens are traditional examples of planting on a
taxonomic theme.   120

Plate 114   An artificial boulder scree with acid soil provides a habitat for
planting design at the Glasgow Garden Festival. Heathers
(*Calluna vulgaris*), heaths (*Erica* spp.) and birch (*Betula* spp.)
not only grow well but also look at home in this kind of terrain.   121

Plate 115   A moist, partly shaded rock garden creates a different habitat
Which will restrict the choice of plants. Ferns are particularly
well suited to these conditions.   121

Plate 116   The development of an hotel and conference centre in an old
quarry at Hagen, Germany, provides the opportunity for
naturalistic planting which reinforces the sense of place.
(Photo: Owen Manning)   121

Plate 117   A waterside theme may be adopted even when the soil is not in
contact with a water body by planting species such as *Alchemilla
mollis* and *Salix matsudana* 'Tortuosa' which we associate with
water but which does not require permanently moist soil
(Lincoln County Hospital).   121

Plate 118   Open woodland is well suited to ornamental planting and, in
many large gardens and parks, provides a habitat theme for
collections of shade and shelter loving plants such as smooth
Japanese maple (*Acer palmatum*).   122

Plate 119   Ash (*Fraxinus excelsior*) and sycamore (*Acer pseudoplatanus*)
woodland has colonised and established itself in an abandoned
chalk quarry. Note the rich shrub and herb growth beneath
the trees.   192

Plate 120   In this high canopy oak woodland (*Quercus robur*) a cross section
of three layered woodland structure has been revealed by felling
in preparation for road construction. An understorey of shrubs
including elder (*Sambucus nigra*) and hazel (*Corylus avellana*) is
well developed and clearly distinguishable below the oak canopy.
Beneath the shrubs a field layer of bramble (*Rubus fruticosus*),
honeysuckle (*Lonicera periclymenum*) and shade tolerant herb

species can be found, although its density is limited by the shade cast by the two strata above it. 194

Plate 121   This high canopy oak (*Quercus robur*) wood, which is located in a country park, demonstrates a two layer structure. The understorey is largely absent, but a field layer of grasses and other herbs is well developed. The spatial qualities are quite different to those in a three layer wood, and the openness beneath the tree canopy is well suited to informal recreation use by comparatively large numbers of people. 194

Plate 122   This wood is being managed as coppice and standard. It can be seen from the age of the standard oak that it is still in its early years. The coppice layer consists mainly of Spanish chestnut (*Castanea sativa*) and rowan (*Sorbus aucuparia*). The birch (*Betula pendula*) in the foreground has also been cut back and is re-growing strongly. 200

Plate 123   The pioneer species birch (*Betula pendula*) and goat willow (*Salix caprea*) have colonised open land to form an extensive stand of low woodland. Note the high canopy woodland developing in the background. 210

Plate 124   A mosaic of young birch (*Betula pendula*) and oak (*Quercus petraea*) woodland and open land where space and vegetation interweave. (Photo: Owen Manning) 210

Plate 125   A plantation containing a woodland scrub mix of shrub transplants and scattered groups of staked ash whips (*Fraxinus excelsior*) immediately after planting. Note that the plantation incorporates and protects a remnant of an old hedgerow. 210

Plate 126   Scattered planting of low thicket scrub transplants protected by tree shelters in an exposed coastal location. Species include burnet rose (*Rosa pimpinellifolia*), gorse (*Ulex europaeus*), goat willow (*Salix caprea*) and sea buckthorn (*Hippophae rhamnoides*). (Photo: Prof. A.E.Weddle, Landscape Architect) 214

Plate 127   Low scrub, including gorse (*Ulex* spp.) and dwarf willo (*Salix* spp.), is now well established on a South facing slope at the wildlife garden site, planted for the 1984 Liverpool International Garden Festival. 214

Plate 128   High canopy woodland in an urban park with an open edge which allows free access between the open space, the path which follows the edge, and the interior of the wood. 214

Plate 129   Gorse (*Ulex europaeus*) and wild roses (*Rosa arvensis* and *Rosa canina*) form a low edge to roadside woodland planting in Milton Keynes. 217

Plate 130   A clipped hawthorn (*Crataegus monogyna*) hedge forms a neat dense edge to this roadside plantation. 217

Plate 131   Outlying groups of self-sown birch (*Betula pendula*) add to the spatial intricacy and microclimatic diversity on the edge of this wood.   217

Plate 132   A woodland belt of ten meters width forms part of the landscape structure of Birchwood Science Park. Low edge species include *Rosa* spp. and snowberry (*Symphoricarpos* spp.).   220

Plate 133   This belt of woodland scrub is no more than four meters wide but provides an excellent screen to extensive car parks. The photograph was taken ten years after planting. In the future, selected coppicing of shrubs and thinning of trees will be necessary in order to maintain the visual density of the belt throughout its height.   220

Plate 134   This broad, medium height hedge of box (*Buxus sempervirens*) provides low level enclosure for bays of colourful bedding. A weaving hedge such as this is an excellent means of structuring a linear planting area and creating well proportioned compartments for planting display. (Photo: Owen Manning)   227

Plate 135   Boundary definition is an important function of hedges in urban as well as rural areas. Yew is a good formal hedging plant for urban locations if we are not impatient for results (Hampstead Garden Suburb). (Photo: Owen Manning)   227

Plate 136   An urban hedgerow of Norway maple (*Acer platanoides*) planted in a hedge of *Cotoneaster lacteus*. The restricted width available for planting made this a suitable means of integrating the decked car park within the planting structure of the office development site. (Photo: Prof. A.E.Weddle, Landscape Architect)   231

Plate 137   Hedge clipping is easier if trees are planted next to rather than within a hedge.   231

Plate 138   An impressive single line avenue of chestnuts (*Aesculus*). (Photo: Owen Manning)   231

Plate 139   Limes (*Tilia* spp.) are traditional avenue trees. This lime avenue is reaching early maturity and its spacing of approximately 8 x 8 meters is now sufficient to give a pleasing sense of enclosure.   233

Plate 140   Poplars (*Populus* spp.) are a suitable avenue tree provided they are not close to buildings or underground services, and are well suited to planting near to water. (Photo: Owen Manning)   233

Plate 141   These closely planted double avenues of *Fagus sylvatica* are part of the great Renaissance park at Het Loo in the Netherlands. The impression is of great green arcades lifted high on sturdy pillars of the beech trunks. (Photo: Owen Manning)   233

Plate 142   Small trees such as (*Robinia pseudoacacia* 'Bessoniana') form intimate, human scale avenues and are particularly successful when found within larger enclosures such as urban squares or streets (Vision Park, Cambridge).   233

Plate 143   Pleached limes (*Tilia* spp.) separate the building from the bicycle park.   235

Plate 144   A laburnum tunnel, such as this famous one at Bodnant in North Wales, can excite not only with its spectacular flower display in May but also with its dynamic spatial qualities.   235

Plate 145   Pleached hornbeam (*Carpinus betulus*), clipped beech (*Fagus sylvatica*) hedges and mown lawns create strong geometric rhythms at Hidcote, Gloucestershire.   235

Plate 146   Some fruit trees are traditionally trained on frameworks of various kinds. Here apple trees form a shady tunnel at Norton Priory, Runcorn.   235

Plate 147   Ornamental shrubs may have a structural role within small spaces. This tree mallow (*Lavatera thuringiaca* 'Kew Rose') separates two seats in the precinct of Leicester Cathedral.   239

Plate 148   Woodland or scrub structure planting consisting mostly of native species may offer detailed decorative interest of flower, fruit and foliage as well as spatial definition and shelter.   239

Plate 149   The wiggles in the edge of this lawn are unnecessary because, in time, the natural spread of the trees and shrubs will provide a soft and varied outline to the planting. Furthermore, this edge is ugly because it is out of scale with the landform and the massing of tree and shrub species.   239

Plate 150   Established shrubs and herbaceous plants spill over the path edge at Knightshayes Court, Devon, to give a delightfully irregular natural outline. Note how the scale of the curves in the outline reflects the size of the plant groupings.   239

Plate 151   The edges of planting beds need protection in busy areas. These sloping walls of stone sets are both a logical extension of the paving and an attractive complement to the decorative qualities of the plant material.   239

Plate 152   Narrow planting beds do not provide adequate soil conditions and are vulnerable to trampling.   240

Plate 153   A traditional edging of stone to a herbaceous border has many advantages. Grass cutting is easier, plants can be allowed to spread over the edge, access and work to the border in wet weather will cause less damage to the edge of the lawn, and crispness of line is visually satisfying. (Photo: Owen Manning)   240

Plate 154   Corners of planting beds of 90 degrees or less are particularly vulnerable to trampling and should be avoided unless pedestrian traffic is minimal. The simplest answer to the problem is a 45 degree paved splay at the path junction. Even a tough ground cover plant like the *Cotoneaster dammeri* shown here cannot withstand more than occasional foot traffic.   240

Plate 155   The monoculture of juniper (*Juniperus horizontalis*) is out of
place by this footpath where much more diversity could be
appreciated. The bleakness of the space as a whole is
exacerbated by the lack of enclosure. The scene is inhospitable
and monotonous.   240

Plate 156   A mixed border of shrubs and herbaceous plants creates an
unusually fresh and colourful decorative planting for an office
development. Herbaceous plants in this scheme include
Bergenia, *Iris*, *Astrantia major* and *Geranium* spp.   243

Plate 157   It is partly the close proximity between the small light foliaged
tree and the building that makes this planting successful.
Harmony of colour and complementary form and pattern make
it a pleasing association of hard and soft materials. (Photo:
Owen Manning)   243

Plate 158   This multiple layered ornamental planting includes a light
tree canopy of *Betula jaquemontii*, a scattered shrub layer of
azaleas (*Rhododendron* spp.) and a diverse low ground cover
including *Tiarella cordifolia*, *Bergenia*, *Polygonum affine* and
Alchemilla mollis.   243

Plate 159   *Tiarella cordifolia* and *Heuchera sanguinea* form a simple unifying
carpet of ground cover below a selection of specimen fruiting
shrubs including *Rhus typhina* and *Euonymus* 'Red Cascade',
and taller herbaceous species including the evergreen *Iris
foetidissima* in the foreground. This kind of planting association
provides both decorative diversity and low maintenance
requirements.   243

Plate 160   The assertive forms of Adam's needle (*Yucca gloriosa*), in the
foreground, and New Zealand flax (*Phormium tenax*), at the far
end of the seat, make them among the most effective accent
plants. Here their role is enhanced by contrast with the fine
textures of the grass, hedge and stone.   247

Plate 161   These specimen groups mark the entrances to University of
Strathclyde Residences. The bold foliage of devils walking
stick (*Aralia elata*) help make a striking composition.   247

Plate 162   This delightful woodland wild garden at Wisley in Surrey
consists of a mix of naturalised exotic herbaceous species
including *Alstromeria*, *Campanula*, *Geranium*, *Astrantia major*,
Aconitum and *Astilbe* mixed with natives such as *Digitalis
purpurea* and *Hieracium*. The utmost sensitivity in management
is required to establish and maintain this kind of planting.   250

Plate 163   Trees such as ash (*Fraxinus excelsior*) often colonise ground cover
and shrub planting and are a benefit, provided they will not
be likely to interfere with buildings or services as they grow to
maturity.   250

Plate 164   Ferns and other small herbs have colonised these stone steps. They give an air of luxuriance and romantic decay and yet will not cause any significant damage to the structure.   250

Plate 165   If they are to promote luxuriant growth, planting containers must be of sufficient width and depth to provide adequate soil volume and avoid rapid drying out. (Photo: Prof. A. E. Weddle, Landscape Architect)   255

Plate 166   A generous width is needed if raised planters are to include standard trees. The soil imported for the planters here rests on natural ground and this allows drainage and water uptake by the plants (standard *Sorbus intermedia* and *Hedera colchica* ground cover).   258

Plate 167   A South West facing wall is an ideal location for growing tender climbers and shrubs such as *Camellia saluensis*, *Cytisus battandieri*, *Acacia dealbata*, *Abutilon* spp. and *Magnolia grandiflora*.   260

Plate 168   A well proportioned pergola well furnished with *Vitis vinifera*, *Wisteria* spp. and *Clematis*.   260

Plate 169   These steel and wire structures are specially designed to introduce vegetation into a busy confined space. The climber is *Wisteria*. (Photo: Owen Manning)   260

Plate 170   This pergola displays a relatively high proportion of structure to foliage, but the balance is successful because of the quality of the timber-work. (Photo: Owen Manning)   260

Plate 171   This decorative fence is designed with climbers in mind. *Hydrangea petiolaris* is able to scramble up the open timber-work with the aid of occasional tying in to the laths. (Photo: Owen Manning)   261

Plate 172   *Vitis coignetiae* rambles through this double row of steel posts with the aid of wires strung between the posts and forms a sculptural combination of hard and soft elements at Broadwater Business Park, Denham.   261

Plate 173   Established trees and shrubs such as this fastigiate yew (*Taxus baccata* 'Fastigiata') can provide natural support for the more vigorous rambling roses (shown here) and climbers such as mountain clematis (*Clematis montana*) and honeysuckles (*Lonicera* spp.).   262

Plate 174   Even the most stately of architectural elements such as this balustrade can be complimented and enhanced by climbers. The species shown is a cultivar of common honeysuckle (*Lonicera periclymenum*).   262

Preface

Planted vegetation is an essential part of our environment. The human landscape which we inhabit is the result of the manipulation of inorganic materials and the cultivation of organic life. As soon as we begin consciously to modify the vegetation in our human habitat, whether for farming, building or to make a garden, then we create possibilities for design with plants. This book is about how to design with plants.

When we design with plants we design with nature. This is true whether we are restoring eroded moorland, establishing a woodland or laying out a herbaceous border because all plants are living, growing, changing things which form part of the dynamic pattern of the natural world. This makes plants quite different to any other medium of design. An understanding of natural forms and processes is necessary for horticulture, but it can also be an inspiration for the art of planting.

In my work as a teacher of landscape design and horticulture, and in my professional activities as a landscape architect, I have become aware of the need for a comprehensive treatment of the aesthetic role of planting within the designed environment. The visual and spatial qualities of planting design are of primary significance to its aesthetic impact, and so this book is an attempt to provide a systematic examination of these effects and, particularly, to uncover the full potential of plants as a three dimensional medium of design.

Planting design plays a primary role in the professions of landscape architecture and amenity horticulture. It is also of relevance to architects, urban designers and civil engineers because it holds possibilities for the solution of some of the aesthetic and technical problems that they encounter and because buildings, roads, bridges and other structures must frequently be integrated with planting in order to achieve successful site planning.

It is no coincidence that many of the principles of spatial and decorative design are shared by planting, architecture and other design disciplines. All are concerned with the fundamental, timeless qualities of form, space and pattern. This book aims to show both what planting designers have in common with other designers, as well as to explore the delightful characteristics which make living plants a unique medium for design. It is hoped that the common ground revealed by this approach will help to foster mutual understanding and shared inspiration amongst everybody who is working for a better environment.

The first part of this book will examine the principles of design with plants. It will explore in depth the visual and spatial qualities of planting, and establish the relationship between these and the ecological and horticultural characteristics of planted vegetation. Planting design is a visual subject and so we shall rely heavily on drawings and diagrams to support and compliment the text. Part two will trace the stages of the design process from the inception of a project to its realisation and show how design principles can best be applied through design procedures. Each stage will be illustrated with examples of professional drawings produced by landscape architects in practice. Readers should note, however, that no attempt will be made to give comprehensive advice on the management of planting contracts or landscape commissions for landscape architects. These matters are fully dealt with in publications on professional practice such as Hugh Clamp's *Landscape Professional Practice*, published by Gower. The final part of the present volume is entitled Practice. This will attempt to identify good design technique and illustrate good practice in the choice and arrangement of species for various kinds of planting. Examples of actual planting schemes prepared by landscape architects will be used throughout to demonstrate the recommendations of the text.

The text contains numerous plant names. Both scientific names (in italics) and common names have been given whenever possible in order to help the reader who is less familiar with botanical latin. Where no common name is given this is normally because no such name is in widespread use, or because the common name is the same as or unmistakably similar to the scientific name (eg. *Rosa* = rose). If the reader has any doubt about the identity or common name of a tree or shrub they are referred to Hillier Nurseries (1991) *The Hillier Manual of Trees and Shrubs*, (6th edn), published by David and Charles. Botanical, ecological and horticultural terms have also been explained as they are introduced into the text, but if further information on such necessary jargon is required *The Penguin Dictionary of Botany* (1984) is comprehensive and can be highly recommended.

NICK ROBINSON
Department of Landscape,
University of Sheffield, UK

Acknowledgements

I am endebted to many people who have influenced and inspired me in my study, practice and teaching of landscape design. Their enthusiasm and ideas have led ultimately to the writing of this book.

I would like to acknowledge my particular gratitude to those people who have had a direct influence on its production. Jia-Hua Wu of the Zhejiang Academy of Fine Arts in Hangzhou, China has made a major contribution with his engaging and informative sketches, and through our many inspiring conversations about design. Many of the plans were drawn by Stella Lewis in her lively, informal but highly effective style. Oliver Gilbert and Owen Manning of the University of Sheffield and Dan Lewis of Sheffield City Council have offered valuable comment on particular chapters of the book, and have helped me to refine and develop these. Kenneth and Jean Warr's editorial advice, word processing skills and enthusiasm for the project have been invaluable, particularly during the more difficult early stages of writing, and many of the students at the Department of Landscape Architecture at Sheffield University have been encouraging and supportive, and have always offered valuable advice when asked what they would hope to find in a book on planting design.

Finally, I thank my partner Kris Burrows for her constant interest and advice despite the long hours I have spent on the mostly private pursuit of writing.

PART 1

Principles

CHAPTER 1

Why Design?

We should start by questioning the purpose of planting design. Why do we do it? And what is its place in environmental design as a whole?

The answer is essentially a matter of the quality of human life and of our relationship with the rest of the living world. Landscape design and, in particular, planting design offer us the opportunity to improve both of these.

In the first place, planting design can help us make the best use of our environment. Good planting design is an essential element in the creation and management of a landscape which is truly functional because it provides for a broad range of uses rather than a narrow exploitation. Secondly, planting design can help us restore the balance between people and nature by recognising and maintaining valuable natural plant communities, and by helping to create new vegetation associations which will provide a healthy, diverse and robust habitat for wildlife. Finally, planting offers many opportunities for enjoyment of the aesthetic delights of both cultivated and wild plants. The sight, scent and sensation of flowers, foliage and fruits, even the sound of wind and rain in the branches of trees, shrubs and other plants: all can add immeasurably to the quality of peoples' daily lives.

These three justifications for planting design, namely its functional, ecological, and aesthetic aspects, are by no means independent. For example, the presence of abundant wildlife in a wood can give great aesthetic pleasure to naturalists and lay people alike: a landscape ordered by a matrix of shelter belts may provide excellent nesting cover and have a distinctive character and visual appeal. But, without forgetting the inter-relationships, let us look a little more closely at each aspect in turn.

Planting Design as an Expression of Function

Throughout history the arrangement and cultivation of plantings has expressed human use of the land. This has been the case not only with the cultivation of food, timber and other crops, but also in planting which is not primarily for economic production. For example, the layouts of the earliest pleasure gardens in Persia were adapted from the functional agricultural landscape of the time with its irrigation canals and regularly spaced plantings of fruit trees. In eighteenth and nineteenth century England the hedges planted to enclose arable and pasture fields were carefully planned to improve farming efficiency. The ability of these hedges to shelter and protect and to give aesthetic pleasure helped to make the English pastoral landscape attractive as well as productive. These same qualities led to the extensive planting of hedges in gardens, ornamental parks and institutional grounds where human comfort and pleasure were essential for the function of the landscape.

Style and technique in planting are as varied as is the human use of the land. The environmental designer may be concerned with planning for almost any land use and for activities ranging from occasional visits to private or near inaccessible landscapes to the most intensive use in urban centres. These uses include domestic activities, play, work, study, and active or passive recreation. They all require an environment which fits the function, that is it must provide the right amount of space, the right microclimate, and the right aesthetic character as well as any specific facilities such as paving, seating and access which may be necessary. Planting can help create an environment which fits the function.

Many human activities require buildings, roads, car parks, waterways and other built structures. Planting design is much more than a cosmetic treatment to be applied to indifferent or insensitive architecture and engineering in order to 'soften' the harsh edges or disguise an awkward layout. It can play a major role in integrating structures into the environment by reducing their visual intrusiveness, by repairing damage to existing vegetation and, more positively, by providing a setting which is attractive and welcoming. New planting, as well as the conservation of existing vegetation, is an essential element in good site planning for many types of land use.

If it is well designed, planting is an apt expression of function and of the needs of the users. Let us take a children's play area as an example. The basic provision of equipment such as swings and climbing structures will allow children to engage in certain play activities, but it does not create the best environment for play. This needs much more. It needs a defined and welcoming place, separation from traffic for safety, segregation of boisterous from quiet play, enclosure for shelter and to give older children a sense of independence, opportunities for discovery and adventure, and the raw materials for creative and fantasy play. Much of this can be provided by planting. A hedge or shrub belt can enclose and shelter and separate. But trees and shrubs also create a whole environment which can be explored, where dens and tree houses can be built, where there are trees to climb and swing from, and where plants and animals can be discovered. This kind of use requires an appropriate kind of planting. It must be robust, resistant to damage, varied and stimulating and it will be quite different from the kind of planting that would be right in a communal garden for the elderly or in a busy urban centre precinct.

One of the major challenges of environmental design is the need to accommodate several different functions within any single area. Modern forestry provides a good example of how recognition of multiple use requirements has led to more sophisticated design. Early plantations had narrow objectives. They were laid out and managed purely for commercial efficiency exploiting the maximum proportion

Plates 1 and 2   Planting design makes an essential contribution to an environment fit for living and working (new housing court, Sheffield and Birchwood Boulevard Technology Park, Warrington).

Plate 4   Generous tree and shrub planting integrates new buildings and structures of Wuppertal University into the surrounding landscape. (Photo: Owen Manning)

Plate 3   Without planting, retaining structures of this scale would be dominating and intrusive. With planting they are well integrated and an asset to the local environment. (Munchen Gladbach. Photo: Owen Manning)

Plate 5   Planting helps to create an environment suitable for children's play by providing a comfortable microclimate, the sense of special place, and plenty of robust trees and shrubs for climbing, swinging and imaginative play.

Plate 6   Natural processes of colonisation have resulted in the vegetation of this urban nature park with little intervention.

Plate 7   No planting or seeding was needed on this cliff face: natural colonisation alone was appropriate.

Plate 8   This verge beside a busy trunk road has developed into an attractive species rich meadow.

Plate 9   The indigenous dune species marram grass (*Ammophila arenaria*) was appropriate for this coastal fill site, but planting to assist establishment was necessary. (Photo: Prof. A.E. Weddle, Landscape Architect)

Plate 10   After 18 months only a few traces of intervention remain visible. The geotextile netting was employed to reduce surface erosion. (Photo: Prof. A.E. Weddle, Landscape Architect)

Plate 11   A high degree of control over natural vegetation processes is demonstrated in this highly manicured display of hybridised and selected flowers at Gruga Park, Essen. (Photo: Owen Manning)

of available land for timber production. Little attention was paid to visual amenity or to habitat conservation. But the increasing recognition of recreational uses, visual amenity and the need for wildlife conservation has led to forestry being more sensitively sited, the inclusion of a diversity of indigenous species along the more visible and accessible edges, and the retention of the most valuable existing habitats within the forest area.

So good planting design endeavours to provide for all the uses of a place and to respect the needs of all the users.

Planting Design as the Management of Natural Vegetation Processes

There are some circumstances in which the natural processes of colonisation and succession of vegetation will be sufficient to provide for human needs or to repair damage done to the landscape by human activities. The spontaneous colonisation of urban wasteland, for example, can result in attractive urban commons which are enjoyed by children playing, dog walkers, blackberry pickers and naturalists; a road cutting in a rural area may be clothed with a prodigious display of colourful cornfield weeds the first summer after construction and would, with time, develop into a diverse meadow or scrub community.

It is more common, however, for landscape designers to be called in when nature requires some assistance. It may be necessary to speed up the process of colonisation and succession, such as on a denuded steep slope which would otherwise erode; or we may wish to purposefully direct the development of spontaneous vegetation, for example, by planting particular tree and shrub species to increase the diversity of an establishing woodland community. These are both examples of managing natural vegetation processes, but our intervention in these processes may be only to the minimum extent necessary to provide for human use. There is no functional reason in these instances to supplant a spontaneous 'natural' plant community with a wholly artificial one. Indeed, there may be good aesthetic reasons for retaining spontaneous, indigenous vegetation, for example, to reflect the local character or provide better habitats for wildlife which can be enjoyed by people.

The majority of planting design involves a much greater degree of control over nature. An extreme case is found in the planting of highly manicured gardens with exotic and tender species which could not exist there without constant horticultural intervention. This kind of completely artificial planting is wanted and needed in some settings; it is not intrinsically better or worse than the minimum intervention, ecological approach.

Good design means choosing the kind of planting and management which is appropriate to the site and its functions. This will often be the one which requires the lowest level of intervention in natural processes necessary for the planting to meet the design objectives. There are two reasons for this. Firstly, it will cost less because less labour and material resources will be used. The second reason is more debatable because it depends upon our perception of the environment and what we value most highly about it. But if we accept the environmental ethic that nature is intrinsically valuable and must be given more respect and more space then we will wish to take every opportunuity to allow it to develop with the minimum of human intervention. This is not to say that we should do naturalistic planting and management everywhere, only that we should not destroy natural vegetation unless there is a good reason.

Both the planting design and its subsequent care can be understood in the broadest sense as the management of natural vegetation processes. Different types of planting merely require different degrees of intervention in order to develop and maintain the desired plant community. Our purpose should be to understand and work with those processes to fulfill the functions of the planting.

Planting Design for Aesthetic Pleasure

The importance of aesthetic pleasure as an objective of planting design should not be underestimated. The idea of pleasure is deliberately and often falsely associated with all manner of consumer products and lifestyles. It appears to be a persuasive and successful technique for stimulating demand, but the products and experiences rarely live up to their billing. In reality our culture is one which often frustrates genuine delight.

In landscape and planting design we are in the business of helping people to live fulfilling and enjoyable lives. The pleasure of a lovingly tended garden or of contact with wild plants and the creatures they support can contribute a great deal to our daily lives and foster a genuine recreation of the spirit.

What is Successful Planting Design?

We have identified three major purposes of planting design: functional, ecological and aesthetic. The extent to which a design serves these purposes can be used to judge its success.

Of course, different planting schemes will have different priorities. These priorities will be reflected in the amount of thought that has been invested in meeting each of the functional, ecological and aesthetic requirements. For example, a shelter belt in a very exposed location will have the shelter function as its primary objective. The character of the indigenous vegetation and the aesthetic qualities of form, pattern and colour will need to be considered carefully but only after establishing the arrangements of species which are able to provide the optimum permeability and profile, and ensure the minimum damage to valuable existing habitats and take any opportunities there may be to create new habitats. A successful shelter belt will thus reduce wind speed and turbulence over the required distance, improve, or at least not damage, the ecology of the locality, and it will be attractive and in harmony with the local landscape character.

The criteria of functional performance and ecological fitness can be judged with a greater degree of objectivity than aesthetic value. That is, there is more likely to be disagreement on aesthetic criteria because opinions about what is visually appropriate and attractive vary enormously. This is the case not only when we consider different people's opinions, but one person's taste may vary markedly during their lifetime or even from day to day according to their mood. When

Plate 12 This successful shelterbelt in North West Scotland combines effective wind speed reduction, ecological diversification and aesthetic harmony with the local landscape.

assessing the aesthetic success of a planting scheme the designer should certainly ask 'Do I like it?' and, if so, 'Why?' or, if not, 'Why not?' But if we are to give full and systematic answers to the questions of aesthetics we need to develop an understanding of the aesthetic characteristics of plants and the effects of these when they are combined in planting composition. This is the subject matter of Chapters 3 to 7.

In addition to a personal analysis of the aesthetics of planting it is essential for the designer to ask 'Does the client like it?' (that is, does it satisfy the person or persons commissioning the work?) and 'Do the users like it?' The taste of the client and other users of a landscape may be different from that of a trained designer and it is essential to understand and provide for their various preferences and needs. As designers we may have a strongly individual style and firm opinions about aesthetics but if we do not achieve planting which is appreciated and enjoyed by the client and the users we are simply not doing our job.

CHAPTER 2

Plants as a Medium for Design

Designers of all kinds share basic principles. The materials with which they work, however, vary widely in their functional and aesthetic properties. Before examining the principles of planting design we should familiarise ourselves with some of the distinguishing characteristics of planting design.

In the first place, our creations have a life of their own.

Plants as Living Materials

Plants are growing, changing, interacting organisms and plant communities are in a constant state of flux. Even a climax community such as mature oak woodland is not static in its composition. Over-mature trees die back, fresh bursts of field layer vegetation are observed as glades open up or the canopy becomes thinner and young trees colonise to begin the next generation. The plant world has its own dynamic, developmental order. We can only manage this, we cannot change it.

In addition to genetically programmed aspects of plant growth and development, vegetation is continually interacting with its physical environment. Many environmental factors cause significant variation in the growth of plants, yet these cannot always be predicted or controlled with precision. The weather, from day to day and from year to year, will influence growth rate, form, foliage density, flower and fruit production. The elevation, aspect and topography of a site and its surroundings are among the factors which modifiy the regional climate and create variations in microclimate among particular locations. A favourable microclimate could promote taller and more luxuriant growth, or more abundant flowering and fruiting; a harsher microclimate on the same site might result in stunted habit and smaller leaves. The changing qualities of light at different times of day and in different seasons, and the amount of moisture in the atmosphere, affect the visual qualities of plants and planting composition. Regional and local variations in soil can also affect growth characteristics such as extension rate, biomass production, leaf and flower colour, ultimate stature, and vulnerability to pests, disorders and weather damage.

The growth of any single plant will be influenced by its neighbours. These can modify the microclimate, introducing shade and shelter, increasing humidity but reducing precipitation at ground level. Vegetation also affects soil conditions, reducing the moisture and nutrients available in the short term but over a period of years increasing the essential humus and nutrient content of the soil. Certain types of vegetation, for example many conifers and moorland grasses, can acidify the soil reaction by the chemical composition of their leaf litter. This can lead to a build up of only partly decomposed organic matter and a reduction in available nutrients. Birch (*Betula* spp.), on the other hand, improves moorland soils by returning leached nutrients to the surface in its leaf litter.

Plate 13 The development of a planting association over its first 10 years: A view one season after planting shows scattered trees and shrubs of a similar size to when they left the nursery.

Plate 14 The same view three years after planting shows a well established thicket.

Plate 15 After ten years the trees and larger shrubs have attained heights of up to ten metres and have begun to have the visual impact for which they were planted.

Plate 17 The dramatic effects of light can give unpredictable yet memorable qualities to planting.

Plate 16 The favourable microclimate provided by a South facing wall allows the growing of plants which would not survive in the open. *Abutilon* and *Ceanothus* spp. (shown in this photograph), *Fremontodendron californicum* and *Magnolia campbellii* are among the shrubs grown successfully in the walled gardens at Newby Hall in North Yorkshire.

Diseases and pests affect the growth and development of planting. In rural locations, animals such as cattle, sheep, deer and rabbits are selective grazers which prevent or restrict the growth of some species and favour that of others which they find unpalatable. This helps determine both individual plant form and the composition of plant communities.

Finally, human pressures are a crucial and often unpredictable biotic factor affecting plant growth and development. In densely populated areas pollution, vandalism and rubbish dumping can seriously interfere with the form and health of plants. Erosion due to excessive foot traffic, pedal or motor cycle riding can destroy or prevent the development of the lower layers of vegetation and the regeneration of shrubs and trees. In addition to these incidental anthropogenic influences we should also consider fashion and taste as important habitat factors (Gilbert, 1989). These significantly influence the management and make up of artificial plant assemblages, favouring those which most closely meet the prevalent cultural preferences and reducing the chances of survival of those which are regarded as 'untidy', 'boring' or 'uncared for'.

Cycles of Plant Growth and Development

The various cycles of plant growth and development are another crucial aspect which the designer cannot control or predict with certainty. These rhythms of change, however, are more of a benefit than a problem. They offer an unfailing source of excitement and interest.

The periods of growth cycles vary enormously, from diurnal rhythms such as the opening and closing of flowers to the annual rhythm of the seasons. The entire life cycle of a plant can occupy a period as short as six weeks, in the case of ephemerals like groundsel or shepherd's purse, or as long as millena for wellingtonias (*Sequoiadendron giganteum*), and the bristlecone pine (*Pinus longaeva*).

It is necessary for designers to be familiar with the distinctive characteristics of the different stages in the life cycle of the species they are using. Competitive young growth, reproductive maturity and senescence are normally distinguished by very different size, habit and form and so, at each of those stages, the role that the plant can play in an association will be quite different.

A further distinctive aspect of vegetation design is the vital role of landscape management. After implementation the young planting requires careful and creative tending over a number of years if the designer's initial intentions are to be properly realised. This is the period during which the original idea is shaped into the finished product, and it brings with it a risk that the planting scheme may fall victim to

MATURE TREE FORM

IN CLOSE WOODLAND   IN OPEN PARKLAND   ON EXPOSED HILLSIDE

Figure 2.1

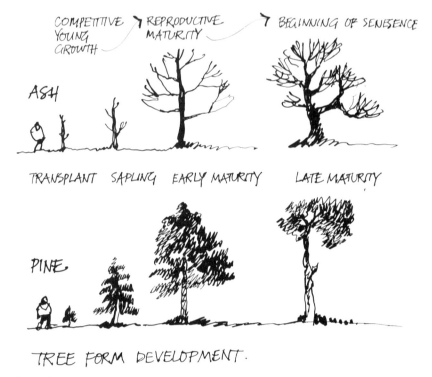

COMPETITIVE YOUNG GROWTH — REPRODUCTIVE MATURITY — BEGINNING OF SENESCENCE

ASH

TRANSPLANT SAPLING EARLY MATURITY LATE MATURITY

PINE

TREE FORM DEVELOPMENT.

Figure 2.2

inadequate or misguided horticultural practice. On the positive side, however, management provides the opportunity to achieve far more than could ever be envisaged on the drawing board because it is able to respond directly and immediately to the variety and vitality of living plant communities.

There are clearly important elements of unpredictability in many aspects of planting design. These range from the inherent nature of the material and the vagaries of climate to the problems of communicating the subtleties of design to maintenance staff over a period of many years. Building a landscape with vegetation is not like building a motor car with steel or even a hard landscape with bricks and mortar. Plants cannot be definitively represented by a precise scale drawing or model because the appearance of planting after a certain number of years can never be fully guaranteed. There will always be an element, however small, of unpredictability. This often causes difficulty to students and designers with limited plant knowledge but, with increasing horticultural experience and understanding, they will begin to gain greater confidence in the results of their endeavours in the studio.

The Landscape Designer's View of Plants

People have always had a functional interest in plants as providers of food, fuel, shelter and tools. Scientific understanding and, perhaps, aesthetic appreciation have developed more recently. There are now numerous technical and scientific disciplines which endeavour to understand plants and to use them in imaginative and profitable ways and there are many arts and crafts in which plants are employed either directly or indirectly through inspiration and metaphor for expression in other media.

The essential question is, what is distinctive about the landscape designer's

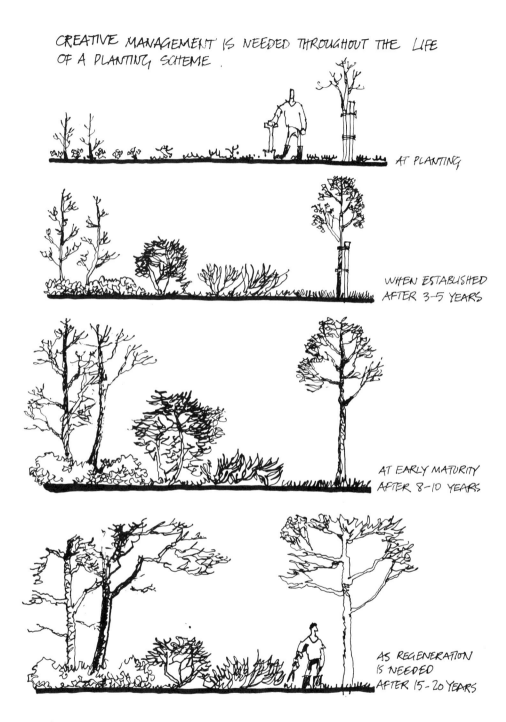

CREATIVE MANAGEMENT IS NEEDED THROUGHOUT THE LIFE OF A PLANTING SCHEME.

AT PLANTING

WHEN ESTABLISHED AFTER 3–5 YEARS

AT EARLY MATURITY AFTER 8–10 YEARS

AS REGENERATION IS NEEDED AFTER 15–20 YEARS

STAGES OF DEVELOPMENT OF TREE, SHRUB AND GROUND COVER PLANTING.

Figure 2.3

PLANTING.

CANOPY CLOSES AT 3-5 YEARS IF DENSELY PLANTED

HEIGHTS OF TREES AND SHRUBS BEGIN TO DIFFERENTIATE

EARLY MATURITY AT 20-30 YEARS AND GLADES CAN BE
CREATED FOR REPLANTING.

STAGES OF DEVELOPMENT OF WOODLAND PLANTING.

Figure 2.4

TREE - BRANCH FORM   TREE - CANOPY SPACE   TREE - FORM   TREE - SPACE

Figure 2.5a

AVENUE - FORM   AVENUE - SPACE

WOODLAND - FORM   WOODLAND - SPACE

Figure 2.5b

understanding of plants? What makes it different from the approach of the botanist, the ecologist, the gardener, the forester, the painter or the flower arranger?

The first part of the answer is that the landscape design approach is broader. As designers we must understand something of botany, be familiar with the basic principles of ecology and use some of the techniques of gardening and forestry. We must also have a painter's eye for line, texture and colour and a flower arranger's ability to combine plants to create a mood appropriate for the occasion.

In addition to the breadth of knowledge required of the landscape designer there is one specialised understanding that no other discipline shares, and which provides the essence of visual and spatial composition with planting. This is the understanding of plants as structural elements in the landscape.

Plants as Structural Elements

Plants provide us with green building blocks which can be assembled in a variety of different ways. An assemblage does not constitute simply a plant collection but rather it forms living and changing 'structures' in the outdoor environment.

But all kinds of three dimensional design are concerned not only with the final shape and form of the solid structures into which their raw materials are moulded, but also with the 'empty' space that the form defines. The edges and surfaces of a building, a piece of furniture and a sculpture limit and thereby define the space around or within it. This defined or enclosed space has both aesthetic qualities and functional purpose such as meeting, sleeping, sitting, exploring and so on.

Plants, in combination and individually, create spaces beneath, between, and sometimes within the bulk of their canopies. The planting designer uses vegetation to create a landscape structure which both defines spaces and helps to create places in order to serve the required human functions.

This planting structure can be observed at a wide variety of scales. At the largest, woodland belts or even forests can build a landscape framework within which large-scale land uses, such as industry, housing and recreation can be accommodated without undue visual intrusion on their environs. The human activities provided for will also benefit from the improved microclimate, wildlife conservation and general appearance that is brought by the enclosing planting. At the smaller scale of individuals and small groups of people, planting continues to play a vital role in structuring the landscape. Facilities such as a play area or a communal or private garden all require definition, enclosure, shelter and privacy in varying degrees. This can be easily and attractively provided by introducing shrubs and trees of suitable size and habit. Even a single tree can define a space and identify a place. Its spreading canopy will give containment above and create a domain of influence below.

So vegetation has the structural role of creating spaces in the landscape and this can be seen to be analogous to the space enclosing envelope of a building, but over a much wider range of scales. For this reason the basic language and concepts of building architecture offer a spatial vocabulary which can be applied to landscape and planting design. Rooms, streets, squares, arcades and colonnades, for example, are architectural spaces which are familiar to us and so can help us to appreciate that similar but looser spaces can also be created with plants.

In his book *Trees in Urban Design*, Henry Arnold summarises the spatial use of trees with particular reference to the urban environment:

> Trees in the city are living building materials used to establish spatial boundaries. They make the walls and ceilings of outdoor rooms, but with more subtlety than most architectural building materials. They create spatial rhythms to heighten the experience of moving through outdoor spaces.... In

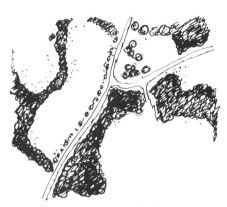

LARGE SCALE STRUCTURE PLANTING
OF WOODLAND BELTS

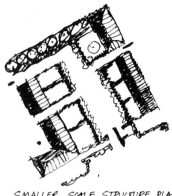

SMALLER SCALE STRUCTURE PLANTING
OF TREES, SHRUBS AND HEDGES

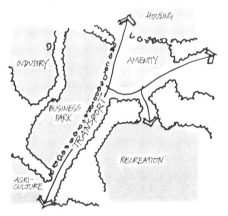

CREATES A FRAMEWORK FOR VARIOUS
LAND USES.

Figure 2.6a

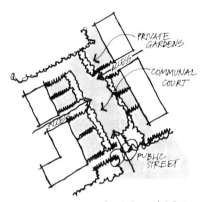

CREATES SPACES FOR VARIOUS PEOPLE
AND USES

Figure 2.6b

Plate 18   The space beneath the canopy of this single beech (*Fagus sylvatica*) is further delineated and emphasised by a circular hedge and a change of ground level.

Plate 19   Hedges of species such as yew (*Taxus baccata*) may be clipped to make green walls of similar form to those built in masonry.

Plate 20   The natural growth of belts of trees and shrubs can create informal walls of vegetation.

Plate 21   Trained and clipped cypress (*Cupressus* sp.) form a wall with windows giving views in and out of a small urban park in Malaga.

Plate 22   Carpets of low ground covering ivy (*Hedera*), blue fescue (*Festuca glauca*) and juniper (*Juniperus*) form an attractive floor to this courtyard. The broad bands between the lines of paving are planted on the roof of a room below. (Photo: Prof. A.E.Weddle, Landscape Architect)

Plate 23   *Wisteria* is trained over supports to form a delightful ceiling of foliage above this patio in Majorca.

Plate 24   The naturally spreading canopies of these silver maples (*Acer saccharinum*) forms a sheltering and screening ceiling above the car park at Leeds University.

Plate 26   Natural gateways and windows are formed by gaps in otherwise impenetrable vegetation.

Plate 25   Plants such as cypress (*Cupressus* sp.) can be trained to form a green gateway of inviting proportions.

Plate 28   A carefully spaced and regularly pruned double row of limes (*Tilia* sp.) gives overhead enclosure to form an arcade of trees. (Photo: Owen Manning)

Plate 27   A single row of small trees forms a green collonade in this residential courtyard in Cologne. (Photo: Owen Manning)

Plate 30   Analogies in both the structural and decorative aspects of trees and built form are employed in the work of Antoni Gaudi in Parc Guel, Barcelona.

Plate 29   Regular street tree planting echoes the rhythms of adjacent architecture.

Plate 31   An overgrown beech hedge *(Fagus sylvatica)* creates a sheltering canopy and a semi permeable curtain of stems at Formakin, Scotland.

addition to actually creating discreet spaces, trees are used to connect and extend the geometry, rhythms, and scale of buildings into the landscape. It is this function more than any decorative and softening effect that is of primary importance to architecture. (Arnold, 1980)

Planting can also create more complex and fluid spatial form. This can be found in spontaneous woodland and scrub, and in nature-like planting where tree and shrub canopies of various heights and densities interweave with glades, paths and open land.

Creating spaces is frequently described as an 'architectural' function of plants (eg. Booth, 1983, Robinette, 1972). This certainly recognises the spatial concepts common to architecture and landscape, but the term 'structural' is to be preferred because it implies only the underlying framework of outdoor spaces and not the ornamentation of structure. For the purposes of design it is useful to distinguish these two functions and, indeed, most planting can be divided into that which is primarily structural and that which is primarily ornamental.

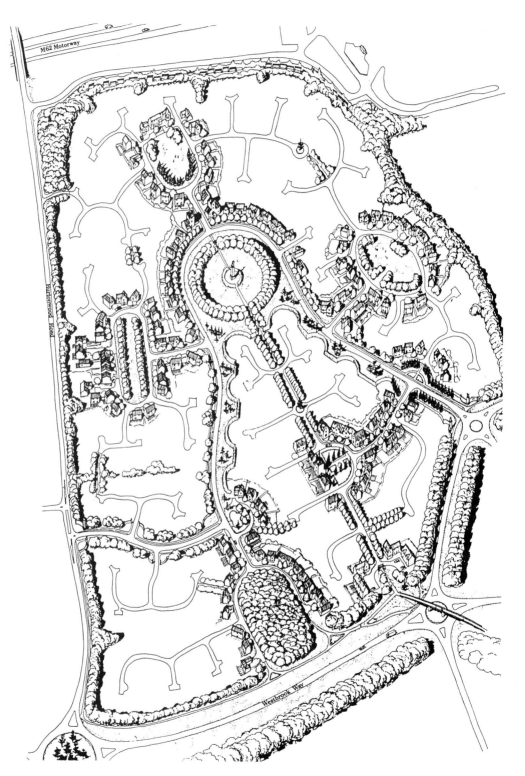

Figure 2.7   This axonometric vividly illustrates how tree planting will form the green spatial structure to a housing development. (Landscape Design Associates)

PLANTING CAN CREATE THE FLOOR, WALLS + CEILING OF INTIMATE OUTDOOR ROOMS

Figure 2.8

Plants as Decorative Elements

Like the architect of a building, the landscape architect is, of course, also concerned with the detailed aesthetic qualities as well as the spatial dimensions of the basic structure. Plants offer an enormous wealth of aesthetic characteristics: the appearance of their leaves, twigs, bark, flowers and fruit; the fragrance of flowers and aromatic foliage; the physical texture of bark and leaves; even the sound they make when stirred by the wind or beaten by the rain.

Trees and shrubs with desirable aesthetic characteristics can be planted to add ornament to the basic structure planting. This would be analogous to the embelishment of a building facade or the decoration of its interior, and could be regarded as specifically ornamental planting. Another approach would be to rely on the aesthetic qualities of the structural planting itself to give surface detail to the space, and additional species would not be introduced purely to give variety or for their ornamental qualities alone. This would produce a landscape of simpler character in the tradition of modernist architecture and landscape. In practice most design utilises the decorative characteristics of both structure planting and specifically ornamental planting to clothe the framework of spaces.

There are two common and often justified criticisms of the decorative qualities of planting design. On the one hand, too much reliance is sometimes placed on a limited number of fail-safe species. This can simply lead to monotony. At the other extreme it is easy to become captivated by variety at the expense of aesthetic order and clarity of purpose. The first fault is usually the result of inadequate plant knowledge, due to insufficient experience or a lack of interest in plants. The second is a product of a genuine appreciation of plants but this enthusiasm must be tempered by an understanding of principles of composition. In order to achieve successful and enduring planting we must choose and combine plants with knowledge and discretion.

Plate 32   Sculptural organic form and fluid space are created by the nature-like planting of clumps of willows (*Salix*) near the water's edge. (Photo: Owen Manning)

Plate 33   The lavender (*Lavandula*), rose and everlasting (*Anaphalis*) play a chiefly decorative role in the spaces created by garden walls and buildings.

Plant Selection

There is an enormous diversity of size, habit, foliage and other characteristics among the range of species and cultivars which are available in the nursery trade. This can make the designer's task of choosing the right plant seem overwhelming.

The efficient and successful choice of plants is best made by a selection procedure in which the designer makes increasingly fine distinctions between groups of plants on the basis of their design characteristics. These characteristics can be conveniently placed under three headings:

1. Functional and structural characteristics.

2. Visual and other sensory properties.

3. Plant growth habit and cultural requirements.

The functional and structural characteristics are those which determine the ability of a species to perform its working role in a designed landscape. For example, a plant's form and foliage density will affect its ability to shelter, screen or shade an area; the density of root growth near the surface will determine its ability to bind the soil and protect against erosion. Functional characteristics allow planting to produce a functional landscape, one which provides a fitting environment for human activities whilst avoiding damage to the ecology of the landscape. A full treatment of the climatic and bioengineering functions of planting is beyond the scope of the present volume. We shall concentrate here on the structural characteristics which determine the spatial functions that can be performed by planting. These spatial qualities are of primary importance to the aesthetic effect of planting and we shall examine this phenomenon in the chapters on creating spaces and composite space.

The visual properties of stems, foliage, fruit and flower are also important ingredients in planting of high sensual quality. Their importance and the care needed when choosing and combining these characteristics will vary according to the importance of the ornamental function on the site and the visual sensitivity of the location. For example, when we plant a garden we expect to spend a great deal of time and effort creating beautiful pictures. In an office courtyard a similar visual impact may be required, especially if the client wants an impressive showpiece for visitors. A shelterbelt or woodland in a national park or other area of scenic value, although it would not require the same attention to detail as intricate planting in a courtyard or garden, must still be designed with sensitivity to the existing character of the landscape and, in particular, the indigenous vegetation; the character of foliage, flower and branch form of the chosen species should harmonise with their setting. Locations such as reclamation sites may, on the other hand, be far less demanding when it comes to the visual and other aesthetic qualities of plants. Indeed, to get anything to grow at all may be a major challenge on sites with difficult or badly polluted substrates. In such cases the technical considerations of establishing plants would far outweigh the visual properties of their foliage and flowers when it came to selecting species.

Growth habit and cultural requirements help determine the habitat and ecological niche a species can occupy. This applies both to spontaneous vegetation communities and to contrived or managed associations. Such characteristics are an essential consideration for the designer if they are to create plant associations which are vigorous, healthy and sustainable.

To summarise, the procedure of design and plant selection consists of first determining function, followed by spatial form, and finally visual character. Only then can appropriate species be confidently selected and arranged to perform each of these roles. It is this sequence that will be adopted in the following chapters.

Functional and Aesthetic Considerations in Design

The use of plants in landscape design always has both a functional and an aesthetic effect. However great the need for a landscape to be convenient to use, the designer must also consider the aesthetic impact. It is the relative priority given to each aspect that should vary according to the demands of the site and the needs of the users.

We should also recognise that functional effectiveness and sensual quality are by no means independent. Indeed Victor Papanek, in *Design for the Real World* (1974), defines the function of an artifact in the widest sense, identifying six aspects which include both use and aesthetic quality. He argues that successful functioning depends on:

1. Good **method** in design and manufacture which employs appropriate tools, processes and materials.

2. Ease and effectiveness of use.

3. Design for genuine **need,** not artificially manufactured fads and desires.

4. The **telesic content** of a design, that is, the extent to which it reflects the economic and social conditions of its time and place.

5. The materials and forms employed having appropriate **associations in** the minds of the users (no product is free from association in both individual and cultural experience).

6. The intrinsic **aesthetic qualities** of the materials and forms employed being appropriate to the function.

Thus, aesthetic character is an essential part of design for function. This notion is different, in a subtle but important way, from the saying that 'if it works well it will

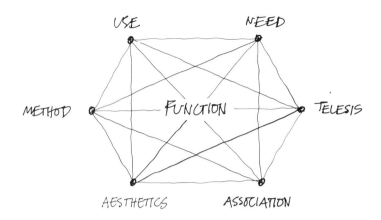

Figure 2.9   THE FUNCTION COMPLEX (AFTER PAPANEK, 1971)

Plate 34   The aesthetic qualities of a planting scheme should be in harmony with the character and the function of the site. Compare the ground modelling and planting of this entrance to an industrial site with the rockery in the next photograph.

Plate 35   This rockery and planting at the entrance to an industrial compound display aesthetic qualities which disregard the character and function of the site.

look right'. The implication is that we cannot leave the aesthetic qualities to be the incidental product of a function which is narrowly defined. There are often a number of potential solutions to a problem of function, especially in landscape design, and aesthetics should be one of the criteria for choosing the best alternative. The aesthetic qualities of any artifact convey some meaning to the users, so that meaning should concur with the function and the purpose of the artifact if we are to design honestly and with proper regard for the real needs of the users.

A designed landscape is not only a large artifact but it also commonly requires a highly complex integration of various uses. Many different functions are normally fulfilled by planting on any one site. These functions are design objectives which arise out of the designer's analysis of the needs of the users and the problems and opportunities of the physical site. In simple terms, design functions are what we want the planting to do. To take a straightforward example, analysis of social data might indicate the users' need for a high level of privacy in a sheltered, sunny part of the site. This would tell the designer that planting functions must include screening for privacy and shelter for optimum microclimate.

Although aesthetic effects are always present and should be considered as one aspect of function, in some landscapes aesthetic pleasure may be a primary design objective. This is clearly the case in parks and gardens, ornamental courtyards and the grounds of institutions such as hospitals where an important requirement might be a strong sense of character in the planting and a high level of aesthetic delight. So an understanding of aesthetics is an essential tool in the repertoire of designers. It helps them fashion landscape that will be truly functional and is more likely to be valued and respected by the users.

CHAPTER 3

The Structural Characteristics of Plants

The structural characteristics of plants are those aspects of form which can contribute to the spatial structure of the landscape. Mature size, density, shape and speed of growth are all essentially structural characteristics, and it is the combination of these that will determine the spatial qualities of the planted environment.

The Spatial Functions of Plants in the Human Landscape

When we are designing spaces for human use the dimensions of plants relative to the dimensions of the human figure are critical. Simply to distinguish planting areas on a plan by canopy height is a major first step in the process of design and species selection because it is the height of planting that determines many of its possibilities for spatial design, namely those related to vision, movement and the physical comfort of people.

Jakobsen (1977) reminds us that the critical heights of shrub and herbaceous planting are ground level, knee height, waist height and eye level, and that the designer needs to break down the range of plant material into size categories based on these human dimensions.

Canopy height	Plants
Ground level:	Mown grasses and other turf herbs, ground hugging and carpeting herbs and shrubs.
Below knee height:	Prostrate and dwarf shrubs, sub-shrubs, low herbs.
Knee-waist height:	Small shrubs, medium herbs.
Waist-eye level:	Medium shrubs, tall herbs.
Above eye level:	Tall shrubs, trees.

When it comes to actual dimensions, these critical heights will of course vary for different people. For adults, this variation will be only marginal and would rarely affect our choice of species. For children of different ages and for people in wheelchairs, however, the height difference will be much greater and so on sites which are to cater for children or the disabled we must take this into account and allow for their rather different spatial experience.

We shall examine the design potential of each canopy level in turn.

GROUND LEVEL PLANTING (CARPETING PLANTS)

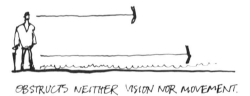

OBSTRUCTS NEITHER VISION NOR MOVEMENT.

IT CAN PROVIDE A VISUAL LINK BETWEEN RELATED AREAS,

CAN MAKE OCCASIONAL CIRCULATION SURFACES,

CAN PAINT PATTERNS ON THE GROUND,

Figure 3.1

Ground Level Planting (Carpeting Plants)

The essential spatial characteristic of this size category is that it offers no obstruction either to vision or to movement.

This lowest growing vegetation forms a foliage canopy which is very close to ground level, and often not more than a few centimeters, thick. It includes grasses and other turf herbs which can be mown or grazed, absolutely prostrate shrubs (eg. *Juniperus* 'Bar Harbour', *Cotoneaster dammeri, Thymus lanuginosus)* and creeping herbs (eg. *Lysimachia nummularia).*

The carpet of vegetation formed by plants such as these follows closely any small undulations in the ground surface. On even, firm ground this carpet can become a circulation surface for pedestrians although of course it is considerably less hard wearing than a hard pavement. The most wear tolerant species are many of the grasses which, when grazed or mown regularly, form not only visually appealing carpets of green sward but also surfaces suitable for walking, play, sport, lying, cycling and occasional vehicles. This accounts for much of the value and popularity of lawns, paddocks and other grasslands in public and private landscape.

Such ground level vegetation also fulfills an important decorative role. Carpets of foliage may be used alone or interspersed with rocks, gravel and paving materials to form a visual tapestry draped on the ground surface. Different species give variations in foliage or flower with which we can paint two dimensional patterns on a canvas of earth.

Shrubs and Herbs Below Knee Height (Low Planting)

Shrubs and herbs which create a higher canopy but still below knee height have further possibilities in planting design. Many of them come within the category commonly referred to as 'ground cover'. This comprises those species which are well enough adapted to the local climate and soils and vigorous enough in their growth to compete with and exclude most unwanted, self-colonising 'weed' plants. Species which form such a dense, long-lived ground cover are often employed in landscape planting to reduce weed control and other maintenance operations which could be prohibitively expensive in many planting projects.

In addition to its labour-saving role, low canopy vegetation has other design functions. It can form a visual platform above which taller trees, shrubs and herbs can be displayed. This is akin to a foundation or wash in painting, a 'ground' against which the 'figure' is seen. It can provide a common ground which unifies the various other elements and incidents in the composition.

Many species which form prostrate ground cover will also trail down vertical or inclined planes to form hanging curtains. Climbers will of course grow up walls, fences and other supports. This enables vigorous climbers to provide screening or green enclosure up to the desired height more rapidly than could be achieved by free-standing shrub planting. A further advantage of climbers over shrubs for screening and separating is that they do not require as wide a planting strip, being much more confined in their spread.

Many trailers or climbers may be planted to form a continuous mantle of foliage over vertical and horizontal surfaces alike. Expanses of foliage will cascade down banks and walls and flow over flatter ground, masking and softening the angles between vertical, horizontal and inclined planes. By clothing new and old alike, climbers can rapidly give a sense of belonging and maturity to structures or earthworks which have been insensitively imposed on the landscape.

We may wish to emphasise rather than subdue the visual impact of ground

PLANTING BELOW KNEE HEIGHT (LOW PLANTING)

ALLOWS UNINTERRUPTED VISION BUT DETERS MOVEMENT

CAN FORM A CARPET OF PATTERNS VIEWED
FROM ABOVE,

CAN FORM A CARPET OF FOLIAGE
BELOW TALLER PLANTS,

Figure 3.2a

MEDIUM SHRUB PLANTING

PLANTING BETWEEN KNEE AND EYE LEVEL
OBSTRUCTS MOVEMENT BUT ALLOWS VISION.

IT CAN SEPARATE PEDESTRIANS FROM HAZARDOUS OR
SENSITIVE AREAS,

CAN EMPHASISE DIRECTION AND CIRCULATION,

Figure 3.3a

CAN DEFINE TERRITORY,

CAN IMPROVE PRIVACY WITHIN BUILDINGS,

AND CAN PROVIDE A MINOR VISUAL FOCUS.

Figure 3.3b

extensive areas of masonry or cladding.

An isolated pair of tall shrubs or a gap in mass planting creates a frame. It can frame a whole vista or attract attention to one focal point or landmark. This kind of arrangement not only guides the eye but also invites exploration. Like an arch or gateway, it is suggestive of a different, perhaps more exciting place beyond, and it is hard to resist going through the gateway to discover what has been withheld from view.

When planted as single individuals or in small groups, the more distinguished tall shrubs have the size and presence to be notable specimens providing a key feature or visual focus within a human scale landscape.

Tree Planting

The sizes of trees are generally of the same order of magnitude as buildings, roads, bridges and all but the largest industrial developments. Tree planting can therefore be used for screening, separating, sheltering, enclosing, accompanying and complementing these larger structures.

The mature heights of trees commonly found in Britain range from about five metres in species such as almond *(Prunus dulcis)* and weeping pear *(Pyrus salicifolia* 'Pendula') to over 40 metres in ash *(Fraxinus excelsior)*, London plane *(Platanus x hispanica)* and beech *(Fagus sylvatica)* when these trees are growing in especially favourable conditions (Mitchell, 1974). For design purposes, it is helpful to divide them into small trees of approximately 5 to 10 metres, medium trees of 10 to 20 metres and tall trees of 20 metres and above at maturity.

Small trees are of similar height or lower than the majority of buildings of two stories or more, and so their impact in the urban environment will be mainly local to the spaces between buildings. Medium trees can create spaces which contain smaller buildings, and therefore have a greater effect on the structure of urban landscape. Tall trees are less common in urban areas because of the space they demand, although naturally tall growing species are often planted in streets and gardens only to be lopped or pruned as they begin to dominate nearby buildings. However, the size of tall trees enables them to contribute to the structure of the largest urban spaces and to form the dominant element in the largest scale of structure planting.

Even in the case of developments such as power stations and other massive industrial sites which are far taller than any tree, medium and tall tree planting can still play a crucial role in the integration of these structures into the surrounding landscape. Extensive belts and plantations which envelop and extend outwards from such development sites can provide complete screening of near distance views. From greater distances such planting cannot obscure structures on the scale of cooling towers or turbine houses, but can visually anchor these structures to their supporting landscape and also screen the lower level development of ancillary and temporary buildings and car parks. This can be a vital role because these structures can often be the most disturbing elements of large-scale industry.

The ability of tree planting to screen and obscure views from a greater distance than shrub planting can be made use of to strictly control those views which are presented to observers as they move through the landscape. Gaps in planting can be carefully located to open up a vista or frame an attractive view at just the right moment. Like a window or an archway, a frame of branches and foliage directs the attention and concentrates the mind on what is beyond it.

A single tree or small group, on the other hand, acts as a focus of attention.

TALL SHRUB PLANTING

PLANTING TALLER THAN EYE LEVEL FORMS
BOTH A PHYSICAL AND VISUAL BARRIER.

IT CAN GIVE PRIVACY AND SHELTER,

CAN PROVIDE A BACKCLOTH FOR DISPLAY PLANTING,

Figure 3.4a

CAN ACCOMPANY SMALLER BUILDINGS,

CAN FRAME A VISTA OR LANDMARK,

AND CAN MAKE A SPECIMEN OR VISUAL FOCUS.

Figure 3.4b

TREES

CAN FORM A BUFFER BETWEEN INCOMPATIBLE ACTIVITIES,

CAN SCREEN AND SEPARATE LARGER BUILDINGS,

CAN INTEGRATE THE LARGEST STRUCTURES,

CAN FRAME AND EMPHASISE LANDMARKS,

A SINGLE LARGE TREE CAN BE A LANDMARK AND MEETING PLACE.

Figure 3.5a

TREES CAN COMPLEMENT BUILDING FORM

CAN INTEGRATE UNRELATED BUILDING STYLES,

CAN GIVE VERTICAL CONTAINMENT TO ROUTEWAYS,

Figure 3.5b

TREE CLUMPS AND WOODLANDS CAN EMPHASISE TOPOGRAPHY,

OR DISGUISE INSENSITIVE EARTHWORKS

AND CAN CREATE A DISTINCTIVE WOODLAND
ENVIRONMENT WITHIN THEIR CANOPY.

Figure 3.5c

Being a relatively isolated object it occupies a comparatively small area within the field of vision, and is an object upon which the eye can come to rest. A tree species with a distinctive character will form a particularly noticeable specimen. A single large tree or a small group can have this effect even at a considerable distance from the observer, and so provide foci and landmarks within the wider, larger-scale landscape.

Single specimens or small groups of trees can be an important balance and accompaniment to domestic scale buildings. In this case, the relationship between the form and character of the tree and that of the building is of considerable importance. Humphrey Repton recognised this and formulated his rule for tree forms to accompany different architectural styles. He recommended that buildings in the classical style with broad, stable proportions and shallow roof angles should be accompanied by the rising lines and upright forms of fastigiate trees such as spruces or firs. Conversely, the sharply rising pinnacles and steeply pitched roofs of the Victorian Gothic Revival should be complemented by the stable rounded or horizontal forms of spreading trees such as cedar of Lebanon, English oak or chestnuts. Although these associations may be particularly satisfying, we need not necessarily abide by Repton's rule, indeed there are many attractive examples which contradict it.

A further architectural role of tree planting might be the unification of visually unrelated building styles. The simple, regular line of a single species avenue can form a linking, uniform frontage or a free-standing structural element in urban design. Its continuity can bind together disparate buildings and leave the variety of the architecture to add interest within a dominant, unifying green framework.

We have seen how the height and habit of plants determine their potential spatial functions. In particular, they allow us to control vision and circulation, and these two factors are fundamental to spatial design. How we can combine plants to create spaces of various characters and for various purposes provides the subject of the next chapter.

CHAPTER 4

Creating Spaces with Plants

When we first visit a site and begin to imagine its potential for design, one of the qualities to strike us will be its existing spatial character, whether it is open and bleak, expansive and exhilerating, intricate and intimate, or introverted and mysterious, and so on. Some of our first ideas about design will include the scale and character of the spaces we might create, and trying out possible arrangements of spaces is the best way to overcome the perplexing problem of what to do on a blank sheet of paper. In short, a spatial understanding is fundamental to all areas of environmental design, especially landscape and planting design.

But before we examine how plants can be used to create spaces we should first ask why spaces are so important for our experience of the environment.

The Experience of Space

Our experience of our environment is the product of all our senses. The smell and feel of the air; the quality of the sound of voices, footsteps, car engines; the texture of the ground under our feet, all contribute a great deal to this experience in addition to our primary visual perception

These perceived qualities of environment result from its physical form and its surface patterns, textures and colours. Pattern, texture and colour give a vast amount of information about where we are: whether it is a natural or artificial environment (eg. a rock outcrop or city paving), whether it is friendly or hostile (eg. rolling pasture or desert sand dunes). The form of spaces around us, however, has a primary but less acknowledged role in our experience.

One explanation for our often subconscious emotional responses to spatial arrangements is offered by Jay Appleton's theory of prospect and refuge (Appleton, 1975). The foundation of this theory is the enduring effect of humankind's pre-agricultural relationship to its habitat. This habitat was a landscape where food needed to be hunted or gathered, but predators also roamed. Thus, enclosure offered refuge from danger and a commanding prospect allowed danger to be anticipated or food to be identified, then caught or gathered. Because of this, an enclosed space felt safe and relaxing whereas a vantage point was stimulating and exciting. An exposed location such as the open plain, although it allowed good vision, also meant that the early humans could themselves be seen and would be associated with a mixture of excitement and caution.

Appleton argues that our responses to the spatial order of the hunter-gatherer landscape were so essential for survival that even today they remain ingrained in the fabric of our experience. Thus varying degrees of exposure and enclosure and combinations of views and screening continue to elicit archetypal responses of anticipation and excitement, caution and anxiety, relaxation and safety, according to their archaic survival meaning. This unconscious meaning of spatial order would help to explain why certain sizes and shapes of spaces feel 'right' and others don't. For example, too confined an enclosure or one without a clear exit route is no longer safe but threatening, whereas a large expansive space is unsatisfactory if it is cluttered with many objects that obstruct views and thereby reduce its prospect value. The right combination of enclosure and outlook will give a balance of welcome refuge and pleasant prospect.

Prospect-refuge theory is of great value for designers, not least by virtue of its basic simplicity and it helps to remind us that when we design spaces we are creating experiences. Although the theory was developed mainly by reference to rural and natural landscapes, it can also be applied to complex urban spaces created by buildings, topography and vegetation. In such cases its foundation in hunter-gatherer ethology should be taken as a starting point. This fundamental person-landscape dynamic is then overlaid with a diversity of social demands and opportunities that are the products of the specific cultural setting of our lives. For example, a residential space such as a housing courtyard will not only be experienced as a familiar refuge from the exertions of the wider world, but also in terms of the opportunities it offers for social intercourse, the degree and type of relationships it fosters between residents, and whether these meet their cultural expectations.

We can consider, then, our perception of space as an integrated whole, a *gestalt* built up from a variety of received sensory information which is interpreted in the context of our biological and cultural heritage. This helps us to understand why space is not simply the gap between objects, the absence that allows us to perceive the presence, but something with an impact and meaning in its own right.

The Use of Spaces

Whether spaces are conducive to the activities taking place within them is determined not only by their functional provision but also by their physical composition. We must endow the space with aesthetic qualities that fit it for its purpose.

Simonds (1983) reminds us that 'a space may be so designed to stimulate a prescribed emotional reaction or to produce a predetermined sequence of such responses.' For example, a space may suggest rest or it may induce a sense of movement, it may enclose and protect, concentrating the attention inwards, or it may frame a vista and call us on. The responses stimulated may be more complex and involve emotions such as gaiety, contemplation, awe. It is important that these responses are appropriate for the use of the space. For example, the insignificance that we feel in the presence of soaring architecture inspires humility and awe at the approach to a cathedral, but between high-rise flats it is uncomfortable or can even provoke anxiety because the feeling of being dwarfed and overlooked is out of place in what should be a safe refuge and a personal environment.

In environmental design vegetation can play a primary role in creating spaces. Outdoor 'rooms' can be enclosed by 'walls' of planting, 'floors' can be surfaced with grass, ground cover or hard materials and the 'ceiling' may consist of a tree canopy, climbers on a pergola, or be left open to the sky. 'Doorways' or 'gateways' may give access to spaces, and 'windows' can be formed by gaps in a closed canopy or merely by the natural permeability of trees and shrubs with an open branching habit. The 'decorating' and 'furnishing' of outdoor rooms with planting is supplementary to the basic spatial form, and will be dealt with in the chapters on the visual characteristics of plants and ornamental planting.

This architectural vocabulary is valuable to the planting designer for two reasons. Firstly, it reminds us that outdoor spaces, just like indoor spaces, should be designed to be used, and secondly, it identifies the structural aspects of planting which are the most important in the composition of space landscape.

The Elements of Spatial Composition

Higuchi, in *The Visual and Spatial Structure of Landscape* (1983), analysed spaces in terms of four aspects: boundaries, focus-centre-goal, directionality and domain. His comprehensive study encompassed all the elements of the landscape, including topography, water and structures, as well as vegetation. Here we shall interpret Higuchi's aspects to identify the aspects of spaces which are of primary importance for planting design.

Higuchi defines 'domain' as 'the total space that is brought together and given order by the conditions of boundary, focus-centre-goal, and directionality.' Domain also has a social connotation. It suggests ownership and territory. It is an important concept for the designer, but it is a composite property of spatial configuration and not a primary dement of composition, so we shall not discuss it further at this stage.

Higuchi's 'boundaries' include both open boundaries as well as endosing edges. Open boundaries which allow free access delineate territory but do not create space. All spatial boundaries are formed by some degree of endosure, and so our first element of spatial composition with plants will be enclosure.

'Directionality' is the sum of all the elements of composition which give directional emphasis or orientation to a space. These include shape, proportion, location of the focus, slope of the ground, even the direction of the wind or sunlight. Directional elements introduce dynamic qualities into the form of a space because they imply movement. We shall examine how the arrangement of planting affects the dynamics of space.

The 'focus-centre-goal' of a space comprises any element which is of sufficient importance to act as a visual focus (eg. a fountain or specimen tree), a natural centre (eg. the stage of an amphitheatre or the intersection of routeways) or the goal for the users (eg. a spectacular viewpoint or an archaeological site). We shall examine the role of plants as a focus.

Enclosure

Higuchi asserts that a barrier 'to be effective ... must be difficult to penetrate. It must also shut the outside world off from view while at the same time have a high degree of visibility within the domain it protects.' In other words, it must enclose, offering protection and refuge.

But enclosure need not be complete: it may be clearly defined but not an impenetrable barrier. Indeed, it is only rarely that complete closure is needed. As Barrie Greenbie (1981) points out in *Spaces*, 'The openings in the walls enclosing a space make the difference between ... an enclosure and a prison.'

The nature and location of these openings will control vision and physical movement within and between spaces. This control is essential to the design potential of enclosure. By varying the degree of enclosure and the permeability of barriers we can create spaces for different uses and moods, ranging from a contemplative enclave to a dramatic prospect point.

Degree of Enclosure

The degree of enclosure is the length of the perimeter that is enclosed by vertical planes. Different degrees of enclosure will result in spaces which vary from introverted to extroverted in their character.

Enclosure on four sides or 360 degrees. This creates the most introverted character. It is appropriate if the space is surrounded by incompatible or hostile environments, for example the earliest gardens in Persia were fully enclosed to protect them from the inhospitable climate and surrounding landscape. The Old Persian word for garden or park, *Pairidaeza is* made up from *pairi*, meaning around, and *diz*, meaning mould. Thus, to mould around an area was of the essence of garden making. A modern counterpart in temperate climates which would need protection would be a town garden in a busy urban location. Other examples are play areas, outdoor exhibitions, outdoor classrooms, music rooms and performance areas. Full enclosure will also be important for land uses which are ugly or otherwise intrusive, in order to minimise visual, sound and atmospheric pollution in surrounding areas. Examples include heavy industry, car parking, storage and service areas.

Full perimeter enclosure may be further extended to overhead enclosure. This is found in places such as dense woodland or a small courtyard shaded by the spread of a large tree. This complete surrounding creates the most private kind of place. But we should be careful because, depending on its proportions, it can be either pleasantly intimate or uncomfortably claustrophobic.

Enclosure on three sides or 270 degrees. This gives a high degree of protection or screening to the space within but also offers a directed outlook. It creates both refuge and prospect. The prospect significantly affects the character of the space by drawing the attention in the direction of the open side and beyond the implied limits of the space. Indeed, a distinct landmark or vista may become part of the identity and character of the space even though it is located beyond it.

Such a 'space with a view' would be appropriate for many gardens and play areas and also specifically for seating in towns, parks and countryside.

Plate 36   Enclosing boundary tree planting creates a protected, warm, sheltered and attractive space for informal games, walking, sunbathing and other recreation in Golden Gate Park, San Francisco. (Photo: Owen Manning)

Plate 37   Tall beech (*Fagus sylvatica*) hedges provide enclosure around the entire perimeter of this quiet rondel set within Gruga Botanical Gardens. (Photo: Owen Manning)

Enclosure on two sides or 180 degrees. This defines space half by implication and only half by actual delineation. The domain of the space will cover roughly the area of ground that would be enclosed if the two omitted sides had formed a mirror image of the actual sides. The space will have an outward looking, extroverted character with completely free access across half the boundary. Yet a sense of place, a feeling of having arrived somewhere, is engendered by the limiting and protecting functions of the two enclosing sides.

Two-sided enclosure may be 'free-standing' in a flowing, wider space. Here it will create a subsidiary protected domain. This combination of protection and orientation is made good use of by farmers in some parts of Japan where L-shaped shelter belts protect farm buildings from winter winds and snow storms.

Semi-enclosed spaces are frequently encountered in the form of niches or enclaves in the edge between open space and solid form. Such enclaves may be quite informal, occurring without deliberate design intent along the edges of dense woodland or scrub where natural undulations in the canopy or irregular, spontaneous colonisation creates a serpentine or broken edge. Despite their unplanned nature, such enclaves are an important part of the spatial structure of informal or naturelike planting where they add variety and vitality to the experience of large-scale landscapes.

In the more formal setting of many urban landscapes a semi-enclosed enclave can provide variety and incident along the edge of an enclosed route or around the boundary of a larger, dominant space. In addition, seating areas, ornamental display planting, building entrances and other gateways can all benefit from the protection combined with ease of access offered by this configuration.

Objects. If enclosure is much less than 180 degrees spatial definition is weakened and soon becomes ineffective. It the structural element is isolated rather than forming part of a structural continuum it will be experienced as a free-standing object rather than a space forming enclosure.

Although no distinct spatial boundary is defined, such an object can create a field of influence around itself. There is a tendency to feel fully under its influence, in its domain, when we are within a radius equal to the height of the object. This is

Plate 38 Informal shrub planting provides a semicircle of enclosure behind the seat giving protection and emphasising its outlook beyond this art gallery entrance court in Essen. (Photo: Owen Manning)

Plate 39 Planting forms seating enclaves along the edge of an enclosed route in Rudding Park. (Photo: Owen Manning)

DEGREES OF
ENCLOSURE

4 SIDES –
INTROVERTED

3 SIDES –
PROTECTED

2 SIDES –
EXTRAVERTED

OBJECT –
FOCUS .

Figure 4.1

only a very rough boundary, but it can be useful to be aware of it when locating key objects. These objects behave, in fact, as foci, and their effectiveness is often greatest if the boundary of their influence is reinforced and defined on the ground by physical enclosure so that they become a focus within a clearly established space. To define the space which focusses on the object can help to avoid the risks of relying on the compound influence of separate objects. This can easily create a landscape which, as a whole, is formless and without boundary; for example, a series of 'island beds' or a collection of specimen trees are in themselves unsatisfactory as a spatial composition, they are objects which need to be located in spaces and play a role within a firm spatial structure.

Permeability of Enclosure

The architecture of green spaces is constructed from plants of the different growth habits and canopy heights described in the previous chapter. These offer various combinations of visual and physical closure and openness. This permeability is as important as the degree of enclosure for the composition and the character of the space.

Visually and physically enclosed. Enclosure is complete. The boundaries of a space consist of impenetrable foliage up to a height above eye level. This will consist of shrubs with a naturally close-knit canopy to near ground level or traditional clipped hedging. There are no significant gaps in the planting, at least not below eye level, and so complete separation is achieved.

The resulting space, if enclosed around more than half of its perimeter, will offer shelter, protection and seclusion. Attention will be focussed on what is within the space rather than what is beyond it unless any openings in its enclosure and perimeter are directed towards a notable view.

Partly visually enclosed, physically enclosed. Openings which extend below eye level in the enclosing planting will form windows which allow visual penetration of the space. These may be small, allowing only carefully controlled glimpses out and in, or they may be more generous, giving a greater degree of connection between inside and outside.

Windows can be created by omitting tall (above eye level) planting in chosen positions to leave clear gaps, or they may be more loosely formed by trees and shrubs with an open habit which allow views through the tracery of their branches.

Partly visually enclosed, physically open. Shrub planting is omitted so there is no barrier to movement, but a narrow band or single line of trees clearly defines the boundary and their boles interrupt and frame views across the boundary. Trees must be managed to form a canopy above head height, and the spacing of the trunks will determine the degree of visual permeability. Comparatively dense tree planting at 1-2 metre spacing eventually forms a frame around numerous tall and narrow 'doorways'. A line of trees at wider, regular spacing would form a 'colonnade,' the trunks becoming columns supporting an arching canopy of branches and foliage above.

The advantage of this kind of spatial definition is ease of communication with surrounding spaces combined with a strong sense of place, of being somewhere.

Visually open, physically enclosed. Full visibility is achieved when planting is restricted

PERMEABILITY OF ENCLOSURE

VISUALLY & PHYSICALLY ENCLOSED

Plate 40   Full visual and physical enclosure may be desirable around visually intrusive land uses such as this car parking at Broadwater Business Park, Denham and will also provide shelter and a pleasant environment for the people using it. The trees are London planes (*Platanus x hispanica*), the tall shrubs bamboo (*Arundinaria*) and the low shrub edge is composed of *Rubus tricolor*.

PARTLY VISUALLY ENCLOSED
PHYSICALLY ENCLOSED

Plate 41   Full visual and physical enclosure gives shelter and seclusion to a public garden at Birchwood Warrington.

PARTLY VISUALLY ENCLOSED
PHYSICALLY OPEN

VISUALLY OPEN
PHYSICALLY ENCLOSED

Plate 42   Partial visual and physical enclosure results when windows and doorways are created in a wall of planting. Here they frame views across Willen Lake, Milton Keynes.

VISUALLY OPEN, PHYSICALLY OPEN

Figure 4.2

to substantially below eye level. Yet shrub planting at around knee to waist height is an effective barrier to movement. A space enclosed in this way by medium height shrub planting will be clearly defined and separated from surrounding ground, and yet allow open prospect in all directions. It will feel open even if there is only one entrance. Because of the exposed nature of such a space it is commonly used as a subsidiary space within a larger, dominant enclosure which offers a higher degree of protection. Nevertheless, medium shrub planting creates a clear boundary and can effectively define a domain where territory must be identified and easy surveillance is required.

Visually open, physically open. Domain can be defined by low planting of knee height or below. This allows complete visibility and, although it discourages movement because the surface can be difficult to walk on, it does not prevent it. Indeed, some ground covers can tolerate a moderate amount of foot traffic. The role of low planting in this kind of spatial composition is not the separating but the visual linking of distinct use areas, giving an uninterrupted flow of space between them.

Enclosure is one key element in the composition of spaces. Its degree and permeability can be manipulated by the designer to control the linkages and interrelationships between spaces. These relationships will be examined further in the sections on composite space and transitions. In addition to the enclosure of a space, the designer must understand and control its shape and relative proportions. These give a landscape composition much of its dynamic quality.

Dynamics

The dynamic qualities of space are those which create a sense of movement or rest within it.

Shape

These qualities are partly a product of the shape of the space, that is its horizontal proportions. One which approaches circular or square, pentagonal, hexagonal, etc. (though it need not be geometric and formal) suggests a place of arrival, for gatherings and focussed activities, a place for stopping and doing or simply for resting. It is static.

In contrast, a space which is longer than it is wide implies movement. It appears to lead somewhere like a street or corridor. It is dynamic, motive. The more elongated a space, the greater the directional emphasis and the desire to move through it. A familiar analogy would be that of water in a pipe. Given the same water pressure, the narrower the pipe, the faster the flow of water. Space, like water, is fluid. It is formless without containment and the shape and dimensions of that containment determine the dynamics of its flow.

The dynamics of an enclosure which is intermediate between static and linear may be ambiguous if the circulation is not defined separately by a path or other routeway. This kind of shape will have a quality of restlessness without leading anywhere in particular, but the ambiguity could be resolved by introducing a feature such as a specimen tree or other focus which creates a goal within the space.

The pattern of a shape also influences the implied speed of movement. Maurice de Sausmarez in *Basic Design: the Dynamics of Visual Form* (1964) notes that 'Rectilinear shapes and curvilinear shapes appear to have differing potentials in terms of suggested movement - in general the latter appears to move more swiftly

Plate 43　A stopping and gathering place is most successful if its shape is of largely similar horizontal proportions such as a square or a circle. This example is in museum precincts, Brussels. (Photo: Owen Manning)

Plate 44　A pond and clearing provides a natural stopping and gathering place in the woodland at Risley Moss, Warrington.

Plate 45　The extended shape of linear spaces express the functions of communication and movement. The photograph shows footpath, cycleway and carriageway firmly defined by trees, shrubs and walls in Leuven.

Plate 46　A watercourse creates a natural linear space in dense woodland at Green Park, Aston Clinton, Buckinghamshire.

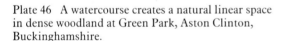

than the former', though he recognises that this is not always the case: 'For example, a star shape of a certain kind has as great an apparent speed as almost any curvilinear shape.' The star shape implies greater speed because it is made up of diagonals and acute angles. Elements of this kind of pattern are encountered in landscape in what Higuchi (1983) calls 'opening' and 'closing' spaces. An opening space has a clear beginning from which attention or movement is drawn out, for example a deeply cut valley head. A closing space funnels attention or movement into the apex which becomes a focus of the space.

Static spaces are of necessity reasonably regular. Motive spaces may be regular and symmetrical, for example a formal avenue or boulevard. But straight, uninterrupted linear spaces such as these can be either grand and impressive or dull and even daunting depending on their scale, the vistas they frame and the detail along their length. An excellent example of grand formality is the double avenue in

STATIC SPACES

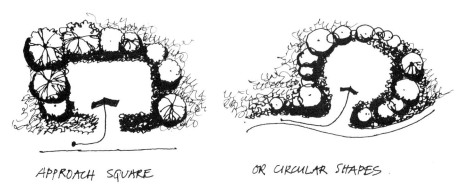

APPROACH SQUARE   OR CIRCULAR SHAPES.

MOTIVE SPACES

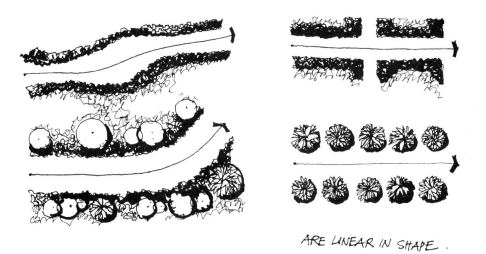

ARE LINEAR IN SHAPE.

Figure 4.3

Plate 48   If an avenue is very long and has no visual focus it may be daunting for the traveller, especially if they are on foot (Central Milton Keynes).

Plate 47   This mature avenue of plane trees (*Platanus*) leading to Castle Arenberg, Belgium is a grand and dynamic element of landscape structure.

STATIC AND MOTIVE SPACES MAY BE COMBINED

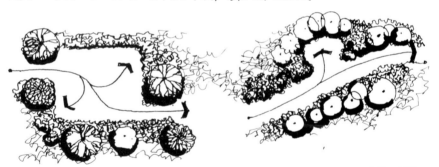

STATIC SPACES MAY BE LOCATED ON THE ROUTE OF LINEAR SPACES.

INTERMEDIATE SHAPES CAN BE AMBIGUOUS

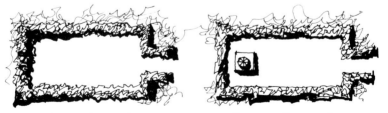

IF THEY HAVE ONLY ONE ACCESS THEY BENEFIT FROM A FOCUS OR GOAL.

Figure 4.4

LINEAR MOTIVE SPACES

WHICH ARE STRAIGHT AND SYMMETRICAL CAN BE GRAND AND IMPOSING.

IRREGULAR MOTIVE SPACES SET UP A DYNAMIC TENSION BETWEEN CONCEALMENT AND REVELATION.

Figure 4.5

Plate 49 The gate at the end of this *allee* at Hidcote, Gloucestershire provides a focus and also anticipates what may be revealed beyond it.

Plate 50 Curving linear spaces create curiosity and anticipation by concealment. The gentle curve and the flow of the landform are further enticements to explore (Ashridge, Hertfordshire).

Plate 51 This hillside promenade is fully closed
along one side but visually open along the other
giving an outlook over the distant landscape. The
waist height hedge prevents distraction by foreground
detail on the slope below the path and emphasises the
distinction between here and there. Although the view
is at once spectacular, the concealment caused by its
curving alignment promises further rewards and
draws the observer along its length
(Muncaster Castle, Cumbria).

Windsor Great Park which leads the eye gently but purposefully over the undulating parkland to focus on the impressive statue beyond.

Motive spaces may, however, gain much of their dynamism from the tension set up by the irregularities of shape. The enclosing sides may approach one another and then recede; they may be interrupted by sudden changes in direction or their density may vary along their length. The visual length of the space may be limited by bends, corners and changes in level. The concealment and anticipation that results can create a strong desire to explore and the designer can deliberately shape the space to incorporate progressions, incidents, surprises and arrivals which will create a varied and intense experience for the participators.

Vertical Proportion

The height to width ratio of a space also influences the motive forces. If it is too low, physical containment and orientation are lost. If it is too high, the impression of a deep well or trench is created and the mood is one of claustrophobia. One way of understanding this effect is to imagine that the motive pressure brought into being by the shape of the enclosure is multiplied by a factor which expresses the height to width ratio. Thus, the higher and narrower a linear space, the more urgent the sense of movement. In a static space taller enclosing sides create stronger motive forces and, although they may still be in balance, these forces have greater potential energy. If the height to width ratio is too great the space will be experienced as oppressive.

Empirical studies of architectural spaces have observed that certain proportions are generally experienced as the most satisfying. For a street these are between 1:1 and 1:2.5, and for a square between 1:2 and 1:4 (Lynch, 1971, County Council of Essex, 1973, Greater London Council, 1978). There are well-known exceptions to these rules including the deep cleft-like streets of Florence and other Italian Renaissance and mediaeval towns which give pleasant shade from the summer sun, but such narrow canyons would not be successful in the colder, greyer Northern European climate.

Although these proportions were derived from the study of spaces enclosed by buildings, they can also be considered when designing green spaces enclosed by vegetation. The ratios represent a range of proportions which feel inviting, satisfying and comfortable. They should not be taken as a hard and fast rule. The limits of comfort might be stretched in order to dramatise the contrasts felt between different spaces. For example, the designer could deliberately induce a temporary feeling of claustrophobia in order to heighten the experience of release as the participator

HEIGHT TO WIDTH RATIO OF A STATIC SPACE :

IF TOO LOW - SENSE OF ENCLOSURE IS LOST

IF TOO HIGH - THE SPACE BECOMES CLAUSTROPHOBIC

HEIGHT TO WIDTH RATIO OF A LINEAR SPACE :

IF TOO LOW - ORIENTATION IS LOST

IF TOO HIGH - ESCAPE IS URGENT.

Figure 4.6

Plate 52 The ratio of height to width of a linear space influences its dynamic qualities. A 1:1 ratio gives a strong, purposeful character (Generalife, Granada).

Plate 53 A linear space with a height to width ratio of greater than 1:1 can create a pressing sense of urgency and expectation and a consequent desire to move quickly towards its goal (Generalife, Granada).

enters a generously proportioned, warm, sunlit space beyond. Conversely, the feeling of refuge in an intimate enclosure is all the more welcome after a journey through an expanse of comparatively featureless space.

Slope

Steeply graded land may itself give enclosure and thereby define space, but the slope of the ground will also affect the dynamics of a space which is defined by planting or structures.

Sloping ground will introduce a directional quality. It may encourage ascent to a point of prospect or descent to the protection of a hollow or, if the slope is greater than approximately 1 in 3, movement will be generally restricted to the direction of the contours. Thus the orientation of the ground plane will be a dynamic element which may help determine the placing of the elements of enclosure and the shape of the space.

Focus

The focus of a civic, architectural space is often provided by a dominant building, monumental statuary or water. In a space enclosed by planting the focus could be any of these, a structure such as a pergola or arbour supporting climbers, or simply a specimen tree or group of plants. Whatever constitutes the focus it must be clearly distinct from its surroundings and of strong character. Indeed, its special character may imbue the space with much of its identity.

In large-scale spaces or in the composite landscape a focus may be perceived as a landmark. Lynch (1971) and Greenbie (1981) both report the significance of local landmarks such as churches, old buildings and parks for the identity of districts or urban areas. A single grand old tree might have equal presence and renown as a landmark.

Symmetric Focus

A static space with an internal, more or less central focus which terminates sight lines is described as centric (French, 1983). The axes of symmetry inherent in the shape of the space will be emphasised by the location of the focus at or near their intersection.

The motive forces remain evenly balanced and a sense of calm and often of strict formality will result. Such an arrangement is very simple but is found in some of the finest examples of spatial design in history, eg. Piazza of St. Peter, Rome and Islamic courts and gardens. Although the design of a formal, centric space is distinguished by its apparent economy of effort, it is far from easy to accomplish. Inexperienced designers frequently place foci and other objects in the middle of a space and the result is often clumsy and prosaic. Successful design of a centric symmetrical space requires as much flair and sensitivity as for asymmetric, informal

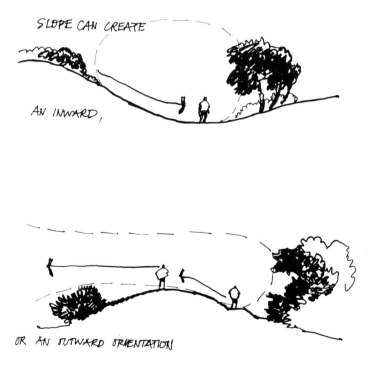

Figure 4.7

Plate 54 The focus of a space can be provided by a single specimen tree of sufficient stature. In this urban space in Brugge it also makes a natural informal gathering place.

design. The space must be of appropriate, simple layout of classic proportion, and the greatest attention to detail is needed throughout.

Asymmetric Focus

When any object is located in a defined space motive forces are brought into being between the object and the boundaries of the space. The strength of those forces depends on the proximity of the object and boundaries, and on the overall geometry of the space. This principle is understood in the visual arts (de Sausmarez, 1964) and in architecture (Ching, 1979).

If the focus of a static space is located off-centre the sum of the motive forces introduces a dynamic quality to the spatial composition. The imbalance gives a directional emphasis. Another way of understanding this is to picture the implied

A FOCUS OR LANDMARK

BY CAREFUL LOCATION CAN IMBUE A SPACE WITH ITS OWN SPECIAL CHARACTER.

Figure 4.8

A SYMMETRIC FOCUS

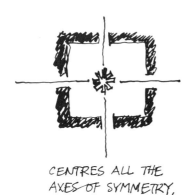

CENTRES ALL THE
AXES OF SYMMETRY,

OR SELECTS ONE
AXIS OF SYMMETRY.

Figure 4.9

AN ASYMMETRIC FOCUS

ADDS DYNAMISM TO
A STATIC SPACE

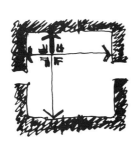

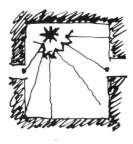

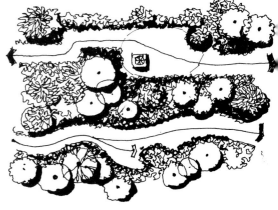

Figure 4.10

OR ADDS TO THE DYNAMISM OF A LINEAR SPACE

division of the space by its focus. Asymmetric focus implies division into unequal parts and so creates a progression through sub-divisions, normally in order of magnitude, and the place of arrival is the focus itself or somewhere within its immediate zone of influence.

Thus, an asymmetric focus introduces movement and rest within a space. This dynamic tension contributes much to the character of a space and yet is independent of the nature of the focal element itself. The dynamics would be the same if the focus were an obelisk, a fountain or a specimen tree.

Focus on the Boundary

The focus of a space may be part of, or located on, its boundary. For example, an entrance, by virtue of its function as an access point or because it allows attractive glimpses into an adjacent space, may be the centre of attention. In the absence of another focal element the main entrance will become the focus of the space.

Part of the enclosing boundary structure, if it is sufficiently distinct, may act as the focus. For example, planting which encloses may also be spectacular in colour or form, providing the main eye-catcher from within the space.

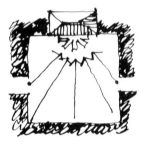

ON THE BOUNDARY.

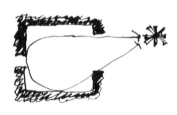

BEYOND THE SPACE

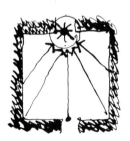

THE ENTRANCE MAY
BE THE PRIMARY FOCUS

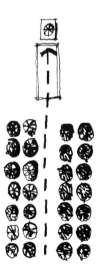

Figure 4.11a   Figure 4.11b

A focus which is located within or on the edge of a space clearly belongs to that space because it is an integral part of its composition and is chiefly or only visible from within. An internal focus emphasises the feeling of arrival, of achieving the goal, of completeness.

External Focus

A prominent landmark which is visible from most of a separate space can act as a focus of that space even if it is some distance away. It will give orientation by creating

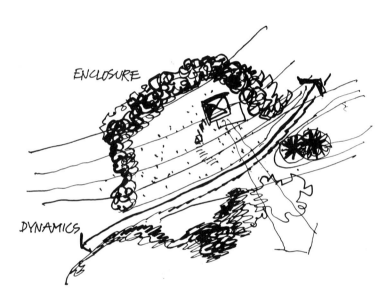

Figure 4.12

a visual axis between it and the space, and it will also help to endow the space with a particular identity, a sense of place because it is visually included within it. The external focus will be part of the experience of the space.

An external focus can be used to emphasise orientation which is already inherent in the shape or degree of enclosure. A common example is the placing of a monument, statue or fountain beyond the end of an avenue where it terminates the long, straight vista.

So far we have examined the composition of single spaces. But no space exists in isolation. It will always be part of a sequence through which we pass and which gives relative meaning to each particular space. We shall now examine how the relationships between spaces determine our experience of the landscape as a whole.

CHAPTER 5

Composite Space

Movement is fundamental to our experience of landscape. Out of doors we spend much of our time on a journey of one kind or another, either casually passing through whilst *en route* to somewhere else or deliberately exploring. To view an unchanging scene from a fixed position is the exception rather than the rule.

Our interaction with the outdoor environment consists of a myriad of sensory events. These include the most common everyday sights, sounds and smells and also the unexpected - a surprise view, or a shrub opening its first flower of the season. As we move through the landscape we enter and leave spaces, we pause to examine something unusual, and we encounter people, animals and plants. These are events which happen in a chronological sequence. The experience of landscape is a journey in time as well as in space. The structure of the composite landscape which consists of the spaces created by the arrangement of landform, built structures and vegetation, also controls the unfolding experience of the participant. Because our perception of an event is affected to some extent by everything that has gone before, the position of a space in sequence will affect our experience of it.

In the design process we begin to synthesize ideas by determining the kind of spaces required by the character of the site and the activities of the users. The next step is to understand the place of each space in the composite landscape, to determine its relationship with other spaces. There are two keys to this relationship, the kind of organization we adopt for a related group of spaces and the nature of the transitions between adjacent spaces.

Spatial Organisations

If we observe spaces as we move through the landscape we see that there are a number of fundamentally different kinds of organisation. These depend on the relative locations of spaces and the circulation patterns which will link them. The architect Francis Ching, in *Architecture: Form, Space and Order* (1979), describes various types of organisations of rooms, courtyards, squares and streets. If we study these carefiflly we see that three of his types: linear, clustered and centralised organisations, are 'primary' organisations, that is, they cannot be made up from or subsumed under any other type. All of these primary organisations can be found in landscape as well as architecture and they offer a means of analysing and understanding composite landscape space.

Linear Organisations

A linear organisation is a serial progression of spaces. It is associated with a single circulation route which may either pass through each space in turn, or may follow the line of spaces in parallel and give separate access to each space. The direction of the progression may be straight, angled, curved or irregular, but the line is unbroken with a beginning and an end.

The form of each space within the series may be similar, or size, shape and enclosure may vary according to function and symbolic status. The spaces at either end of the line will have a special importance because they initiate and terminate the sequence. The significance of intermediate spaces is articulated by their location in relation to the overall direction of the series or by their size, shape and focal elements.

A linear organisation of spaces is experienced as a progression of limited but separate places in a definite order and building up to a climax at some point within the line. The climax or goal is often, but not necessarily, at one end.

This kind of organisation is well suited for the approach to an important place or building. It allows careful control of the design elements to promote anticipation, excitement and a strong sense of arrival. Examples of how vegetation can achieve this are found in the wooded approach to the J.F.Kennedy memorial at Runnymede, near Windsor, and in the sequence of land and tree formed spaces which are strung together along the valley of the River Skell and culminate in the view of and appoach to the ruins of Fountain's Abbey at Studley Royal, North Yorkshire. Both the outward and the return journey may, of course, include other incidents and interest, but these should support rather than compete with the primary objective.

Clustered Organisations

Ching (1979) shows that a cluster of spaces forms a different kind of organisation in which its constituent spaces are related primarily by their proximity to one another or to an entry point or a path. He also introduces the role of symmetry as a means

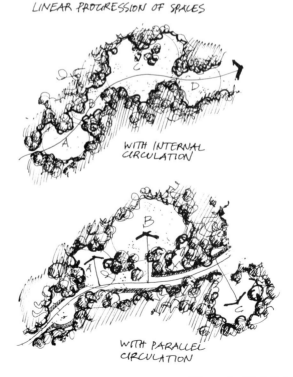

Figure 5.1   (Drawn by Nick Robinson)

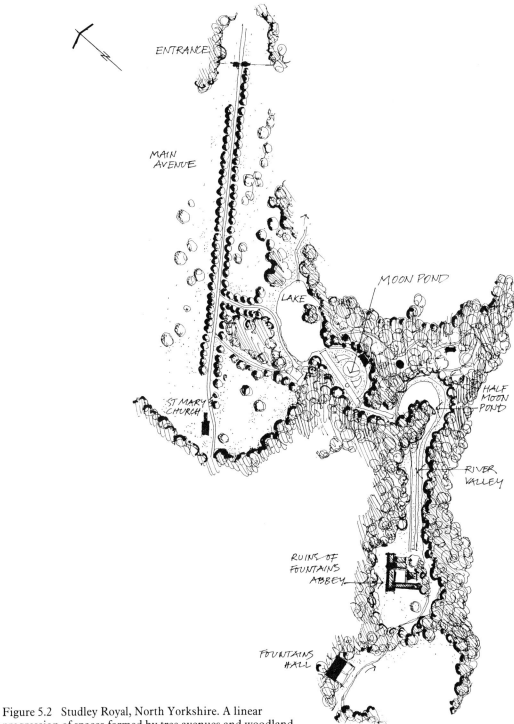

ENTRANCE

MAIN
AVENUE

MOON POND

LAKE

HALF
MOON
POND

ST MARY
CHURCH

RIVER
VALLEY

RUINS OF
FOUNTAINS
ABBEY

FOUNTAINS
HALL

Figure 5.2 Studley Royal, North Yorkshire. A linear
progression of spaces formed by tree avenues and woodland
clearings along the valley of the River Skell, culminating in
the ruins of Fountains Abbey. (Drawn by Nick Robinson)

Plate 56   A linear progression of spaces in an urban park in Sheffield. The enclosing structure planting is edged with ornamental shrubs and the path provides both a connecting route and a strong visual element in the composition. (Photo: Owen Manning)

Plate 55   Woodland glades separated by groves of birch (*Betula pendula*) in a Bristol park form a linear progression of spaces explored by a sinuous path. (Photo: Owen Manning)

Plate 57   The impressive view from the lawn in front of the house at Stowe in Buckinghamshire penetrates a series of three parkland spaces enclosed by belts and clumps of trees and focuses on the Corinthian Arch on the horizon.

CLUSTERED SPACES
RELATED BY PROXIMITY

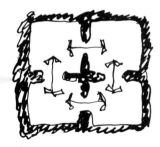

TO EACH OTHER

TO A SHARED ENTRY

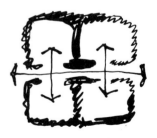

TO AN ACCESS PATH

Figure 5.3

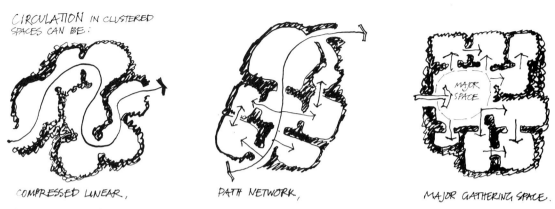

CIRCULATION IN CLUSTERED SPACES CAN BE:

COMPRESSED LINEAR,   PATH NETWORK,   MAJOR GATHERING SPACE.

Figure 5.4

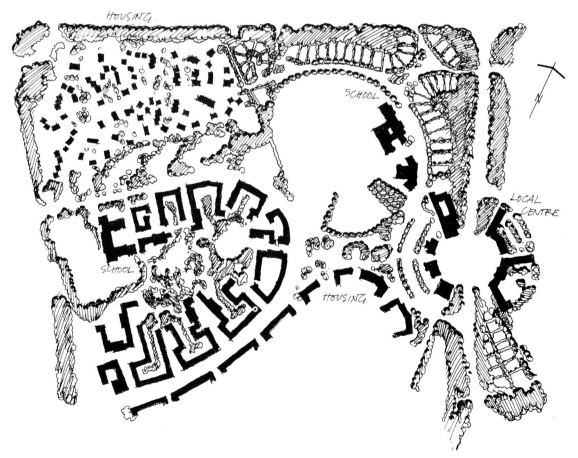

Figure 5.5   Neath Hill, Milton Keynes. Residential, park and garden spaces cluster around a central open space.
(Drawn by Nick Robinson)

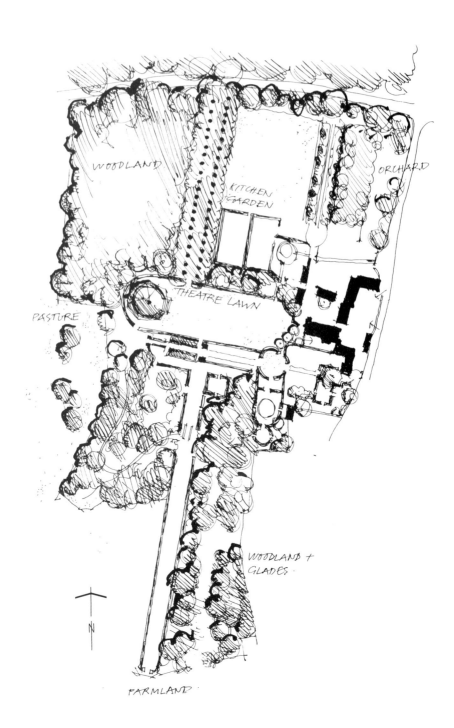

Figure 5.6   Hidcote Manor, Gloucestershire. A complex of spaces clustered around the Theatre Lawn and organised about two major axes at right angles. (Drawn by Nick Robinson)

of ordering clustered spaces. The axis of symmetry acts like a perceptual, if not physical, path linking as well as reflecting the spaces it divides.

Circulation among clustered spaces can take a variety of forms. If each space leads on to only one other, the effect would be of a linear organisation which has been compressed into a concentrated area. A more common and more useful arrangement is a network of paths connecting spaces according to their function and significance. A primary path might give access to the main spaces and the remainder are entered either by way of intermediate spaces or secondary paths. Another method is to create a major gathering and distribution space such as a city square or performance arena which, although static not linear, gives access to all the spaces adjoining its perimeter. The gathering space is often the largest and most important due to its strategic position and close proximity to all the other spaces. A fine example of such a gathering space is the Theatre Lawn at Hidcote Manor in Gloucestershire. The Central Gathering Space at the Glasgow Garden Festival of 1988 was designed to help people orientate themselves on the festival site and as a place for rendevous as well as being a venue for various entertainments.

A clustered organisation of spaces is suited to a number of similar or related activities but which require their own separate domains. A common example is

TYPES OF CONTAINED SPATIAL ORGANISATION

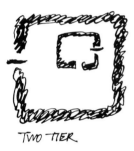

TWO TIER

TWO TIER CONCENTRIC

TWO TIER ASYMMETRIC MULTIPLE SUBDIVISION

THREE TIER

THREE TIER ASYMMETRIC MULTIPLE SUBDIVISION

Figure 5.7

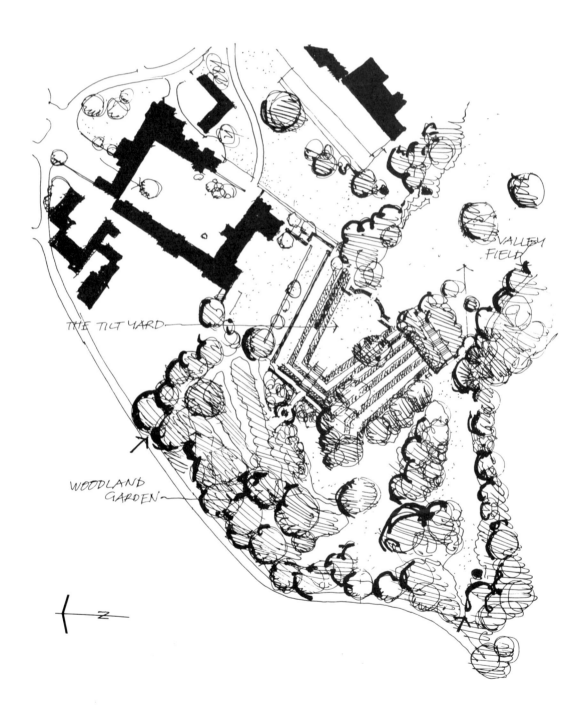

THE TILT YARD

VALLEY FIELD

WOODLAND GARDEN

N

Figure 5.8 Dartington Hall, Devon. The Tilt Yard is the focal space contained within enveloping woodland. (Drawn by Nick Robinson)

provided by the private gardens, public courts and streets, play areas and neighbourhood parks within a residential area. The circulation network should allow the resident or visitor to choose whether to include or exclude some of the spaces. This is different from a linear sequence which would offer only one path, only one prescribed sequence of experience. Intricate and varied sequences of clustered spaces can be found, for example, in Chinese gardens where indoor, outdoor and intermediate, covered spaces are gathered together within the confines of the enclosing boundary wall.

Contained Organisations

One or more spaces may be contained within a larger, all embracing enclosure. Ching's 'centralised organisation' is one kind of contained organisation. The contained spaces may be fully enclosed themselves and so separate from the surrounding space, or they may be only partially enclosed yet still possess a domain which is clearly differentiated from that of the larger space. A fine example of a contained space is found in the Tilt Yard in the gardens of Dartington Hall, Devon. This beautifully proportioned space is defined by grass terraces, yew hedges and shrub planting, but resides within the protection of a woodland belt of forest trees on rising ground which bounds and encloses the gardens as a whole.

A contained organisation may be two tiered (a space within a space), three tiered, four tiered and so on, although in practice it is rare to find contained organisations with more than three tiers out of doors. Any tier within the containing space may consist of more than one space.

The organisation may be concentric (a centralised organisation) or the contained spaces may be distributed asymmetrically according to the requirements of circulation and other usage.

Unlike linear series and clusters of spaces, a contained organisation depends for its effectiveness on the relative sizes of the constituent spaces. If a contained space is very much smaller than the containing space, it takes on the character and role of a focus of that larger space. It is perceived from the dominant space like an object rather than a second domain which can be entered and explored. On the other hand, if the smaller space is too large then the larger, containing space will have insufficient domain, and will lose its separate and dominant identity. In this case, either the two sets of boundaries simply reinforce one another to form a double boundary, or a space of linear form is created between the boundaries which becomes an encircling path.

The experience of contained spaces is of deepening involvement, of progressive penetration of boundaries, of gradual approach towards the heart of the composition. Any of the spaces making up a contained organisation may be dominant by virtue of the relative size, the strength of its enclosure, or the influence of the focus. However, it is often either the largest space or the innermost space which dominates. The largest space because of the extent and height of its enclosure, or the innermost space because it is the goal of the composition. The remaining, subsidiary spaces should play a supporting role, adding diversity and incident, subdividing domains or offering protection for and a prelude to the innermost space.

Hierarchy of Spaces

Linear, clustered and contained organisations will all have some degree of hierarchy in their constituent spaces, that is, there will be differentiation in the status and function of spaces. Like a hierarchy of positions within a company organisation, a

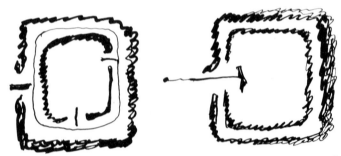

A CONTAINED SPACE
WHICH IS TOO SMALL
BECOMES AN OBJECT

A CONTAINED SPACE WHICH IS TOO LARGE CREATES
EITHER A CIRCULATING PATH OR A DOUBLE,
REINFORCED BOUNDARY.

Figure 5.9

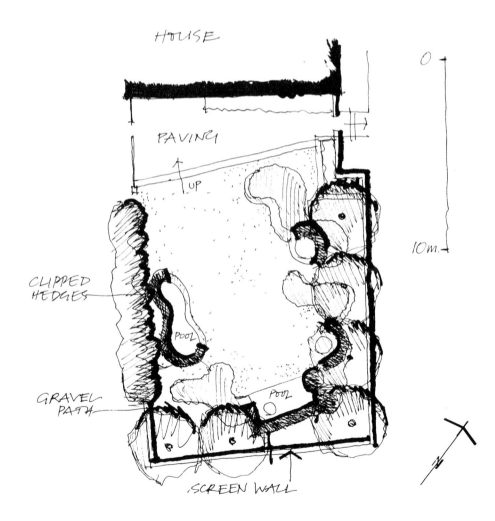

Figure 5.10 Garden at Newport Rhode Island by Christopher Tunnard, 1949. The lawn, enclosed by clipped hedges, is contained within the boundary wall and tree planting. (Drawn by Nick Robinson)

hierarchy of spaces may be 'vertical' or 'horizontal'. The number of levels in the hierarchy will depend on the purpose and the character of the spatial organisation.

Hierarchy According to Function

Ashihara, in his book *Exterior Design in Architecture* (1970), describes the hierarchical order of spaces in terms of their uses. He lists the following pairs of functional opposites:

exterior ....interior
public..private
big groups..small group
amusement..quiet, artistic
sport ....non-movement, cultural

Any single space will occupy a position somewhere along the continua between these opposites. The successful design of composite space will depend on understanding and articulating the position of each of its constituent spaces in the hierarchy.

The hierarchy of space between exterior and interior may be well developed such that moving between outdoors and indoors we pass through a sequence of spaces in which each is more sheltered and more enclosed than its predecessor. This would allow us to adapt gradually to the change, or to choose a place to pause or rest which has just the right combination of indoor and outdoor qualities for the weather and our mood at that time. Traditional Oriental gardens provide a delightful example of this kind of spatial hierarchy with verandahs, covered walkways, sheltered terraces, walled enclosures and roofed pavilions linking the larger outdoor spaces with the intimacy of indoor rooms.

At the other extreme, the transition from an extensive exposed outdoor space to complete protection within a building might be made, literally, in one step. This simplest of hierarchies, containing only two opposites, can be found, for example, in rural cottages and other buildings standing alone in an expansive landscape There is drama in such a sudden exposure to the elements or the plunge from sunlight into dimness and intimacy within. Although it lacks the variety of a multi-levelled hierarchy, a single threshold can offer impact and excitement.

The hierarchical organization of outdoor-indoor space is articulated primarily by degree of enclosure. The extension of structures from a building to enclose the surrounding space is the most effective way of creating 'semi-outdoor' spaces, because these structures are obviously associated with the building. Plants are more strongly associated in our minds with the outdoors so, in the creation of intermediate spaces, plants are best employed in a supporting or furnishing role, eg. climbers on a trellis or an overhead pergola.

The hierarchy of public-private spaces is a hierarchy of territories which belong to increasingly small numbers of people. It is expressed in its most elaborate form in complex urban areas where it can provide a vital framework for social interaction, a way of giving shape to and bringing together what Greenbie (1981) calls the 'community of strangers'. Entirely public places are found in city squares and shopping streets. Complete privacy is found in the home and its immediate, enclosed curtilage. A number of writers (primarily Newman, 1972) have shown that positive social interaction and responsibility is facilitated by a hierarchy of spaces which make a staged transition between these two extremes. Each stage is a different domain with clearly identifiable ownership. People need defensible space between their private domain and the anonymous crowd. Although the importance of

SPATIAL HIERARCHY:

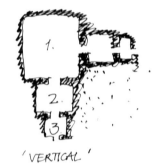

'VERTICAL'

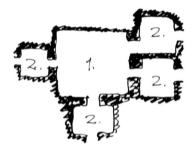

'HORIZONTAL'

Figure 5.11

HIERARCHY OF CLUSTERED SPACES

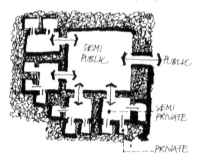

Figure 5.12

HIERARCHY IN CONTAINED
ORGANISATIONS:

THE INEVITABLE DOMINANCE OF THE
CONTAINING SPACE IS EMPHASISED BY
ITS GREATER HEIGHT OF ENCLOSURE

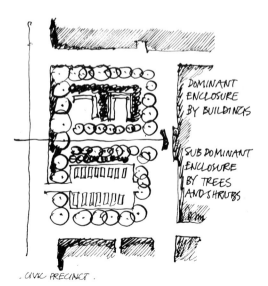

. CIVIC PRECINCT .

Figure 5.12

Figure 5.13

territorial hierarchies has been discussed in an urban context, the spatial structure may be found in part by planting as well as built elements of landscape. As we have seen, planting can create boundaries with different degrees of permeability to suit the need for separation between spaces. The hedge is one of the oldest ways of marking the boundary of a territory.

Outdoor-indoor and public-private hierarchies provide two examples of how the form and relative location of spaces helps to clarify and facilitate the kind and intensity of use.

Transitions

As we move through and explore our environment we are constantly crossing boundaries of one kind or another. Many of these are so familiar to us that we take them entirely for granted; for example, entering our own front garden or turning into our own street. Other boundaries assert their presence with more force; we may think twice before crossing them and the experience of penetration may be quite dramatic, such as when we enter an enclosed courtyard visible and accessible only through a gate in a wall, or enter the shelter and darkness of a wood from an exposed sunny meadow.

The transition between one space and the next can take many forms, but its precise nature will do much to influence our experience of the space we are entering. Our first view of a place, like our first impression of a person, sets the scene for an acquaintance. The transition is formed by the arrangement of the planes which separate and enclose the two spaces. This will determine how much of the domain of space is visible before crossing the boundary, and how quickly the full extent of its domain is revealed.

At one extreme, overlapping enclosure forms the most abrupt transition which completely hides the space until we have crossed the boundary and its domain is suddenly revealed. This creates suspense and surprise because we do not know quite what to expect until we have arrived. It offers an unknown territory to be explored, and requires a sense of curiosity and commitment on the part of the visitor. In contrast, two spaces might flow gently and gradually into one another such that most of the domain is visible before it is entered. The boundary between these spaces is only suggested, not rigidly defined, so a less definite intention is needed to enter. Between these two extremes can be found a variety of transitions which are more or less abrupt. In general, the more abrupt the transition, the more deliberate the act of entry must be.

The transition between two spaces will also vary according to what Ching (1979) calls the relationship between the two spaces. He identifies four conditions: a space within a space, interlocking spaces, adjacent (abutting) spaces, and spaces linked by a common space. The first of these is an example of two-tiered contained spatial organisation.

The remaining three relationships can be understood as a condition of the transition between spaces. Thus, the shared domain of interlocking spaces plays the role of a transitional zone; the threshold between adjacent abutting spaces will be at the 'neck', where the passage between them is narrowest; and a common space linking two other spaces is a specifically transitional space analogous to the lobby or porch of a building. We will now examine some of the variations which these spatial relationships offer for the imaginative design of transitions.

Transitions Between Abutting Spaces

This may be a simple gap in a separating hedge or other screen planting. The gap

TRANSITIONS AND ENTRIES:

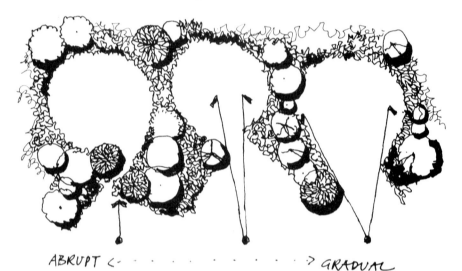

ABRUPT <- . . . . -> GRADUAL

Figure 5.14

Plate 58   A gap of a little more than the path width in tall and medium shrub planting creates an informal but concise transition between intensively detailed building curtilage and the more extensive parkland beyond (Hounslow Civic Centre and park, London).

may be emphasised or elaborated by 'pillars' or an overhead canopy to create an archway rather than simply a gap. Changes in level of the ground plane can further articulate the transition, separating the two spaces by height as well as by enclosure. The width of the gap will determine the conciseness of the transition. An overlapping screen can be added within one of the spaces in order to prevent any view into the adjacent space. Abutting spaces could be separated by a permeable enclosing plane which allows visual and physical penetration over a wider area but still clearly distinguishes one domain from the other.

Transitions Between Interlocking Spaces

The zone which is shared by two interlocking spaces may be defined by low planting, in which case a gradual transition is created which allows a prospect of both spaces as we approach the boundary. Because the two spaces overlap, not one but two boundaries will be crossed. We enter the domain of one space before we leave that

ENTRANCES

OVERLAPPING ENCLOSURE GIVES COMPLETE SURPRISE

A NARROW GAP ATTRACTS INTENSE ATTENTION

ITS IMPORTANCE CAN BE ENHANCED BY OVERHEAD ENCLOSURE

OR A GREATER VISUAL CONNECTION MAY BE DESIRED.

Figure 5.15

Plate 59   A simple narrow gap in an enclosing hedge overhung with the branch of a nearby tree provides a concise transition. The point of entry is precisely defined and a glimpse of what is within is revealed. This public park was once the Bundesgartenschau at Mannheim. (Photo: Owen Manning)

Plate 60   An overlapping entrance ensures complete surprise on entering the space (Bodnant, North Wales).

Plate 61   A gradual transition is made between two distinct spaces but dynamic tension is created by the sinuous curve of the grass path, by the gap which first narrows and then widens, and by the locations of the clumps of trees being offset either side of the opening (Askham Bryan College, York).

Plate 62   This transition is made in stages. As the observer skirts the lake at Stowe, Buckinghamshire new views are opened and the far paddock is revealed in carefully controlled sequence. Finally the focus of the space, the Palladian Bridge, will come into view.

of another so the transition is made in stages. If the shared zone is defined by a continuation of the visual and physical enclosure which delineates the spaces proper, then an overlapping screened entrance is created. If the size of the overlapping zone is large enough and it is clearly distinguished from its parent spaces it could legitimately be called a transitional space in its own right.

Transitional Spaces

An intermediate, transitional space is separated from the spaces it links by some

Plate 63   Trees and shrubs create a small but well defined transitional space between the precinct in the foreground and the courtyard beyond the arch at Leuven, Belgium. (Photo: Owen Manning)

form of enclosure and it has it own distinct character. Yet because it is primarily a routeway and it is subsidiary to the spaces it links, its character should be comparatively subdued; it should prepare us for the next space and link the two in our minds as well as physically. The three spaces will form a linear organisation, and will include two entrances or subsidiary transitions.

Entrance Zones

The more concise transitions which form distinct entrances are strategically important parts of a space. They are a visual focus, and become gathering and meeting areas for people; for example, the main doors leading into a building, and a gateway leading into a courtyard. The entrances to larger spaces give rise to zones of confluence, where people come together and into close proximity with the enclosing elements of the space; for example, the entrance to an auditorium or stadium, or a large public park. Because it will come under close scrutiny, the detail of an entrance zone must be given careful attention, and may be designed at a more intimate scale than general boundary planting. Entrances and transitional spaces offer great scope for the eloquent expression of the relationship between spaces and, in hierarchical arrangements, of the relationship between the people that use them.

On a particular site we may be blessed with a landscape which benefits from a strong existing spatial structure and organisation. This existing structure may need to be strengthened, modified or added to in order to accommodate fully the changes in land use. Many sites, on the other hand, have little or no existing spatial structure; for example, some derelict land and demolition sites. Here spaces must be created and organised anew to suit the new uses planned for the site. To meet the functional brief, however, is only part of the design objective.

The form and character of the site itself, the spirit of the place, should determine what uses and spaces are appropriate. The site may suggest spatial form and organisation. For example, a site with a fine prospect would suggest an outward looking space or spaces, while hostile environs would require a more defensive, inward looking arrangement. A site with small scale, undulating topography would

Plate 64 A larger transitional space enclosed by beech (*Fagus sylvatica*) hedges and pleached lime trees (*Tilia*) forms the entrance zone to a public park in Oakwood, Warrington.

preclude uninterrupted extensive space, and would suggest a more intimate, human scale organisation of enclosures. A steeply sloping site would most easily accommodate a series of elongated spaces strung out along the contours.

In the next chapter we shall return to the characteristics of individual plants and examine the visual properties and decorative qualities of forms, foliage, flowers and fruits which clothe the skeletal structure of outdoor spaces and bring them to life.

CHAPTER 6

The Visual Properties of Plants

Planting which is primarily structural, as well as creating spaces, will also endow plants with some of the visual properties which they possess. The character of the foliage, bark, flowers and fruit of avenue trees, for example, all contribute to the aesthetic qualities of the space, even though they may be secondary in importance to the structural characteristics of form and spacing. Other planting within a space may have a more strictly ornamental role being used to provide aesthetic highlights and special details which add to the spatial and visual character created by the structure planting. A display border within a hedged enclosure is an example of stictly ornamental planting. For this the decorative characteristics of the plants will be of primary importance.

Before we examine these characteristics in detail it should be stressed that decorative does not necessarily mean elaborate. Just as the decoration of a room in a house can be plain and simple, even minimal at times, the decoration of an outdoor space might rely on the simplest of plantings for its effect.

Subjective and Objective Responses to Plants

We all have personal responses to particular plants and combinations of plants. As designers, however, we should have a model of planting aesthetics which will help us to provide for the whole range of people, places and functions that we are likely to meet in the course of our work. It is possible to analyse the aesthetic qualities of plants in a systematic way and to use the understanding gained to construct a model which both explains certain observed effects and helps us create the effects that we want.

Firstly, we can separate subjective responses to plants from their objective qualities which we can be confident will be perceived by all observers, albeit with varying degrees of sensitivity. Tanguy and Tanguy (1985) distinguish what they call the 'objective plant' and the 'subjective plant'. The objective plant consists of all the features or physical attributes which can be described and agreed upon by different people. Those people may have different interpretations and preferences but they will largely agree on features such as plant habit, leaf shape and leaf size.

The subjective plant, however, consists of the observer's interpretation of the objective plant. Many plants have strong associations and symbolic meanings both for individuals and for groups of people with a common culture. For example, the red rose is given as a symbol of love and respect. It has many other associations and symbolic roles, for example as a tribal or political emblem: the white rose of York, the red rose of Lancaster. The rose is one of the oldest of cultivated ornamentals, and so has many associations throughout the Western world. Its association with the rites and rituals of human societies probably dates back as far as the Minoan civilisation in Crete around 2000 BC. A fresco unearthed by Sir Arthur Evans near Knossos included a rose resembling the Holy Rose of Abyssinia, a form of *Rosa damascena* (Thomas, 1983).

A more recent example of the power of association to influence people's choice of plants is provided by the common evergreen laurels. Cherry Laurel (*Prunus laurocerasus*), Portugal Laurel (*P. lusitanicus*) and Japanese Laurel (*Aucuba japonica*), along with a number of other common evergreens, including Holly (*Ilex aquifolium*) and the hardy hybrid group of rhododendrons, were much planted by the Victorians in large private gardens and in public parks. Because of the general resilience of these species and their ability to tolerate the severe atmospheric pollution prevalent in industrial areas until the 1950s, they have survived in large numbers and thrived where the choice flowering shrubs have been lost. The unrelieved evergreen shrubberies of these species now create a distinct atmosphere of dark, often gloomy enclosure, and have come to be associated with the more melancholy and oppressive aspects of Victorian culture. As a result they are now planned less often than is merited by their objective characteristics of growth and appearance.

Let us leave the realm of associations and fashions and return to some of the important attributes which attract people to plants. In the countryside we admire the rugged and picturesque forms of wind sculpted trees. We notice the wealth of colour to be found simply in the greens of summer foliage and, later, the fruit and leaf colours of autumn shine brilliantly and dramatically, a poignant climax to the season. The whole landscape is enlivened through the year by the changing weather and light, and its green mantle is soothed by gentle breezes and exhilarated by gusts of wind.

In gardens and other ornamental planting we discover spectacular exotic species and the extravagant creations of plant breeders. These ornamentals are grown and celebrated for the sheer beauty of their flowers, their powerful fragrance and the decorative qualities of their leaves and bark. Features such as these are all memorable aesthetic attributes, and they can make the individual plants objects of great character and beauty. Indeed, the majority of plants, when regarded as individual living things, offer much aesthetic pleasure. Even the most gaudy hybrids or the strangest sports give pleasure to some people.

The ornamental highlights of flower and fruit can be regarded as special effects because they are enjoyed for only a short period. More subtle, but no less delightful, are the sight and sound of plants moving in the wind, and the changing patterns of shadows cast on walls and ground. These are especially welcome in built up environments where they offer a lively complement and contrast to the unyielding geometry of much architecture and engineering. In addition to these delightful but transient effects, planting should be designed to look good throughout the year, and regardless of the weather. The best way to achieve this is to create a permanent visual foundation using the enduring qualities of foliage, bark and habit. These esssentials should form an attractive composition in their own right, as well as support the transient displays of flowers, fruit and other special effects.

In planting design a keen aesthetic sense is needed to create a composition which both brings out the best qualities of the individual plants and is effective as a whole. This may be partly intuitive for the designer, particularly if they have a wide plant knowledge, but design intuition is strengthened and can be further developed by an understanding of the aesthetic characteristics of plants and the principles of composition; that is, by a knowledge of what to look for in plants and how to make the most effective use of these qualities.

The Analysis of Visual Characteristics

The appearance of a plant or association of plants can be analysed in terms of certain visual properties. Form, line, texture and colour are the basic elements of visual composition. Although they are more abstract than the special effects of flowers, fruits and the like, these properties are fundamental to understanding composition. They allow us to describe both the aesthetic character of a particular plant, and to arrive at principles for the combination of plants to form an effective whole. We shall begin by examining each element in turn.

Form

The form of a plant is its three dimensional shape. It can be observed from various directions and distances and these affect the shapes presented to the eye. It can be explored at close quarters, or rather the space around the plant can be explored. This space may become in places quite small and intimately entangled with the solid form of the plant.

For example, the form of a mature oak in open parkland will appear, from a distance of around 500 metres, as a spreading dome with some gentle irregularity in the outline with part of the bole visible below the canopy if the lower branches have been grazed. At medium distance, say 100 metres, the sheaves of foliage arising from the main limbs will be visible as more or less distinct, projecting parts of the canopy and the major branches within will be discernible in places. Thus, from this distance the form will appear as a rough dome with an undulating surface penetrated by gaps. If we approach within a few metres of the tree or under the spread of the canopy, the form of the oak will be understood to be far more complex than could be appreciated from afar, and to include quite different shapes and qualities. The rugged, cylindrical shapes of bole and branches will be dominant and the spaces between the branches and bunches of foliage will form an important part of the character of the tree. Details such as the shape of a typical spray of foliage or individual leaves will be more clearly perceived than the overall shape of the tree.

Form is an important aesthetic criterion for species selection. Although plant form is wonderfully varied, we can group them into a number of major types, and each of these has a distinct role in composition. These categories of form will now be described with a view to exploring their aesthetic potential. It is not an attempt at a rigorous classification of plants. In the examples given we will assume reasonably favourable growing conditions and a sheltered but not crowded location. It is essential to remember that the actual form of a particular plant depends to a considerable extent on environmental conditions, especially light and wind exposure, and that overall form can be one of the most variable characteristics within a species.

Prostrate and carpeting forms. A number of shrubs and herbaceous plants have a distinctly prostrate form. These include ground hugging creeping plants which spread by the layering, or rooting, of their prostrate stems at intervals, and which rarely produce ascending stems (eg. *Hedera* spp., *Cotoneaster dammeri*, *Lamiastrum galeobdolon*). There are also a number of shrubs which produce woody stems held above ground level but which constitute low, horizontally spreading masses of foliage (*Juniperus horizontalis*, *J. sabina tamariscifolia*, *Cotoneaster horizontalis*, *Prunus laurocerasus* 'Zabelliana').

Carpeting plants are those which form a neat canopy of constant height, close to ground level (eg. *Hypericum calycinum*, *Pachysandra terminalis*, *Lamium maculatum*).

Many carpeting plants are fast spreaders, increasing by means of vigorous underground stems (see Chapter 8). Although the shoots of carpeting plants are more or less upright, these are mostly hidden by leaves and the plant presents a dense plane of foliage parallel to the surface of the ground. Prostrate and carpeting forms hug the ground surface and so express rather than hide its shape. For this reason they can be used to emphasise ground modelling. In addition, their low stature makes them successful as a foundation or foil to more dynamic plant forms and taller specimens.

Hummock and dome forms. Many low growing plants spread by means of a gradually increasing rootstock (see Chapter 8) rather than vigorous, searching propagative stems. They form enlarging clumps which, if planted as a monoculture, will eventually unite. These clumps are often rounded in form and create a hummocky ground cover (eg. *Festuca glauca* and other grasses, *Geranium* spp. and *Nepeta faassenii*). A similar ground covering hummock form is typical of many sub-shrubs (plants with a woody stem base below herbaceous growth which may die back in a cold winter) and dwarf shrubs. These spread by lateral growth of branches from the main stems or, in some cases, propagate new plants by the layering of these stems (eg. *Lavandula spica*, *Erica* spp. and the lapponicum rhododendrons).

A domed, rounded form is perhaps the commonest found amongst larger, broadleaved shrubs and trees. In the case of trees this dome is normally supported on a single massive bole from which lateral branches arise. The canopy of a shrub normally develops from a number of main stems arising at, or very close to, ground level. Domed form is often found in the mature form of species which at earlier stages display more upright habit. We should also remember that the forms of trees in particular are dramatically modified by environmental factors. The canopy dome is held high aloft both in dense woodland as a result of suppression of the lower branches and in urban settings where the crown has been raised to allow circulation below. Competition for light or exposure to wind can cause the development of an asymmetrical canopy.

Common examples of distinctly dome shaped shrubs include *Hebe* spp., *Choisya ternata* and *Viburnum davidii*. Among the many trees with distinctly dome shaped umbrageous mature canopies are *Quercus robur*, *Acer platanoides*, *A. cappadocicum*, *Sorbus aria*, and pendulous species such as *Pyrus salicifolia* 'Pendula'.

Hummock and dome forms are valuable for their visual stability. Such plants can be used as anchors in composition, balancing and anchoring the more lively and dramatic forms. They can act as 'full stops' at the end of a border or any assemblage which requires containment or conclusion. Because the canopies of dome shaped plants tend to be compact with well defined boundaries, the smaller shrubs can form a good edging to a planting area.

Erect form. Whereas domed, rounded trees and shrubs produce a high proportion of branches which spread horizontally or at obtuse angles to the stem, those with erect form are characterised by a majority of vertical or near vertical main stems. Erect shrubs are often multi-stemmed with comparatively short, wide-angled side branches. This habit gives the individual plant an overall shape which is taller than it is broad and frequently a strong component of ascending line. The overall appearance can be rather stiff with the mature canopy held aloft. Examples of notably erect shrubs include *Mahonia japonica*, *M. x media*, *Aralia* spp. and *Decaisnea fargesii*.

Erect shrubs may remain as distinct individuals as they mature, or in a number of cases they display the suckering habit which leads to the creation of dense thickets

Plate 65   The quite prostrate form of this Juniper (*Juniperus*) provides a base to display the startling white trunk of Himalayan birch (*Betula jaquemontii*).

Plate 66   Prostrate dwarf shrubs such as this *Cotoneaster adpressus* hug the ground and follow the shape of whatever they cover.

Plate 67   The hummock and dome forms of herbaceous plants such as *Liriope muscari* and shrubs such as *Hebe rakaiensis* and *Viburnum davidii* anchor this gateway, reflect the curve of its arch and contrast with its rectilinear outline.

Plate 68   Many trees in temperate climates ultimately develop a spreading dome-like form if allowed to grow unhindered in an open location and free from a high degree of environmental stress. This photograph shows a group of widely spaced Norway maple (*Acer platanoides*). (Photo: Owen Manning)

Plate 69   *Isoplexis canariensis* is a tender shrub with a distinctively erect form, seen here growing out of a low cover of ferns at Tresco Abbey in the Isles of Scilly.

of stem growth which can spread over considerable areas (eg. bamboos). Erect branching trees fall into the oval or fastigiate form categories and will be described later.

Because of their ascending habit, erect shrubs, if planted singly or in small groups, can be a forceful, assertive element in composition. If erect form is combined with other eye-catching qualities, the shrub can provide an accent or focal point in the planting assemblage. When planted *en masse* shrubs with erect form create the impression of a small dense forest of stems which may become quite bare of foliage near the base and the plants may become quite 'leggy' as they are drawn up towards the light. Under these conditions the plants can lose much of their more distinguished qualities and become merely fillers of space at an upper canopy level, leaving bare stems and bare soil near the ground.

Erect form is found at a smaller scale amongst some sub-shrubs and herbaceous plants in which linear leaves are held stiffly upright. Examples include *Phormium tenax*, *Celmisia spectabilis*, *Yucca* spp., and *Iris* spp. Plants such as these can have such a striking appearance that they are the most dominant elements in a plant grouping despite their moderate or small stature.

Arching form. Many shrubs make vigorous erect stems which, after their initial burst of growth, produce lateral branches and arch over under their own weight. The overall shape is akin to a sheaf of wheat with the stems gathered in at the base but sprayed out towards the top. The initial vigour of the stems helps the plant 'forage' for light, then arching and lateral branching, produce a broad, elevated canopy to exploit this light. Examples of arching shrubs include *Buddleja* spp., *Cotoneaster salicifolia*, bamboos such as *Arundinaria nitida* and many shrub roses such as *Rosa* 'Nevada'.

The arching form is also common at a smaller scale amongst herbaceous plants

Plate 70 New Zealand flax (*Phormium tenax*) has numerous large, linear, erect leaves which make it a dominant element in plant groupings. (Photo: Owen Manning)

Plate 71 Shrubs with arching form such as this graceful bamboo (*Arundinaria nitida*) can make fine specimens.

where the stems or linear leaves adopt this configuration. Examples include *Carex pendula, Hemerocallis* spp., *Polygonatum multiflorum, Miscanthus sinensis* and other grasses. Arching form is not well expressed amongst trees because they generally produce sturdier main branches which strengthen as they grow, rather than leaning or drooping under their own increasing weight.

Shrubs and herbs of arching form play a similar role in composition to that of erect shrubs, although often with a little less impact because of their rather looser habit. They can be, nonetheless, extremely valuable as specimens, or where a canopy of foliage is required at an elevated level rather than furnished to the ground.

Oval upright form. A number of shrubs and trees have a generally erect habit of growth but a crown which also spreads laterally and, unlike erect and arching forms, is consistently furnished with side branches and foliage to near ground level. The form which results is oval or egg-shaped. It is encountered more commonly in selected cultivars than in wild tree species, largely because an oval upright form is desirable in many urban and garden locations where lateral space is restricted. Examples include *Carpinus betulus* 'Fastigiata', *Acer platanoides* 'Columnare', *Malus tschonoskii,* and *Sorbus x thuringiaca* 'Fastigiata'). This form is less common amongst shrubs than trees, mainly because shrubs, being generally multi-stemmed, assume a broader habit even when their branching is erect.

Oval form brings an ascending element to tree and shrub planting. It possesses some of the qualities of the erect form but, due to its normally compact rounded outline, is more contained, less straining and soaring than the spires and slender columns of highly fastigiate forms and clean vertical trunks. Oval form can be used to punctuate less regular forms and, rather like the related dome shape, its restrained nature can help it to provide a clear stop to a run of mixed planting. Unlike the hemispherical dome form, however, the canopy of an oval upright tree or shrub is less closely associated with the ground and so it may need anchoring with lower dome or hummocky planting.

Conical form. Conical form is common amongst coniferous trees and also found in some deciduous species. A conical crown is generally taller than it is wide and tapers from a broad base to a sharp apex. It is the product of a distinctly regular branching habit. A single straight bole gives rise to a comparatively larger number of first order branches (those arising directly from the bole) and these are regularly arranged in whorls or in a spiral with regular vertical intervals between nodes. In many cases the branches are nearly horizontal, and thus the cone is made up of horizontal tiers of diminishing diameter towards the top of the crown. Notable examples of conical trees are *Picea omorika, Picea sitchensis, Psuedotsuga menziesii, Sequoiadendron giganteum* and *Corylus colurna.*

The effect of conical form is similar to that of oval and erect forms. The main difference lies in the distinctly tapering crown which ends in a leading shoot pointing upwards. It thus shows more dynamically ascending qualities, and is more dramatic and inspiring although it can be rather austere. A strongly conical form, particularly if it is narrow and acutely pointed, can add a striking accent to planting composition.

Fastigiate and columnar forms. The narrowest of upright crowns are normally referred to as fastigiate or columnar. This form is rare in the wild state and most fastigiate trees and shrubs are selected clones of species which may show a very different habit in their normal range of expression. The crown of fastigiate trees consists of

Plate 72   The hornbeam cultivar *Carpinus betulus* 'Fastigiata' has, in its early years, an upright oval form. Its restricted spread makes it convenient for planting next to roads which carry high vehicles. Its visual effect here is to punctuate the linear mass of domey and arching shrub planting.

Plate 73   The conic form of the two coniferous trees in the foreground is in striking contrast to the long low building at Stirling University.

numerous short, ascending branches which usually form a dense, well defined crown. When this fastigiate habit produces a very narrow cylindrical shape it is often referred to as columnar. The top may be more or less pointed (eg. *Juniperus* 'Skyrocket') or flattened (eg. *Libocedrus decurrens* and *Taxus baccata* 'Fastigiata' as a young plant).

Examples of shrubs with a fastigiate canopy are less common than trees, but include *Juniperus communis* 'Hibernica', and *J.* 'Skyrocket'. The best known fastigiate trees include Italian cypress (*Cupressus sempervirens*), incense cedar (*Libocedrus decurrens*) and Lombardy poplar (*Populus nigra* 'Italica').

Fastigiate form has an uncompromising visual influence, and can easily be the dominant element in composition. Trees such as Lombardy poplar and Italian cypress appear like exclamation marks amongst other vegetation. They rise out of the mass in an assertive and dramatic way. The smaller the number of fastigiate trees the more they draw attention and so, if they are to be accents and eye-catchers, they should be used with restraint.

Lombardy poplar, because of its rapid growth as well as its narrow crown, has been thoroughly exploited as a screen tree, particularly in urban areas where space for lateral spread is restricted. Unfortunately, a single row does not provide an effective screen, especially in winter, as Lombardy poplar possesses a rather open crown. The visual effect of a 'screen' line of Lombardy poplars, regardless of spacing, is rather like a serried rank of stiffly upright sentries standing guard over some ugly installation. It draws attention to what it is meant to screen. However, despite its poor screening ability, Lombardy poplar does have wonderful potential in compositions with contrasting and complementing forms.

In our discussion of fastigiate form we should include a number of shrubs and herbaceous plants which have a highly distinctive vertical flower spike or raceme, which has a similar effect to a narrowly fastigiate foliage canopy. Examples of these include Yucca, *Acanthus* spp. and *Verbascum nigrum*. These can be used within ornamental planting as accent or emphasising plants.

Tabulate form. Many trees and shrubs posses branching habits in which foliage is held in layers held horizontally away from the main stem. In some species and cultivars this form is particularly well developed, and creates distinctive horizontal 'tables' of foliage. The effect may be further accentuated by the display of eye-catching flowers on these spreading layers. Tabulate branching trees include *Cedrus libani* and *Cornus kousa;* shrubs include *Viburnum plicatum* 'Mariesii' and 'Lanarth', and *Acer japonicum* 'Aureum'.

Horizontal, tabulate form gives such trees and shrubs a stable, restful quality. They are light rather than heavy and earthbound in character because the tiers of foliage are held aloft and may admit plenty of light and air between the branches. The sharp contrast between tabulate and erect or fastigiate forms can be quite spectacular. When combined with rounded or looser canopy shapes, tabulate trees and shrubs can still be quite striking due to the distinctiveness of their form.

Open irregular form. In the descriptions above, species have been chosen which can show the clearest expression of a particular type of form. We have noted that many plants, especially when growing in the wild, only approximate to these types due to environmental factors, and are more or less irregular in form as a result of environmental factors.

There are, however, some species which inherit rather than aquire what can best be described as an open irregular form. Their overall shape is broken and unpredictable, the crown does not produce a well defined outline to its surroundings, nor a densely leafy surface to capture sunlight. The most distinctive feature of such plants is their strong growing, searching extension shoots which thrust out in various directions, carrying with them smaller side branches and clusters of foliage but leaving considerable space between them. These gaps in the canopy can be exploited by other plants searching for light, and so open irregular plants are gregarious in their nature, growing well amongst the other plants to form a mixed canopy. Examples of distinctly open irregular trees are *Populus alba* and, as a young tree, *Prunus x yedoensis.* Shrubs with this kind of form include *Pyracantha rogersiana, Hippophae rhamnoides* and *Cotoneaster simonsii.*

The visual qualities of open irregular form are liveliness and movement. As individuals they can be rather ungainly or refreshingly anarchic depending on the context.

Trained form. Not only do plants grow spontaneously into a wide range of forms, but many species lend themselves to the sculpting of quite unnatural shapes by training, trimming and clipping.

The most common green sculpture is the clipped hedge. In addition to its functional purpose a formal hedge brings an element of control and precision to visual composition which cannot otherwise be achieved with vegetation. The elementary form of the rectilinear slab may be elaborated with changes in height and in width. The whole slab or 'box' may be raised above ground level as in pleaching of tree species such as lime *(Tilia* spp.) or hornbeam *(Carpinus betulus).* Other angles and shapes may be created without excessive labour such as castillations or curves in profile or in plan. A memorable example is the serpentine beech hedges *(Fagus sylvatica)* at Chatsworth, Derbyshire.

The most flamboyant and curious shapes are those created by the practice of topiary which dates from Roman gardens. This includes the sculpting of birds and other animals or abstract geometric shapes out of bushes of yew *(Taxus baccata),* box *(Buxus sempervirens)* or cypress *(Cupressus* spp.), but is a method of ornamentation

Plate 74   Some conifers such as Italian cypress (*Cupressus sempervirens*), as well as some broadleaved trees, show a narrowly fastgiate or columnar form. In this scene at Bodnant, North Wales, the contrast between the rising, spire like tree form and the solid, stable cube of the old mill is dramatic.

Plate 75   The ascending flower raceme of mullein (*Verbascum*) has, on a smaller scale, a similar effect to a fastigiate or columnar tree canopy. (Photo: Owen Manning)

Plate 76   Tabulate form is seen in the spreading branches of trees such as this young deodar (*Cedrus deodara*) and Japanese maple (*Acer palmatum*) which give a serene quality to this composition in Sheffield Botanical Gardens.

Plate 77   This young specimen of Yoshino cherry (*Prunus x yedoensis*) demonstrates the open irregular habit that is found to a greater or lesser extent in many trees and shrubs.

Plate 78   Artificial geometric form is crisply defined in this immaculately maintained yew (*Taxus baccata*) hedge at Bodnant, North Wales. It echoes the built form of the terrace and throws into sharp relief the rising branches of the *Magnolia x veitchii* behind.

which is not widely applied in landscape or garden planting today due to the labour intensive nature of the task. Traditional topiary does, however, play an important role in historic garden management, and sometimes as an occasional feature in prestige planting schemes for which a generous maintenance budget is available. The creation of simpler, but not necessarily less effective, sculptural forms is better suited to the majority of budgets.

Suitable species for clipping are those which respond to frequent light pruning by producing dense twiggy growth at an even rate over the whole canopy. This allows the creation of an even surface to the desired shapes. Smaller leaved species are ideal because the damage caused the leaves themselves is less noticeable, and evergreens are preferable because of their ability to retain the sculpted surface throughout the years. Traditional hedging and topiary species include *Taxus baccata, Buxus sempervirens, Fagus sylvatica, Ilex aquifolium* and, in the milder areas of Britain, *Cupressus* spp. and *Laurus nobilis*.

Because of its controlled precision, trained or clipped geometric forms can introduce a strong sense of order to a composition. They can bring a calming regularity in contrast with the luxurience and unpredictabiliy of free growing vegetation. This very contrast can be delightful and bring out the best in each of these opposites.

Line and Pattern

Line is to some extent an abstraction from three dimensional reality, being the selection of one visual effect of form, that of edges. These may be the edges of a whole plant mass (its silhouette), or of its constituent branches, stems, leaves, or petals, or the edges between different materials or colours and between light and shadow falling on the surfaces of plants.

A single line is essentially a one dimensional phenomenon because at any one time it is moving in only one direction, but the composite patterns created by lines can be understood as a two dimensional element of composition. These are formed on the surfaces of things and, although these surfaces may be curved or bent, they can be percieved from one viewing point as a two dimensional plane. A pattern of lines can, by means of perspective, convey information about the three dimensional shape of objects, but this requires interpretation of the two dimensional pattern based on the experience of the observer.

The essence of line is direction. A line is the result of the movement of a point in space. In visual composition the primary effect of line is to direct the eye. Although we do not necessarily follow each line in a pattern faithfully and right to its end, our eyes will nevertheless tend to move backwards and forwards along the stronger lines, and to follow the compounded direction of weaker and shorter lines. Our attention will tend to rest at the places where lines converge. So line can be used to direct the visual exploration of a scene.

Different directions of line, as found in different patterns and in different plants, have intrinsic aesthetic qualities which can be deliberately exploited in planting composition.

Ascending line. Ascending or vertical line is most strongly expressed in the outlines of plants with columnar or fastigiate shapes (eg. *Juniperus communis* 'Hibernica' and *Cupressus sempervirens*), in the trunks of strong growing trees, particularly when clearly visible through light foliage or leafless winter canopy (eg. *Poplar* spp., *Betula* spp. and *Sequoiadendron giganteum*), in the vigorous stems of shrubs and herbaceous plants (eg. *Cornus alba* and *Rubus cockburnianus* when cut hard back, *Perovskia atriplicifolia,* and the flower spikes of *Verbascum nigrum* and *Stachys lanata),* and in

Plate 79 Trained and clipped form can be treated as sculpture in the landscape. This green wave also has the funtional role of a hedge (Castle Arenberg, Belgium). (Photo: Owen Manning)

Plate 80 The topiary at Levens Hall, Cumbria, creates an intriguing interplay of form and space.

Plate 81 This planting composition depends for much of its impact on the form of the trees and shrubs. The tabulate branches of *Viburnum plicatum* 'Lanarth' are picked out with sprays of brilliant white flower heads and form a striking contrast to the dark fastigiate yew (*Taxus baccata* 'Fastigiata') and the rising branches of the tree in the background. These strongly expressed forms are set within a softly flowing mass of more informal foliage which saves the composition from stiffness.

Plate 83 The ascending outlines of these fastigiate junipers (*Juniperus* 'Sky Rocket') punctuate and regulate the soft billowing masses of roses and herbs below.

Plate 82 Line can be a dominant element in planting composition, especially when we can only see the silhouettes of plants. It is only our ability to interpret perspective that tells us the depth of field in this photograph of an avenue of elm trees (*Ulmus*). (Photo: Owen Manning)

the leaves of a number of monocotelydons (eg. *Iris pseudacorus*, *I. sibirica* and *Curtonis paniculata*).

The character of ascending line is assertive and emphatic. It can be stately or grand when of sufficient scale. Ascending line gains its prominence from the opposition to the direction of gravity. It is the result of growth against gravity, and therefore an assertion of the force of life. Yet a vertical line by itself exists in a state of tenuous balance. The least movement in any lateral direction will offset its alignment and realise its considerable potential energy. This sense of delicate balance lends an air of achievement and distinction to a strongly expressed vertical line. If used without discretion and order, however, vertical line can be restless and overbearing.

Pendulous line. Pendulous or descending line is found in the branches of trees (eg. *Salix* 'Chrysocoma', *Pyrus salicifolia* 'Pendula'), in shrubs with stems that hang vertically when planted above a wall or rock face (eg. *Cotoneaster dammeri*, *Buddleja alternifolia*, *Parthenocissus quinquefolia*), and in plants with hanging leaves or flowers (eg. *Viburnum rhytidophyllum*, *Wisteria* spp., *Garrya elliptica* and *Carex pendula*).

Pendulous line is characteristically restful, lending serenity and peacefulness to a scene. This is because it suggests some letting go of the struggle with gravity. Weeping branches hang in a position of minimum effort. Perhaps because there is less resistance, less vitality in their habit, pendulous plants can reflect or even engender a melancholy mood in some people. This can be particularly strongly felt when the pendulous habit is combined with sombre, dark colours, or with the weighty foliage of the larger leaved *Rhododendron* spp.. The atmosphere created by the delicate, sparkling foliage of *Betula pendula* 'Tristis' or the golden yellow twigs and wispy foliage of *Salix* 'Chrysocoma' is much more lively whilst still gentle. *Picea breweriana* can suggest very different moods; in grey mists it may have a mournful aspect, in sunlight it can glisten like a green cascade.

Weeping foliage or branches draw our attention down to the ground, and this can imbue a sense of heaviness. Indeed, the plant itself can appear overburdened and forlorn. So the presence of a contrasting light, lively element, such as water, below the canopy is the perfect complement to a weeping tree or shrub. One can also note that there is an afinity with the character of water in the flowing, cascading forms of weeping trees. Hence the traditional association of the two.

Horizontal line. Horizontal line is found in the level, spreading branches and foliage (eg. *Cedrus libani*, *Cornus kousa*, *Juniperus x media* 'Pfitzerana ' and *Viburnum plicatum* 'Mariesii'), along the tops of clipped hedges (of many species including *Taxus baccata* and *Buxus sempervirens*), in the browsing line which forms the base of tree canopies in grazed pasture, and in level groundform articulated by mown grass or compact ground cover.

Horizontal line represents a state of stability and rest. Its character is calm and passive, as in a body reclining. It contains no potential energy, and so implies no movement or effort. Because of its visual stability, planting with strong horizontal line can act as a foundation which will support the more active elements of composition. Indeed, without these it can appear featureless and lifeless. The stable simplicity of a clipped hedge is most effective when it acts as a foundation or background to more exuberant planting such as a herbaceous border or a grove of trees.

Diagonal line. Diagonal line is encountered in sharply ascending branches found

Plate 84   Vertical line is also common in the ascending linear leaves of monocotyledons such as *Iris* and rushes (*Juncus*), here contrasting with the horizontal slab of the stone bridge.

Plate 85   Pendulous line is found in the hanging branches of weeping willow (*Salix* 'Chrysocoma'). (Photo: Owen Manning)

Plate 86   The tabulate branching cedar of Lebanon (*Cedrus libani*) produces a strong horizontal component which reflects the lines of the brickwork pattern and building eaves.

Plate 87   Dynamic diagonals are strongly expressed in the linear leaves of New Zealand flax (*Phormium tenax*).

occasionally in many species of trees and shrubs, but more consistently in a few cultivars and species such as *Prunus* ' Kanzan' and *Sorbus sargentiana.* The stiff linear leaves of a number of monocotelydons (eg. *Phormium tenax, Yucca* spp. and *Cordyline australis)* characteristically adopt both vertical and diagonal alignments.

Diagonal line is energetic, dynamic and exciting. It expresses a state of tension, of high potential energy. It is thrust out against gravity, moving upwards and forwards. This forceful quality makes it a powerful element in composition, and it is seen at its most effective when used in contrast to more stable types of line. Too much strong diagonal line would result in a disintegration of the composition into a disturbing chaos. A solid foundation is needed to support the dynamic character and eye-catching qualities of diagonal line.

The quality of line. Because the medium of design with which we work is living vegetation it is rare to find pure line direction except where the human hand has imposed simple and geometrical form on planting. Geometric line which is quite straight or evenly curved is perceived as formal and controlled. It displays conscious intent, the imposition of an order conceived by the human intellect rather than the forces of nature. The majority of form and line found in nature, although directional qualities are clearly discernable, is more varied and irregular in its character.

A meandering or irregular line, whatever its overall direction, can have a spontaneous and playful quality, and this is perhaps best expressed in the darting, weaving growth of branches and twigs as they seek the light. Indeed, some plants have been selected specifically for their unusually twisted and picturesque branch habit (eg. *Salix matsudana* 'Tortuosa' and *Corylus avellana* 'Contorta').

Texture

Plant texture can be defined as the visual roughness or smoothness of any part of the plant. It is akin to the texture of a painting, the grain of a photograph or the consistency of materials such as fabric, stone, brick or wood. Texture is a function of the scale of differentiation and division within a material. It may be the result of a pattern of lines, but, if so, it is determined only by the scale of the pattern and not by the direction of the lines. A plant is commonly referred to as having coarse, fine or medium texture.

Texture, like form, depends on viewing distance. When seen from a moderate distance a plant's visual texture is the result of the size and shape of its leaves and twigs. The larger the leaves and the stouter the winter twigs, the coarser the texture. The petiole also affects texture because a long and flexible petiole allows considerable movement of individual leaves in the breeze. This movement tends to break up the outlines of leaves and give a softer appearance.

If we move far enough away the visual effect of individual leaves and twigs will be lost and the canopy will appear to be made up of clusters or sprays of foliage. Under these conditions it will be the size and arrangement of these clusters or branches which determines texture. Plants made up of large, clearly differentiated branches will appear more coarsely textured. If the viewing distance is so great that the only visible differentiation of vegetation is between whole plants or between clumps of trees or shrubs, texture will depend on the spacing of individual shrubs and trees or clumps. Widely spaced clumps will give the landscape a coarse grain, whereas dense interlocking planting will appear as a fine, even texture.

Under the closest inspection it will be not the combined mass of foliage or stems which give texture, but the nature of the surface of the leaves and bark. Some species have coarse textured leaf surfaces (eg. *Rosa rugosa* and *Viburnum rhytidophyllum),* and some have rough bark (eg. *Quercus suber* and *Sequoia sempervirens)*, whilst others possess smooth leaves (eg. *Fatsia japonica)* or smooth bark (eg. *Fagus sylvatica).*

Texture, like form and line, has specific visual effects, and so also plays an important role in composition. In our discussion of these properties we shall concentrate on the textural effects of plants when viewed from medium distances of between about two to 20 metres, because it is within this range that detailed composition of most ornamental planting is most fully appreciated.

Fine texture. The finest textured plants are those with the smallest leaves or leaflets and the finest, most closely packed twigs. These include most species of *Erica*, many *Genista* and *Cytisus* and many grasses, rushes and sedges. A number of trees also have comparatively fine texture, for example *Taxus bacatta*, *Cupressus* spp., *Chamaecyparis* spp. and *Pinus*, especially those with slender needles such as *Pinus strobus* and *P coulteri*. Fine textured broadleaved trees include *Betula pendula* and *Robinia pseudoacacia.*

Fine textured plants tend to be easy to look at, that is, relaxing rather than stimulating for the eye. They give the impression of being at a greater distance than coarse textured plants, and are said to recede in the field of vision. As a result, a high proportion of fine textured plants increases the sense of spaciousness within an enclosure, rather like the effect of fine textured or small patterned wallpaper in a room. Their character is light and airy, expansive and soft.

A final and very important effect of fine textured foliage is that the overall outline and form of the plant is strongly expressed and easily picked out. The shape of the plant as a whole will usually dominate the shapes of individual leaves and stems, which may be barely noticeable. For this reason, fine textured plants are valuable in formal composition where strict control of form and pattern are the essence of design. Here, the outlines of planting areas, the grouping of plants into geometric patterns and the shaping of hedges and clipped specimens are all expressed with the greatest elegance by fine textured species. Yew makes a magnificent clipped hedge or topiary specimen with the sharpest of edges; lavender and box are traditional low edging plants which delineate and contain planting beds, and the fine even texture of mown grass is not only soothing to look at but also accentuates the shape and grading of the lawn.

Coarse texture. The largest leaves and the stoutest twigs appear to have the coarsest texture. These include the huge rough leaves of *Gunnera manicata* which can be up to 2 metres across, the broad, lobed foliage of *Rheum alexandre* and *Peltiphyllum peltatum*. Other species with bold foliage and coarse texture include trees such as *Catalpa bignonioides* and *Acer macrophyllum*, shrubs such as *Phormium tenax*, *Rhododendron sinogrande* and *Fatsia japonica*, and herbaceous plants such as *Bergenia cordifolia* and *Cynara cardunculus*. In winter the sturdy stems of *Aralia* spp. or coppiced trees such as *Catalpa bignonioides* and *Paulownia tomentosa* provide coarse texture among the deciduous plants.

Plants with bold foliage and stems attract attention and invite closer inspection, because the form and detail of their foliage is clearly visible from a distance. Indeed, the shapes of individual leaves tend to break up the outline of the plant and distract attention from its overall form. In this case the plant's qualities of line arise from the edges of leaves and twigs rather than from the mass of the canopy.

The boldness of coarse textured plants makes them appear to advance within the field of vision. This effect can be employed to increase the sense of depth in planting composition if coarse textures are placed in the foreground and finer textures kept mainly to the background. In a confined area, however, too much

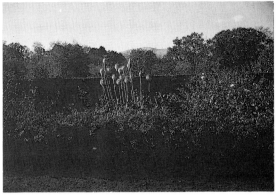

Plate 89 (above)   Line can be crucial to composition: the crossing of horizontal and vertical lines is one of the most dominant aspects of this view.

Plate 88 (left)   Much of the line found in nature is lively and irregular in character such as the branches and twigs of this birch (*Betula*). (Photo: Owen Manning)

Plate 90   Grass, whether mown or long, and yew hedging both have fine visual texture which add to the feeling of simple spaciousness in this orchard at Hardwick Hall, Derbyshire.

Plate 91   The bold foliage of *Acanthus* draws attention to the steps and balustrade and harmonises with the similar, coarse texture of the stone work.

bold, advancing foliage can create an oppressive and claustrophobic character, so care is needed when using coarse texture in small spaces.

The large leaves of coarse textured plants throw large shadows and create patterns of light and shade which can be quite striking. If the plant possesses glossy leaves, areas of deep shade contrast particularly strongly with the reflected light. These strong contrasts add to the visual impact of coarse textures, and help to make many of them fine specimen plants. Very coarse textured specimens accentuate their position within a composition, particularly if their bold foliage is combined wilh forceful ascending lines (eg. *Phormium tenax* and *Agave* spp.). Accent plants such as these provide a focus or emphasis within composition. They can provide a visual goal or, with their distinctive eye catching character, they can provide markers to identify and emphasise the key locations within a composition.

Plate 92 A wide range of textures and forms
contribute to this composition. The fine lawn and
domed *Hebe* harmonise with the fine texture of the
sawn stone. The coarse textured *Drimys winteri* in the
foreground and *Yucca gloriosa* are well displayed in
this subdued setting.

Plate 93 This plant grouping at
Newby Hall, North Yorkshire,
relies on strong form, dynamic line
and textural contrasts for its eye-
catching effect.

In addition to the exciting, energetic qualities of coarse textured plants, their
substantial foliage and sturdy stems give them visual weight and solidity. This allows
them to act as 'anchor' plants in composition the role of which is to stabilise or
ground the more floaty, insubstantial fine textured plants. The most effective
anchors combine coarse texture with the stability of domed, hummocky or
prostrate form.

Viburnum davidii and *Fatsia japonica* are good examples of coarse textured, domed
shrubs which can be used as an emphatic anchor or 'full stop' to a run of planting.
Bergenia cordifolia, with its spreading habit, is often used as a low edging, or
sometimes as a solid foundation carpet to taller planting. *Hedera canariensis* and *H.
colchica* can also be used as a coarse textured carpet. They perform these roles best
when there is a contrast in texture between the weighty lower layer and the higher
canopies which it supports. Thus *Bergenia is* successful as an edging to mixed
foliage and flower borders, and the excellent ground covering properties of *Hedera*
help it to create a firm visual foundation which will support and unite areas of taller
more varied planting.

Medium texture. Between the extremes of plants such as *Gunnera* and *Erica* there
are numerous species which could be described as of medium texture. But even
amongst these considerable contrast can be achieved. Because texture is a relative
characteristic it is the degree of contrast between relatively fine and relatively coarse
texture that determines the aesthetic impact. The starkest contrasts, however, are

generally not the most effective. Some element of linkage to bridge the gap between the coarsest and the finest foliage will help to unify the composition. Intermediate textures allow the eye to absorb the range of variety more easily by making it a progressive rather than too sudden a variation.

Colour

The development of modern colour theory began in a systematic way with Goethe's *Theory of Colours* published in 1840. Certain scientific principles are generally accepted although some aspects of the perception of colour remain enigmatic. We shall not attempt a full exposition of colour theory, but will confine ourselves to the principles which are of most practical use to the planting designer.

As Lancaster (1984) reminds us, colour is light. Differences in colour are differences in the properties of light, mainly wavelength, amplitude and energy. These differences are caused both by the nature of the light source and the reflection, refraction and absorbtion of the light before it reaches the eye of the observer. The colour of light received by the eye can be described in terms of three fundamental qualities: hue, value and saturation.

Hue. Hue is the quality which is popularly referred to as colour, that is, whether an object appears red, blue, yellow, etc. The natural spectrum is conventionally perceived to have seven hues: red, orange, yellow, green, blue, indigo and violet, although on close inspection each is seen to grade continuously into its neighbours through intermediate hues. The hues of the spectrum are as pure as can be observed within the Earth's atmosphere because they arise from the refraction of the sun's light rather than from absorbtion by pigments.

The colours of plants and other natural materials are the result of absorbtion by pigments contained in these materials. The light that is not absorbed is relected back from the surface and almost always contains a mixture of hues. Plant colours are also modified by the other two qualities of value and saturation.

Value. Value, often referred to as tone, is the quantity or luminosity of light relected from the coloured surface. This is most easily understood as the degree of lightness or darkness. A black and white photograph shows the differences of value but not of hue or saturation. The most reflective surfaces have a high value or light tone, and the least reflective have a low value or dark tone. If we study the possible variation in value of a single hue, say red, we note that if the red reflecting pigment is diluted with white pigment (ie. one reflecting all hues equally), the total quantity of light reflected is increased, that is the colour is paler and its value is increased. In the extreme case, the red pigment becomes imperceptible and the colour is pure white. Conversely, if the red pigment is mixed with black pigment (ie. one absorbing all hues), the total quantity of light reflected is reduced and it appears darker, its value is reduced. As increasing proportions of black pigment are added, all red light would eventually be absorbed and the colour would become black. It is interesting to note that some hues are intrinsically paler than others, the palest being yellow.

The values or tones of colour seen in the landscape depend on the pigmentation of materials but also on the amount of light available. In areas of shadow or as dusk approaches all tones will be darker, and the apparent difference between tones will be reduced because of the reduction in the reflected light.

Saturation. Given constant hue and constant value, variation in colour can still be perceived. This is variation in the degree of saturation of the hue, that is, in the degree of redness or blueness of the colour. Saturation gives us a measure of relative colourfulness. A bright red and a dull red may have the same value, but the bright red will be distinguished by its greater saturation. The spectral hues are pure, fully saturated colours, but the majority of colours we see in nature are more or less muted or dull. In these colours the pure hue is in effect muted with a proportion of greyness of the same value as the pure hue. This reduction in saturation could be pictured as the red hue in a colour photograph gradually fading to the grey of identical value which would represent it in a black and white photograph.

Terminology in colour theory can at times be ambiguous or confusing. Saturation is also known variously as intensity, purity and chroma. The term saturation might be preferred because it directly suggest the origin of this quality of colour. It is the proportion of the reflected light which is made up of the hue in question. In the case of a coloured object, this results from the degree of saturation of the surface of the object by the pigment.

Ambiguity can also arise from the use of the word tone. It has been employed by some authors to describe degrees of saturation, and this usage is supported by the expression 'to tone down a colour'. It is more commonly understood, however, to refer to the quality of lightness or darkness, to distinguish tints and shades: thus it can be taken as synonymous with value.

The three qualities or dimensions of colour: hue, value and saturation, allow us to fully describe any colour. For example, a dark dull red or a pale bright green. They also help us to understand the visual effects of colour and to employ it with awareness in design.

Colour perception. The actual colour observed, that is, the characteristics of the light reflected from an object, depend on the light source and, if this is the sun, on the climatic conditions. For example, in the soft bluish light common in humid, temperate climates, pale and muted colours can be fully appreciated, whereas in the strong sunlight of Mediterranean summers and tropical climates, these subtleties are lost, but the most saturated, brilliant colours are seen at their best. Moreover, no colour exists in isolation. The perception of colours is influenced by their context. 'Colour behaviour is relative' Penelope Hobhouse (1985) explains, 'depending on neighbouring colours and the quality of light.' She describes the phenomenon of simultaneous contrast:

> Juxtaposing two hues has the optical effect of exaggerating the difference between them and 'driving them further apart'. Each colour appears to be tinged with the complementary of its neighbour; paired complementaries seem more brilliant. The other two dimensions, value and intensity [saturation], further affect the apparent changes in the pairs of pure hues.

The vast majority of natural objects, including plants, possess a mixture of hues, a range of value and varying degrees of saturation. Because of the complexity of colour, it is unwise to attempt to draw up rules for its use in design. A number of aesthetic effects, however, can be identified as these will influence the choice and combination of colours in planting.

Colour effects. It is mostly accepted that colour hues produce reasonably predictable effects on the observer (Birren, 1978). Indeed, the meaning of colour is reliable enough to have been used as an effective measure of exploring personality, eg. in the Luscher colour test (Scott, trans. 1970). Thus, colour hues can be understood as aesthetic materials, rather like different sculptural media or different paving materials. What follows is a summary of their main qualities:

- Red is the hottest colour. It is energetic and powerful, often dramatic and can be exciting or alarming. Because of its energy it is advancing and instantly perceived, even when present in small patches amongst other hues.

- Orange is also warm and advancing. It is lively and vital, possessing much of the energetic quality of red, but this is tempered by the yellow it contains.

- Yellow is warm but without the passion of red. It is stimulating and so tends to advance when combined with recessive hues. It has a clear, fresh and cheerful character.

- Green is a neutral colour in many ways. It is neither warm nor cool, neither receding nor advancing. It is soothing and balancing but also stimulating. Green light is the most easily focussed by the eye and so to look at green objects requires the least effort by the ocular muscles. Green allows the sharpest distinction of contour and outline.

- Blue is the coolest hue and most recessive in the field of vision. It is calming and serene, but is also expansive and inspiring. It can be airy and even ethereal.

- Indigo and violet contain both blue and red. Like blue, they are cool and receding but less so than pure blue. The power of red gives them an uplifting quality and at times they can be quite mysterious.

- White is the combination of all the hues of the spectrum. It is neutral, favouring none of its composite parts; it is neither advancing nor receding and neither warm nor cool but, because a pure white surface would reflect all of the incident light, it takes on the qualities of that light. A white flower would appear warm and advancing in the golden or reddish light of sunrise and sunset, but cool and receding in the bluish twilight.

Intermediate and mixed hues have combined qualities according to their composition, and hues mixed with white to produce tints show a moderation or refinement of the qualities of the pure hue.

The effects of colour depends on value and saturation as well as hue. Saturated colours and dark shades tend to advance like warm hues, whereas dull colours and pale tints tend to recede along with cool hues. Thus, dull, pale and cool colours provide good backgrounds and saturated, warm colours make striking highlights. Dark shades, rather like coarse textures, are comparatively heavy in their character and so can successfully anchor or stabilize large areas of pale tints and cool, recessive colours which might otherwise appear insubstantial and floating.

Warm, saturated colours, because of their intensity and energy, tend to distract attention from form or texture and so dominate composition. An example of this is the intense red of the common field poppy which, especially when exaggerated by juxtaposition with complementary green foliage, can make the flowers appear disembodied and formless, mere splashes of colour. The outline and size of the poppy flowers and their exact location in space are difficult to establish under these conditions.

Visual Energy

We have noted that the aesthetic characteristics of line, form, texture and colour are all capable of producing certain related effects. For example, diagonal line, fastigiate form, bold texture and bright colours all share the properties of dynamism, drama and stimulation to some degree. They can all produce eye-catching, striking elements in composition. Conversely, horizontal line, prostrate or domey form, fine texture and pale or dull colours are all characterised by restful, unimposing qualities and so play a more recessive, quieter role in composition.

These effects can be understood with the help of the concept of visual energy (Nelson, 1979). The more active, vigorous visual characteristics have a higher visual energy than the more passive, quieter characteristics. The idea of visual energy helps to explain why too many saturated colours or too much bold texture and diagonal line creates a composition which is chaotic and tiring to look at. These high energy elements will all fight for attention and struggle amongst themselves for dominance. To gain the full impact from a striking plant, and to be able to appreciated its unusual qualities, its visual energy should be complemented with areas of quieter, visually undemanding planting.

Planting composition may be designed to be of high or low visual energy overall. The choice should be influenced by the setting and purpose of the planting. For example, in a quiet meditative garden or in borders which complement fine architectural detail, much of the planting should be of low visual energy, whereas in a display garden in a park or in a dreary urban setting it may need to be energetic and spectacular.

Combining Plants

A particular plant may be of attractive appearance and may have the benefit of easy culture. But, when we come to combine it with other plants, these recommendations will come to little if it is placed where its beauty is eclipsed by conflicting demands on our attention, or if it is rapidly overcome by invasive neighbours. The next two chapters will deal with different aspects of plant combinations. Chapter 7, 'Principles of Visual Composition', will discuss how we can combine the decorative characteristics of form, line and pattern, texture and colour to achieve successful composition. Chapter 8, 'Plant Associations', will examine the effects of growth habit and cultural needs on plant combinations. We will see how shoot and root habits, soil and climatic requirements, mode of spread, speed of growth and longevity all help to determine a plant's ecological compatibility with other species, and therefore its ability to form part of a plant association.

CHAPTER 7

Principles of Visual Composition

Our analysis of the aesthetic characteristics of plants gave us a basic visual vocabulary. When this is put to work in a plant association it will convey a visual message of one kind or another. So composition might be regarded as the visual grammar of planting design.

Five Principles of Visual Composition

Painting, photography, sculpture and other visual art forms can all be analysed by composition, and certain principles are found to be common to them all. In the art of planting the most important are the principles of harmony and contrast, balance, emphasis, sequence and scale. An understanding of these will allow us to analyse the visual grammar of any plant association, and can also help us with both design method and with creative inspiration.

Harmony and Contrast

Harmony is a quality of relatedness. Harmony is found between similar plant forms, similar textures, similar qualities of line and closely related colours. The closer the relationship between the aesthetic qualities of associated plants, the greater the harmony. As this relationship becomes increasingly close it approaches identity but, in identity, harmony would be lost because it depends for its aesthetic impact on the simultaneous perception of both similarities and differences. The pleasure of harmony rests not simply in the similarities between things, but in the balance between identification and differentiation. The experience of identity and of difference is of primal importance in the human psyche. We understand everything we perceive in terms of similarity or difference to that with which we are familiar. The sense we make of the world is a pattern of similarities picked out as different from its background, or conversely could be understood as a pattern of differences arising from the undifferentiated. So harmony and contrast go together. They are not mere polarities, neither can exist without the other.

Contrast is found between different plant forms, strikingly different qualities and directions of line, texture and colour. But contrast does not necessarily imply conflict. It may be an attractive, happy contrast arising from a complementary, mutually supportive relationship between widely different characteristics. Conflict is only perceived when the contrast creates strain, when it is not contained within order and aesthetic purpose. Indeed, without a binding, unifying aesthetic purpose contrast is likely to create confusion.

In planting composition we must aim to achieve the right balance of harmony and contrast. The contrast between two species will be more visible and have a

CONTRAST IN FORM,
HARMONY IN TEXTURE.

CONTRAST IN TEXTURE,
HARMONY IN FORM.

CONTRAST IN LINE,
HARMONY IN TEXTURE.

Figure 7.1

greater impact if there is also a measure of harmony. This relationship is particularly successful when a contrast in one aesthetic characteristic such as leaf texture is combined with harmony in another, such as leaf colour. Conversely, the careful choice of closely related harmonious flower colours will appear more engaging if they are used to link varied and contrasting form and texture.

Too much contrast is illegible, because there are too few related elements and we cannot perceive a pattern in the whole. A combination of plants with strong contrast in all its aesthetic characteristics would appear chaotic, and we would find it difficult to appreciate either the qualities of individual plants or of the composition as a whole. The restlessness of such a composition would cause constant distraction. This is why restraint is one of the keys to enduring and refreshing design.

Balance

Balance is a function of the relative magnitude and position of vegetation masses and features of high visual energy.

The possibility of visual balance implies two things: that the elements of a composition have visual force or energy; and that there is a fulcrum or axis about which that force acts. This fulcrum or axis is brought into being and given importance by the way in which plant masses and other elements are positioned around it, and because of its vital role of attracting and ordering surrounding elements it may well become the focus of the space or composition.

The simplest expression of balance is bilateral symmetry in which the arrangement of planting on one side of an axis is repeated in its mirror image on the opposite side. Most commonly, there are one or two axes of symmetry within a composition, but there can be any number (a circle possesses an infinite number of axes of symmetry).

Symmetry has long been associated with a strict formality in design. Its ordered patterns are an expression of rational thought, and the precise control of form is a demonstration of the power of human technology to shape the materials of the landscape. Symmetrical form is remarkable because it contrasts with the natural, organic forms that develop when no conscious plan is imposed. Yet pure symmetry can be seen to emerge from natural forms. It is an intellectual refinement of the underlying patterns of the microscopic world and of the elements of a more relaxed symmetry found in all living things.

Balance can also be achieved in the absence of symmetry. In an asymmetrical composition visual stability arises not from bilateral replication but by the balancing of the visual energy of different qualities about an axis or fulcrum. For example, prominent form may balance coarse texture, and assertive line may balance intense colour. In addition, a small quantity of one prominent characteristic may balance a greater quantity of the same characteristic which is less strongly expressed. For example, a single plant with striking, sword-like leaves would balance a group of three or five smaller plants with ascending linear leaves of similar shape but finer texture.

The visual energy of balanced elements may be the potential energy which results from the positioning of plant masses. This potential energy is a product of both the mass itself and of its relative height or prominence, and allows a smaller plant mass in a dominant location to balance a larger mass in a subordinate position.

When planting composition is balanced about an axis or centre, either by symmetry or by the asymmetrical equality of energy, a state of visual stability is achieved. Such a stable composition may include dynamic elements and exciting contrasts, but its parts are held together in a unified whole.

Emphasis

Important elements and locations in a landscape can be emphasised by associating them with planting which has aesthetic qualities of high visual energy. This is often called accent planting and it can be used to draw attention to elements such as entrances, steps, seating or water. Alternatively, the planting itself may provide the *raison d'etre* of a space, and the points of emphasis may lie within a picture created

Plate 94   Visual harmony can be found amongst natural forms as diverse as trees and clouds.

Plate 95   Harmony of leaf form and colour supports the strong contrast in texture between *Bergenia* and *Saxifraga*.

Plate 96   The close relationship between form and texture of *Choisya ternata* and *Acer palmatum* 'Dissectum Atropurpureum' emphasises the contrast in foliage colour.

Plate 97   The decorative characteristics of plants can be delightful when related by harmony and contrast to hard landscape materials. In this office courtyard the rectilinear geometry of the pool and edgings contrast with organic forms of the plants, and the texture and comparative softness of the pea gravel provides a visual link between 'hard' and 'soft' landscape. (Photo: Landscape Design Associates)

Plate 98   On this Victorian Italianate terrace at Tatton Park, Cheshire, the strictly symmetrical layout of grass and floral bedding denotes absolute control of form and articulates the central axis of symmetry. (Photo: Owen Manning)

SYMMETRICAL BALANCE

ASYMMETRIC BALANCE

PROMINENT FORM BALANCES COARSE TEXTURE

SINGLE STRONG FORM BALANCES SEVERAL
WEAKER FORMS.

PROMINENT POSITION — BALANCES — GREATER MASS.

Figure 7.2

EMPHASIS CAN BE GIVEN BY:

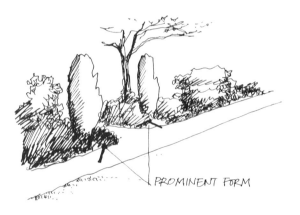

PROMINENT FORM

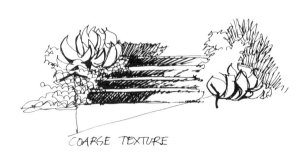

COARSE TEXTURE

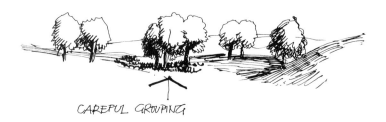

CAREFUL GROUPING

Figure 7.3

Plate 99 Symmetry is observed in the repetition of trees, shrubs and ground modelling either side of the path. By emphasising the axis of symmetry which arises from the building the planting leads the eye to the entrance to these apartments at Kingston Dock, Glasgow.

Plate 100 The drama of a single *Agave* brings a point of emphasis to the remarkable stone work of the viaduct and steps at Parc Guel, Barcelona.

Plate 101 The steady rhythm of the yew bastions reflects the buttressing of the church at Ashridge, Herts.

Plate 102 A regular sequence of spaces is experienced as one moves between the serpentine hedges at Chatsworth, Derbyshire. (Photo: Owen Manning)

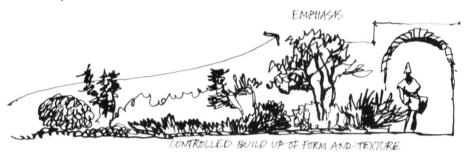

Figure 7.4

Plate 103   In this forestry planting the scale of the species drifts is in harmony with the patterns of the vegetation and landform in the surrounding landscape (Snowdonia, Wales).

Plate 104   The largest structures in the landscape, such as the Humber Bridge, near Hull, require plantations and tree clumps of generous size to maintain good generic scale relationships.

by plants alone. In this case, a striking accent shrub or specimen tree would provide the focus of a space.

Emphasis or accent planting can be effective by virtue of its intrinsic striking qualities, such as bold foliage or dynamic form, as part of a plant assemblage displaying dramatic contrasts or, less ostentatiously, by careful arrangement and grouping which brings the eye to rest at the chosen location.

Sequence

Sequence is the manner in which the appearance of a planting composition changes or unfolds before the observer. Sequence may be visible from one observation point, as in a build up of colours, textures or forms within a single vista terminating at the primary point of emphasis, or it may be experienced as a progression of vistas and views which unfold as we move through the landscape.

Sequence is essential to the dynamic qualities of composition. It is an expression of change. It relates the parts to the whole, not only within a static picture, but also

PERCEPTION OF PLANT GROUPINGS DEPENDS ON VIEWING DISTANCE

AT THE SCALE OF A BUILDING COMPLEX THE MASSING OF TREES DOMINATES

AT THE SCALE OF A SINGE BUILDING INDIVIDUAL TREES AND THE MASSING OF SHRUBS DOMINATE

AT AN INTIMATE HUMAN SCALE INDIVIDUAL SHRUBS AND SMALL GROUPS OF HERBACEOUS PLANTS DOMINATE.

Figure 7.5

over time. Sequence in visual composition can be likened to rhythm in music or meter in verse; it provides a temporal structure to the composition. Just as with musical rhythms or poetic meter, planting sequence may be ordered simply and with regularity, or it may be more complex including various overlapping patterns of repetition. It may, if the designer wishes, be deliberatdy chaotic or arbitrary, allowing expression to forces of disorder.

Scale

Scale can be understood most simply as relative size. Ching (1979) defines scale as either 'generic', that is '... relative to other forms in its context', or as 'human', that is '... relative to the dimensions and proportions of the human body'. In landscape design generic scale refers to the size relationships between the various parts of a whole space, and within a plant association the relative sizes of single plants and of plant groupings determine the generic scale of the composition. These are the aspects of scale which tend to be perceived as separate from the observer. Human scale, on the other hand, refers to the relationship between the size of the parts of the composition and the observer. This means that human scale depends on the participation of the observer. Because we are designing for people we must take account of the human scale relationships of landscape, and we need to allow for the effects of different patterns of viewing.

The amount of detail which we can perceive depends on the viewing distance. As distance increases so we see less detail but a greater area, and although the content of our view changes, the amount of information that we can assimilate remains constant. At close quarters, the finer characteristics of leaf, stem and flowers and the textures and forms of smaller plants hold our attention. At a distance of, say, 25 metres these details will be barely visible, but the form of larger individual plants and groupings of colours and textures will dominate the composition. If we move back to 100 metres only trees can be appreciated as individuals, and smaller plants will contribute only in as far as they form part of the combined mass of woodland, shrubbery or meadow.

The different scales which are inherent in a particular plant association cannot all be perceived at once. Our attention tends to focus on one scale of patterns at a time and so, in design, we must understand the different scales which predominate from different viewing positions or regions.

Viewing scale is reliant not only on distance but also on movement. The rate of travel through a landscape determines the field which will be visible within a given time, and it also determines the amount of information which can be absorbed from an area of given size. For this reason the scale of planting should reflect the likely speed of travel of the observer. Planting to be viewed repeatedly from a fixed vantage point and which can be perused at leisure will do justice to a much smaller scale of design and much greater aesthetic diversity than planting which will receive only brief glances from passing vehicles.

It is, unfortunately, quite common to see planting design that is either too complex or too simple for its setting. On the one hand the designer is often well motivated but misguided in attempting to provide too much richness and diversity within restricted planting areas. It may be that they are attempting to compensate for poverty of planting elsewhere in the locality, or to relieve the dullness of the surroundings, but aesthetic diversity is wasted if it cannot be properly appreciated from the normal viewing distance and in the normal viewing period. Further, the generic scale relationships of planting to space and to architecture and hard landscape are often ignored in the desire to plant for planting's sake. Too much

Plate 105　Only variation in tree and shrub species of sufficient scale will be perceived from fast moving vehicles on a trunk road.

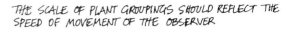

THE SCALE OF PLANT GROUPINGS SHOULD REFLECT THE SPEED OF MOVEMENT OF THE OBSERVER

AT A LEISURELY WALKING PACE INDIVIDUAL TREES AND SMALL GROUPS OF SHRUBS CAN BE APPRECIATED

Plate 106　When vehicles are passing at slower speeds more variation in shape and smaller groups of species can be appreciated.

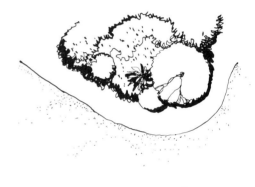

AT A MODERATE VEHICULAR SPEED GROUPS OF TREES AND SHRUB MASSING CAN BE APPRECIATED.

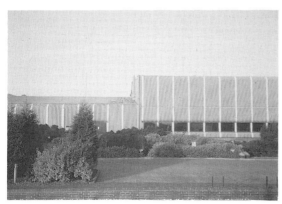

Plate 107　This shrub planting is of suitable scale for stationary or slow moving vehicles and is also in generic scale with the patterns on the buildings' cladding.

Figure 7.6

Plate 108 Planting in a garden, whether public or private, should be of sufficiently small scale to invite prolonged observation and enjoyment. (Photo: Owen Manning)

Plate 109 On this business development at Broadwater Park, Denham, a personal style and scale has been introduced into planting of roadside scale and institutional character. Note its location next to the gate lodge.

diversity in plant associations wastes much of the care and thought that has been put into other aspects of composition.

At the other extreme we find large expanses of shrub monocultures in pedestrian areas. These can appear monotonous, even depressing, because they offer too little diversity to satisfy close inspection, or even to maintain interest whilst we walk alongside. They possess only two scales of interest: the minute detail of leaf, flower or fruit and, when seen as a whole swathe, they can appear in generic scale with large structures such as roads and unadorned buildings.

These are fundamental failures which can overshadow any other attractive qualities the planting may have. When working on the drawing board, the designer needs good imagination to anticipate the effects of the scale relationships of the planting in its setting, and to match that scale to the distance, speed and period of observation.

Movement and viewing angles. The designer must also take into account the angles at which planting will be viewed. These are affected by movement through the landscape, because whilst the observer is in motion the range of focussed attention is more restricted than when static. The greater the observer's speed of travel, the narrower this range will be. For example, the attention of a pedestrian walking purposefully will be confined within a horizontal spread of the order of 90 degrees unless they deliberately pause to examine objects bordering the path. For a motorist on a fast road this horizontal angle will be further reduced to the order of 45 degrees due to the need to maintain close attention on a small, but rapidly changing, visual area.

It is important to note that the angles mentioned above refer to the general spread of focussed attention which allows for head as well as eye movements. It is not the same as the commonly quoted 60 degrees 'cone of vision' which is determined by the optimum angle of eye rotation of 30 degrees either side of the horizontal axis of the head (Dreyfuss, 1959).

The most common viewing angles of planting which borders paths or roads will thus be acute, and the apparent dimensions of planting in the direction of travel will be foreshortened in perspective, whereas the dimensions perpendicular to the direction of travel will merely undergo diminution as they become more distant.

Just as road markings are painted on the road surface in an elongated shape in order to give the appearance of normal proportions, so plant arrangements should be stretched along the axis of movement in order to achieve the perceived scale which is desired.

Unity and Variety in Planting Design

The achievement of unity and variety in design is sometimes treated as one of the principles of planting composition. However, we will deal with it as an objective which underpins all the five principles discussed above. Unity and variety are fundamental to all design, and all materials, methods and principles of design can be dedicated to the achievement of these twin goals.

The need for unity should need little explanation. The desire for wholeness, for oneness, is an essential motivation of the human psyche and the perception of unity in the outer world guides the psyche, on its inner journey. The principles of composition can be seen as guidance towards unity and variety in design. Unity can arise from a pervasive harmony of aesthetic characteristics; from an overall balance of composition which binds the various parts into a whole; from the emphasis of linking or dominant elements in the composition; from an ordered sequence of spaces and planting; and by a choice of planting scale which links the scales of its landscape setting to that of its human participants.

Variety is easier to provide than unity. The range of species and cultivars available includes all the diversity we are ever likely to require under most circumstances. Even a single plant can show great variety as it develops and changes through the seasons. It is achieving unity that offers the real challenge to the designer.

Design Ideas

Over and above the binding functions of good composition, an all-embracing unity can be provided by the dominance of a single design idea or theme. This approach has been adopted with great success in many well known gardens and other ornamental plantings. Memorable examples are the white garden at Sissinghurst Castle in Kent, the red borders at Hidcote Bartrim Manor, Gloucestershire, and numerous well designed rose gardens, herb gardens, woodland gardens, rock gardens and water gardens across the country. By singularity of purpose and strength of composition these gardens create a lasting impression on those who visit them.

A design idea can also be of great value to the designer. Once chosen it provides both an inspiration and a framework for the detailed development of design, and it helps to reduce the overwhelming array of possible plant species to a manageable palette.

A theme may be historic, such as for the recreation of a period landscape or the incorporation of historic features in a contemporary design. It may be inspired by human usage of the landscape and plants, such as in herb and medicinal gardens and *jardins potager* (gardens which intimately mix flowers and vegetables). Historical and usage themes, however, although they provide an objective and a character for the designer to work towards, do still require a guiding aesthetic idea, so we will concentrate on a discussion of aesthetic themes. These can be employed in ornamental contemporary planting as the primary organising principle, or in period and historic landscapes, as a secondary theme.

Aesthetic themes are many and diverse, but can usefully be divided into those based on the visual characteristics of plants, on taxonomic relationships or on a distinctive natural habitat.

Colour. Many beautiful garden plantings have been created by restraining the colours of flowers, fruits, stems and foliage to a limited, related range. For example, gardens of white flowers and grey and silvery foliage are found in many famous UK gardens, such as Newby Hall in North Yorkshire, Hidcote Bartrim Manor in Gloucestershire, and Sissinghurst Castle in Kent. The careful control of colours creates a pervasive mood stimulated by the character of the chosen range of hues. In addition, many subtleties of shade and tint and chroma can be appreciated which would be lost in a more diverse and contrasting colour assemblage. Walking in the white garden at Hidcote we immediately begin to appreciate the gentle diversity of tinted whites, creams, greys, silvers, all offset against the range of foliage greys and greens. The dominant and unifying character is cool and restful, light and gentle.

The contrast with the red borders is dramatic. Here we enter a sultry, almost tropical extravagance. The intense, rich reds of hardy and tender flowers melt into the dark bronzes and purples of foliage, and the whole effect is quite unfamiliar in the soft light typical of the British climate.

Other single colour themes have been used to great effect; for example, yellows can bring vitality to areas in the shade of buildings, and many yellow flowered and foliage plants in fact prefer the low light of such locations.

The majority of blue flowered and silver or grey foliaged plants, on the other hand, need full sun and warm conditions to grow well and develop their most effective foliage colours. This is because the grey or silver leaf colour which arises from a woolly or tomentose leaf surface is an adaption to moisture stress and intense sunlight in the plant's natural habitat.

On the subject of single colour themes Gertrude Jekyll (1908) sounds a note of caution:

> It is a curious thing that people will sometimes spoil some garden project for the sake of a word. For instance, a blue garden, for the beauty's sake, may be hungering for a group of white lillies, or for something of palest lemon-yellow, but it is not allowed to have it because it is called the blue garden, and there must be no flowers but blue flowers. I can see no sense in this; it seems to me like fetters foolishly self-imposed. Surely the business of the blue garden is to be beautiful as well as blue. My own idea is that it should be beautiful first, and then just as blue as may be consistent with its best possible beauty. Moreover any experienced colourist knows that the blues will be more telling – more purely blue – by the juxtaposition of rightly placed complementary colour.

Well balanced dual colour themes can also unify a planting scheme. The contrast and mutual enhancement of complementary colours is displayed most powerfully if each hue is restricted to a narrow range. Yellows and purples offer a striking contrast of hue, and also of value because yellows are generally lighter and fresher than purples of a similar intensity. Blue and orange, however, is often a less successful combination, as the contrast in value is much less than between yellow and purple, and because both colours can appear rather heavy in the presence of their complement. Colour themes can be based on value and intensity rather than only on hue. For example, a planting of pastel flower colours and grey or silver foliage is given a sense of unity by the grey or white which unites the various hues. Pale pinks and pale purple blues can make a particularly effective pastel colour scheme.

An important reason for the success of restricted colour ranges is that a degree of variety and contrast will inevitably be provided by the colours of plant foliage. This contrast is strongest for a red colour theme in which the flower hues will be complementary to the foliage greens. But in other colour ranges there will normally be enough contrast with foliage to enliven the composition as a whole. It is particularly important to include a proportion of dark green foliage to anchor and dignify the paler colours in pastel compositions.

Texture, line and form. Textured qualities may provide the aesthetic inspiration for composition but, again, we must ensure that the balance of harmony and contrast is right.

An association which consists largely of bold textured plants will appear overbearing unless sufficient relief is provided by softer, calmer elements. Yet bold texture can provide an exciting and attractive theme in a space which is large enough to avoid a feeling of claustrophobia, and provided that enough contrast in line, form and colour is also included. A number of dramatic 'tropical' or foliage gardens have been created in this way which have an exotic atmosphere reminiscent of the tropical jungle, despite the fact that the species planted are all hardy in their locations.

The extensive use of bold textures plants is also common, and often successful, in association with modern buildings. This kind of planting is sometimes called 'architectural' planting because the plants have a boldness and consistency of habit and foliage which reflects the purity of form and line found in much modern architecture.

A concentration of fine plant textures would, on the other hand, risk appearing weak and empty unless the lack of stimulation provided by texture was compensated for by bold use of pattern and form. This approach is traditional in formal gardens including parterres, hedging, pleaching or topiary.

Seasonal themes. We commonly strive to provide continuity of interest throughout the year in all our planting. This is often necessary and is certainly admirable, yet there is a place in larger planting schemes for areas which are reserved for seasonal display. Indeed, an area which is wholly committed to spectacular and exhaustive display at one time of year can be all the more memorable for its transience.

In seasonal plantings the great majority of species are selected to be at their peak in the chosen months. A traditional example from English gardens is the herbaceous border which is at its best from July to September when its colourfulness and luxuriance make the most of the short English summer. Other tried and tested seasonal displays include autumn foliage and fruit, winter evergreens with flower and stem colour, and spring blooming bulbs and shrubs. Each has its own distinctive charm.

Scent, sound and touch. Non-visual aesthetic qualities may provide the main inspiration for planting. Emphasis on scent, sound and touch is normal in planting for people with visual disabilities, but any of these could also provide a unifying theme in less specialised plantings.

The fragrance of flowers and aromatic foliage is a source of delight, and planting which is carefully planned to provide an attractive blending and continuity of scents throughout the year would have great distinction and character. Blending of scent is no easier than combining colours, and a garden of scents would require as much skill and sensitivity as one based on a colour theme.

Sound and touch are less obvious characteristics of plants. Sound is dependent on the wind or rain to sway branches, rustle leaves or clatter stems. The physical feel of plants requires our participation and so is less often appreciated. However, either could provide an exciting and unusual theme for planting which would be appreciated by at least the more adventurous and imaginative observer.

Plate 110 The inspiration for this planting is made explicit. A stream of blue, white and purple pansies (*Viola* hybrids) tumbles down an artificial hillside at the Stoke National Garden Festival. The moorland grasses and rushes not only reinforce the suggestion of an upland stream but their subdued browns and greens provide a gentle colour compliment to the brighter colours of the pansies.

Plate 111 Use of bold foliaged species can create a jungle-like character in temperate regions by echoing the macrophyllus plants characteristic of tropical rain forest.

Plate 112 The spring garden is a common seasonal theme. This woodland walk at Dartington Hall, in Devon, is designed to be at its peak in spring with carpets of naturalised woodland flowers and shrubs such as *Camellia* and *Magnolia*.

Plate 113   Rose gardens are
traditional examples of planting
with a taxonomic theme.

Taxonomic themes. In many botanic gardens and horticultural collections plants are arranged by genus, family and order. But taxonomic themes can also provide inspiration for purely ornamental purposes. The prime example is the rose garden, but other genera are also sometimes displayed in their own separate garden or beds. Examples include *Cistus, Iris, Viburnum, Rhododendron* and *Magnolia*. The taxonomic and morphological relationship between the species gives a unity to the planting and a sense of identity to the place. Families or other plant taxa can also be brought together. For example, *Compositae* (daisy family) borders, *Rosaceae* (rose family) plantings and *Ericaceae* (heather family) gardens. Conifer gardens *(Coniferales)* and fern gardens bring together a number of related families as well as species.

Taxonomic relationships can provide an effective theme to help both inspire and unify a planting design. They are perhaps most successful when the environmental conditions are particularly suited to one genus or family which includes a range of species all adapted to a similar habit. For example, a *Cistus* garden would be most effective on a hot, dry, sunny bank.

One significant risk with extensive planting of closely related species, however, is that of pests and diseases. Not only are a large proportion of the species likely to be vulnerable to the same infestations, but its spread will be more rapid than if the host species are more widely distributed among resistant plants. Fireblight on Rosaceae and hypericum rust are diseases which demand caution in the planting of those plant groups.

Habitat themes. Natural habit is a common organising principle in ornamental displays. Rock and scree gardens, wall plantings, woodland gardens, water and marginal plantings are all familiar ways of displaying a variety species which are perceived to belong together. This is because of a shared adaption to similar environmental conditions resulting in similar morphological characteristics, or because we associate these plants together from our knowledge of wild and semi-natural landscapes.

The constraints on species choice imposed by a particular habitat, especially if it is a demanding one for plant growth, allows the designer to introduce considerable contrast and variety in aesthetic qualities without losing the sense of natural affinity between the plants. That affinity and the character of a distinctive habitat will help to create a strong sense of place and a natural logic to the choice and arrangement of plants.

In nature no single habitat, however distinctive, is completely isolated from others. Woodland grades into scrub or meadow or alpine communities; open water

Plate 114   An artificial boulder scree with acid soil provides a habitat theme for planting design at the Glasgow Garden Festival. Heathers (*Calluna vulgaris*), heaths (*Erica* ssp.) and birch (*Betula* spp.) not only grow well but also look at home in this kind of terrain.

Plate 115   A moist, partly shaded rock garden creates a different habitat which will restrict the choice of plants. Ferns are particularly well suited to these conditions.

Plate 116   The development of an hotel and conference centre in an old quarry at Hagen, Germany, provides the opportunity for naturalistic planting which reinforces the sense of place. (Photo: Owen Manning)

Plate 117   A waterside theme may be adopted even when the soil is not in contact with a water body by planting species such as *Alchemilla mollis* and *Salix matsudana* 'Tortuosa' which we associate with water but which does not require permanently moist soil (Lincoln County Hospital).

Plate 118   Open woodland is well suited to ornamental planting and, in many large gardens and parks, provides a habitat theme for collections of shade and shelter loving plants such as smooth Japanese maple (*Acer palmatum*).

adjoins emergent marginal plants or marsh, and so on. Likewise, when we create artificial habitats for planting or establishing particular communities we can build a sequence of related conditions, an ecotone, and thereby encompass more diversity within our planting theme. Indeed, we might even go as far as to represent a whole landscape in microcosm from rocky peaks and tumbling streams to still lakes and tranquil pastures.

Inspiration

The principles of composition consist of an ordering of visual phenomena. These effects can be perceived by anybody, regardless of culture and personal experience. The ability to distinguish harmony and contrast, to experience sequence, to respond to scale, etc. are fundamental to human interaction with the environment because ultimately, they are essential for physical survival.

But this understanding of the visual environment does not, by itself, cause us to manipulate that environment, to create and re-create the cultural landscape around us. To design requires stimulus and inspiration. The stimulus may be a functional necessity such as the need for food or shelter; or it may be a more sophisticated aesthetic need. But what gives rise to an aesthetic need? What inspires the designer to manipulate the elements of composition with aesthetic purpose?

The inspiration for design arises from three major sources. First, the ethos of a particular time and place is an inescapable influence which underpins the work of individual designers. Such cultural influences may be unconscious, as is the case with much popular design, but trained designers should have studied and developed an understanding of the philosophy of design both in their own and also in other cultures and periods. This kind of cultural inspiration marks all the great movements and styles of landscape design. The English Landscape Movement of the eighteenth century was inspired by a new appreciation of nature and influenced by the Italian paintings of Rossa, Poussin and Claude Lorrain. These portrayed a harmony between human activity and natural forces which together moulded a benign, pastoral landscape populated with architectural symbols of European humanist culture. The Gardenesque, to take a later example, was inspired by the vast array of exotic species which were being introduced during the nineteenth century, and was also influenced by the Victorian penchant for orderliness and authority. These influences were more or less grafted onto a scaled down version of the flowing lines and topography of the English Landscape School, and the result successfully reflected the mood of the times.

Individuals have been crucial in practising and propagating new ideas about design which we now clearly identify with their contemporary culture. But designers such as Lancelot Brown (1715-1783) and John Claudius Loudon (1783-1843) were not only vehicles for the birth of embryonic ideas but they also brought their own personal experience and inspiration to design. Their own individuality was stamped on their work.

The value of the individual is enshrined in Western humanism, and the expression of personal freedom and values has become a particularly powerful motivation in design in the late twentieth century. It has perhaps become an end in itself and, regardless of whether we believe this to be enriching or divisive, could certainly consider individualism as a distinctive inspiration of our time. A balancing influence, however, is the growing consciousness of global responsibility, and the maxims 'think globally, act locally' and 'think socially, act personally' may succeed in uniting these two apparently disparate tendencies.

The mark of individuality, although it may be quite conspicuous, is more superficial than the underlying cultural generators of style. It is important to remember that although the designer's personal inspiration and ideas may lead to a design with a strong sense of character and identity, there is also the risk that it will appear too contrived, too mannered, to carry real conviction. This can happen if designers try dogmatically to impose their own will on the site. The result will appear inappropriate and 'over-designed'.

This brings us to the third source of inspiration - the site itself. The *genius loci* or 'spirit of the place' has long been recognised as something which should be deeply respected in design. The term was first coined by the writer and gardener Alexander Pope in 1731 whilst advising on the layout of landscape gardens, most of which would be located in a rural setting. However, the spirit of the place can be just as strong in urban landscapes or small private gardens. If we seek to express this essential nature of the site then the resulting design may be quite unassuming. It may simply build on the best elements and character of what already exists, and it may be difficult for the untrained observer to detect the work of a designer at all. Indeed, some of the best landscape architecture conceals the influence of the designer not by deliberate disguise but because imposed ideas and personal touches are simply unnecessary. In such cases one could say 'the site has designed itself', though with a little help from its friends.

CHAPTER 8

Plant Associations

This chapter will examine some of the key ecological and cultural factors which determine the horticultural success of plant associations. An understanding of these will give us the confidence that our plant associations will develop along the lines that we have in mind, and can be sustained without making onerous demands on maintenance resources.

Plant Communities

In spontaneous, that is natural or semi-natural, plant associations each member of the community earns its place by its ability to compete for light, moisture and nutrients. Each species is adapted to a particular ecological niche, but interacts directly or indirectly with the other members of the community.

Let us take as an example mature temperate deciduous woodland. One characteristic which is typical of the plant associations found here is the manner in which they occupy the physical space above the ground. The range of species present is distributed in two ways. Different species may occupy different areas of ground, that is they are distributed in the horizontal plane, and their canopies may occupy different levels above the ground, that is they are also distributed in the vertical dimension. Distribution in the horizontal plane is determined by ground conditions (especially variations in soil type) and by atmospheric conditions (variation in exposure, light and humidity). The vertical distribution of species is determined by inherent growth form (physiognomy) and stature as well as by the atmospheric conditions.

Pedunculate oak woodland is an example of this formation found in Britain and other parts of Europe. Here the tallest plants are pedunculate oak *(Quercus robur)* commonly mixed with other tall forest trees such as ash *(Fraxinus excelsior)*, sycamore *(Acer pseudoplatanus)* or alder *(Alnus glutinosa)*. The species associated with the oak will depend on local ground conditions and, where these conditions become more extreme, the other species may replace the oak altogether to form specialised societies.

This mixture of tall forest trees forms the dominant canopy, the first layer of foliage to intercept sunlight. In dense woodland this layer may be only several metres deep, although it can be carried at a height of 20 to 30 metres above the ground. Below and between this smaller trees such as field maple *(Acer campestre)*, rowan *(Sorbus aucuparia)*, holly *(Ilex aquifolium)* and wild service tree *(Sorbus torminalis)* may form an intermittent, sub-dominant tree layer.

Below this we find a distinct shrub layer. Its extent and density will depend primarily on the amount of light which penetrates the tree canopy above, and it will be made up of saplings of tree species and mature shade tolerant shrubs including hazel (*Corylus avellana*), midland hawthorn (*Crataegus oxycantha*) and elder (*Sambucus nigra*). A well-developed sub-dominant tree layer together with a dense shrub layer would occupy much of the space below the upper canopy, and create a woodland which is both visually and physically difficult to penetrate. Sparse understories consisting of only occasional small trees and shrubs develop where very low light conditions prevail, and this will leave a much more open space within the body of the woodland.

The third and lowest stratum is known as the field layer. This comprises herbaceous and woody species which commonly grow up to about 0.5 metres in height (occasionally to 1 metre or more). Like the understory layer, the field layer's depth and density will depend largely on the light which is able to penetrate the upper stories. Tree and shrub species also affect the vegetation below by other means such as root competition and leaf litter (Sydes and Grime, 1979). In oak woodland field layer species include shade tolerant prostrate shrubs such as ivy (*Hedera heluix*), honeysuckle (*Lonicera periclymenum*) and bramble (*Rubus fruticosus*), and herbaceous species such as dog's mercury (*Mercurialis perennis*), lords and ladies (*Arum maculatum*) and ground ivy (*Glechoma hederacea*). Because oak is deciduous and comes into leaf relatively late in the season (late May to early June), the ground layer is also likely to include vernal herbs. These flower and make the majority of their vegetative growth in early and mid-Spring before the tree and shrub canopies have reached their greatest density. Wood anemone (*Anemone nemorosa*), bluebell (*Endymion non-scriptus*) and primrose (*Primula vulgaris*) are familiar examples of oak woodland species which take advantage of this seasonal 'window of opportunity'. Vernal herbs are less well developed in beech (*Fagus sylvatica*) woods, where the foliage canopy expands earlier in the spring and casts a heavier shade, and in ash (*Frasxinus excelsior*) woods where the window of opportunity is long enough for an excessively dense shrub layer to develop and restrict the growth of the field layer.

We have sketched only the briefest outline of a woodland plant community, but this should be enough to bring our attention to two principles which can be applied to the design of planted associations of all kinds.

The first is that complete cover of the ground area at one level or more is a sign of a well-developed association growing under reasonably favourable conditions and making good use of the energy available in sunlight. The ground surface is covered throughout the year by living vegetation or a thick layer of leaf and twig litter and other debris. Bare soil, on the other hand, indicates a high degree of stress in the growing environment. This may take the form of low levels of water, soil air, available nutrients, toxicity, excessive compaction or frequent disturbance of the ground surface.

The second principle is that plant communities tend to become increasingly complex as they develop over time. This complexity can be assessed by three main criteria:

1. The variety of species present: **species diversity.**

2. The number of canopy layers present: **structural diversity.**

3. Diversity through the seasons: **phenological diversity.**

Species and structural diversity act as a buffer against environmental pressures such as climatic or microclimatic change and variations in biotic factors including disease, grazing and human interference. A wide range of species offers potential for adaptation to environmental change and a well-developed physical structure tends to ameliorate the severity of climatic and edaphic factors.

Designing with Canopy Layers

Too much planting design is done on plan alone. As much, if not more, attention should be given to the vertical arrangement of plants as to their positioning in the horizontal plane. It is the elevations of plant groupings and the three dimensional spaces around and within them that we perceive most readily. It is the exception to view planting from much above normal eye level, most people never see it in plan view from directly above.

When we design a plant association we must aim to create an arrangement of canopy layers which provides the functional and aesthetic qualities that are needed. A complex community structure of the kind outlined above represents only one possibility for design, we need not necessarily aim to immitate this and, indeed, there will be many circumstances where a simpler canopy and spatial structure will suit the needs of design. In planting design a variety of different structures is often more valuable than a single vegetation structure; however, great a variety of species this may contain.

If we observe a wide range of plant communities, both natural and artificial, in different stages of development we can see many different combinations of canopy layers. In fact, it is possible to find all the possible permutations of tree, shrub and field layers. These permutations consist of either three (or occasionally more) layers, two layers or a single layer.

Three Layer Canopy Structures

Tree canopy – shrub layer – field layer. Multiple layer woodland is the climax vegetation wherever the ground provides sufficient moisture and root anchorage, and where conditions of exposure and temperature allow. But large planted or managed woodlands of this kind are not very common in urban areas and in managed rural locations because it can provide for only a limited range of economic needs. However, it is valuable for shelter, wildlife conservation, aesthetic improvements, environmental education and informal recreation. Small scale multiple layer woodland is more common in both countryside and cities because it can occupy pockets of land which could less easily be put to other, more financially profitable, uses. It may be spontaneous in origin, being the result of secondary succession in areas released from human interference, or it may be deliberately planted.

Ornamental vegetation with a similar canopy structure can be found at the medium scale in woodland gardens, and at a smaller scale in beds of exotic tree, shrub and ground layer planting. These pockets of ornamental woodland, 'exotic groves', can be found in parks, gardens and other urban planting. They may be as small as 100 square metres but still show a distinctive canopy structure of three or more overlapping, but not necessarily continuous, layers.

This kind of planting, whether naturalistic or ornamental, offers a great diversity of plants and aesthetic richness. It gives the best plant value per area because it makes full use of the space above the ground. Unfortunately, many opportunities for this kind of planting are ignored. There are a number of reasons for this. The most common is the predominace of certain traditional ideas about how to grow and display ornamental plants. These tend to encourage the careful and separate placing of plants as distinct objects of ornament for individual scrutiny rather than their combination as components of a well composed association. In addition, many people feel anxiety about planting trees of any great stature in urban areas, and some designers simply lack the imagination or experience to see the possibilities for richer, more complex, planting associations.

Tree canopy – shrub layer – field layer (woodland edge). The edge of natural and semi-natural woodland is often characterised by a gradation in canopy heights from high woodland canopy through smaller trees and shrubs, dense tall herbs with dwarf or prostrate shrubs, down to grassland or open ground. This edge may be fixed by adjacent land management or it may advance as the woodland colonises open land. In all cases, however, its canopy structure and constituent species are a response to the higher light levels and the greater exposure found at the edge than within the woodland core. Although some species may be common to both edge and understorey, many of these will flower and fruit more abundantly in the light and warmth of the edge, especially if it faces South.

The same canopy layers are present at the edge as can be found in a woodland core. The difference is, firstly, that at the edge canopy layers are arranged laterally along an ecotone and, because of the reduction in shading, each layer is denser than its equivalent in the woodland core and can contain more light demanding species. The width of a woodland edge may vary considerably but cannot be much less than five metres because of the space which would be occupied by even a single line of plants which might constitute each canopy layer.

This edge structure is also common in artificial plantings. It may form an edge to high woodland plantation or woodland gardens, or it may stand alone, divorced from the woodland proper. When planted alone, a woodland edge still offers much ecological and visual diversity. So this kind of canopy structure is often adopted for screens and shelter belts where the planting width available would not be sufficient to allow the development of high woodland.

A woodland edge canopy structure can be developed using exotic and ornamental species, and the gradual build up of height from front to back allows each layer in turn to be displayed to view from eye level. In ornamental associations a larger number of layers are often discernible, and there may be a more gradual build up in height. A typical ornamental edge structure would consist of:

1. Front edging of prostrate shrubs or low herbs perhaps with bulbs and other small herbaceous plants emerging from them at various seasons.
2. Low shrubs and tall herbaceous perennials.
3. Medium height shrubs and, behind these,
4. Tall shrubs and small trees.

Small and medium height trees might be grouped or scattered through the various layers taking care to avoid casting heavy shade which would suppress the layers below. Tall forest tree species would be conrmed to the back of the edge in order to reduce the shade cast by their extensive canopy spread to a minimum.

Layers 1, 2 and 3 can be designed to give ground cover, that is to provide a continuous dense canopy down to near ground level which will prevent most weed growth below it. The tall shrubs in Layer 4 are likely to have a more upright habit with less foliage near ground level, but their bare stems and the ground below them will be effectively hidden by the lower foliage canopies in front.

The width of each layer can, of course, vary along the length of the bed, and some may appear only intermittently or not at all. Because of the greater control we can exercise over the height and spread of exotic species in an ornamental

THREE LAYER CANOPY STRUCTURES

LAYERS IN MATURE OPEN WOODLAND.

IN THE INNERSTAND TO NATURALISTIC OR EXOTIC
PLANTING.

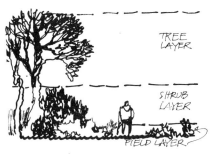

AT WOODLAND EDGE.

Figure 8.1

EDGE STRUCTURES

WOODLAND EDGE STRUCTURE 'BACKED UP' TO
FORM WOODLAND BELT OR WIDE HEDGEROW

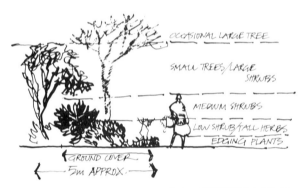

MAXIMUM DEVELOPMENT OF EDGE STRUCTURE USED TO
DISPLAY ORNAMENTAL PLANTING.

MINIMUM EDGE STRUCTURE REQUIRES 2m.

Figure 8.2

association, it is possible to reduce the width of a graded edge type of planting to as little as two metres. In this case there would only be space for two layers, a front edging of carpeting or low shrubs with medium or tall shrubs behind.

The graduated height structure is generally understood and commonly used in planting design, particularly ornamental shrubberies, herbaceous and mixed borders. This kind of planting was advocated as a means of displaying ornamental shrubs by Michael Haworth Booth (1938) at a time when most private gardens no longer had the resources to maintain the more labour intensive herbaceous borders.

Like a multiple layered woodland core, a woodland edge planting is a way of making the most of a limited ground area by including a number of different canopy layers within it. One of these two alternative approaches is likely to be a successful way of achieving structural and ornamental interest in a wide variety of planting schemes. However, we may wish to create a simpler kind of vegetation structure using two or one canopy layers rather than three.

Two Layer Canopy Structures

Tree canopy – shrub thicket. This combination occurs in nature where the tree canopy is sufficiently open to allow a dense shrub thicket to develop in the understory. The thicket is often composed of species which spread by vegetative means to form a tangled 'undergrowth' impenetrable to people and preventing the establishment of any significant field layer.

In artificial plant associations a naturalistic version of this may be created using understory shrubs such as blackthorn *(Prunus spinosa)*, hawthorn *(Crataegus monogyna)* or snowberry *(Symphoricarpos albus)* below a scattered tree canopy of species such as oak *(Quercus robur)* or ash *(Fraxinus excelsior)*. Beneath trees which cast a heavier shade such as beech *(Fagus sylvatica)* only shade bearing understory species would survive: box *(Buxus sempervirens)*, yew *(Taxus baccata)* or holly *(Ilex aquifolium)*, for example.

The ornamental equivalent of this is a planting idiom often seen in large scale landscape projects, rather than those of a garden scale and character. Its popularity derives partly from its low cost. The ground is covered effectively with a small number of thicket forming shrub species which, once established, will require only a low level of maintenance. Suitable species which are shade tolerant and reliable on a wide range of soils include dogwoods *(Cornus alba* and *C. stolonifera)*, cotoneasters (such as *C. conspicuus* and *C. lacteus)*, barberries *(Berberis candidula, B. verruculosa,* and others), and the smaller laurels *(Prunus laurocerasus* 'Zabelliana', *P. l.* 'Angustifolia', and others). Trees are then scattered in drift groups or individually through the shrub thicket, and eventually form a continuous or broken tree canopy above the dense undergrowth.

Tree canopy – field layer. This can be found in nature where a very dense upper canopy precludes the growth of a significant shrub layer, but allows a field layer of shade tolerant herbs to develop. These may include 'shade dodging' vernal herbs. It can also be seen in semi-natural associations such as wood pasture where heavy grazing in open woodland has prevented the establishment of woody seedlings and favoured grasses.

This kind of canopy structure can be useful in artificial plant associations where an open aspect is desired. Space is defined by a ceiling of tree canopy above, and the

TWO LAYER CANOPY STRUCTURES

TREE CANOPY - SHRUB THICKET

TREE CANOPY - FIELD LAYER.

SHRUB LAYER - FIELD LAYER.

Figure 8.3

floor is clothed by the field layer below. The interior of the association would be open to views from its boundaries, and may also include access and circulation. The tree canopy may be dense and unbroken, creating a continuous ceiling, or it may be more scattered giving lighter and more varied conditions within whilst still giving the sense of a distinct ceiling of foliage. The field layer could be a simple ground cover which is tolerant of moderate to dense shade such as ivies (*Hedera* spp.), *Pachysandra terminalis* or rose of sharon (*Hypericum calycinum*). It may, if the shade is not too dense, consist of a grassy meadow or mown grass sward, the ornamental equivalent of wood pasture.

Trees planted in mown grass is such a common sight in all urban areas in Britain that it could easily be taken to be the normal way to plant amenity trees. It is certainly an effective combination where we want trees with free circulation below and a modest establishment cost, but it is slow to take effect and low in visual and ecological interest. Its widespread use is in part due to excessive adherence to one particular idiom, that of the 'English Parkland'. Individual and grouped trees spreading above grazed pasture is a familiar motif of the English Landscape Movement parklands laid out in the eighteenth century, and admiration for these generous sweeps of grassland and fine spreading trees is understandable. The idiom is less appropriate to small scale urban locations which are where factors such as low level shelter, screening and aesthetic diversity are important design objectives.

Shrub layer – field layer. In nature this structure is found in coastal and montane communities where the tree layer is absent because of climatic factors, and in chalk downland scrub and Mediterranean garigue where succession has not progressed to an arboreal stage.

A similar structure can be created in artificial plant associations where trees are not appropriate for reasons of scale, available space, light or views. It can be achieved by planting shrubs to form the dominant canopy at between 1.5 and 3 metres high, and underplanting them with low ground cover species. The shrub layer can be more or less dispersed, but this kind of canopy structure requires shrub species which have a more erect or open habit than would normally be used to form a closed, weed suppressing shrub thicket. The shrub canopy must allow enough space and enough light below for the field layer planting to thrive.

Shrub and ground cover associations are common in small ornamental areas of parks, gardens and courtyards, in planting close to buildings, and where overhead or underground services preclude tall growing or deep rooting trees. It is an excellent method of displaying specimen shrubs, either singly or in small groups because the ground cover avoids the need for close planting of taller shrubs. Even slow growing specimens such as the Japanese maples (*Acer palmatum* and *A. japonicum*) will have the chance to develop their full canopy spread and mature form while the field layer of ground cover reduces weed competion. Exotic shrubs planted as specimens in mown grass represents another example of an artificial shrub-field layer association although one that has certain cultural if not aesthetic drawbacks. Common lawn specimens such as buckeye (*Aesculus parviflora*), stagshorn sumach (*Rhus typhina*) and lilacs (*Syringa* spp.) show off their flowers and form as well, if not better, above a carpet of ground cover. They certainly grow more vigorously in a bed of ground cover than in a lawn of mown grass which is highly competitive for soil moisture and nutrients.

Single Layer Canopy Structures

Tree canopy. Tree growth without associated shrubs or herbs is rare in nature, but not impossible to find. On thin, dry soils xerophytic tree species may be the only plants capable of exploiting ground water at great depth. Under these conditions of extreme moisture stress, individual trees are usually widely spaced, occupying the ground at a density determined by the quantity of water available. Another example can be found on screes and boulder falls, where trees may be the first plants to colonise. Their rapid extension growth at the seedling stage allows the stem to extend into the sunlight from deep crevices which retain the small amounts of soil and moisture needed for tree seedlings to establish.

It is unusual to see trees planted alone in unvegetated ground except during the early stages of establishment of mass tree planting, and in paved urban areas. In both these cases it is human rather than climatic induced stress which prevents the growth of the field layer. Planting trees in pavement areas is a common and valuable means of introducing vegetation to streets, squares, precincts and car parks where space at ground level is limited and pedestrian or vehicular traffic is intense. The spatial structure of this combination is similar to that of trees planted in grass, but the ground surface is of course able to take much heavier traffic. The effect is to create a foliage canopy overhead which defines and partly covers the space but does not significantly restrict vision or circulation at ground level.

Shrub thicket. A shrub thicket which is sufficiently dense to prevent the growth of a significant field layer is not uncommon in natural or in artificial plantings. In nature it is often the sign of an early vigorous stage in the colonisation of an open area by woody plants before a differential age and height structure develops. British hillsides covered in gorse *(Ulex europaeus)* and low maquis in the Mediterranean region are examples. It is also found where extreme climatic conditions prevent the growth of taller plants, that is, beyond the tree line in alpine and tundra regions.

In amenity and ornamental landscapes shrub thickets can be used where ground cover and height are wanted simultaneously. They are best created using densely planted shrub species of spreading or domed form with dense foliage down to near ground level. The commonest species include *Viburnum tinus, Cotoneaster conspicuus* and many barberries such as *Berberis verruculosa* and *B. candidula.* It is, of course, possible to use more light demanding species *than* would grow beneath a tree canopy such as *Senecio* 'Sunshine', shrubby cinquefoil *(Potentilla fruticosa)* and shrubby veronicas *(Hebe* spp.).

The width of a shrub thicket need rarely exceed about 3 metres. This width will be enough to provide any necessary separation and enclosure. Because such planting is dense and its height is close to or above eye-level, views into and across it are very limited, and any planting behind the first 2 to 3 metres is mostly out of sight and contributes little if anything to the composition. Planting areas of greater width can be justified by introducing more visual and ecological diversity with a multi-layered canopy structure.

Finally, we should note that single layer, widely spaced shrub planting with bare soil between, although common in traditional ornamental beds, is laborious to maintain. This is because there is a constant need to suppress the natural establishment of a field layer in the bare ground which provides ideal conditions for spontaneous colonisation.

SINGLE LAYER CANOPY STRUCTURES

TREE CANOPY ABOVE BARE GROUND OR PAVEMENT

TALL OR MEDIUM HEIGHT SHRUB THICKET, OR FIELD LAYER
GROUND COVER .

OPEN FIELD LAYER

Figure 8.4

Field layer. Field layer vegetation with nothing taller than prostrate or dwarf shrubs is found naturally in tundra, alpine and desert communities where plants of greater stature are prevented from growing by the harshness of the climate. Field layer alone is also common where grazing, burning or other biotic factors limit the establishment of trees and shrubs, such as in meadows heaths and moorlands. As climatic or biotic pressure approaches the limit of what plants will tolerate, this ground layer vegetation becomes more open and bare ground appears between plants.

An open community of dispersed low shrubs and herbs is a common sight in traditionally maintained parks and gardens. Here the environmental stress which prevents the canopy from closing is the frequent disturbance of the ground surface by hoeing, forking, or other means of weed control.

Extensive swathes of uninterrupted low ground cover are seen in artificial plantings where visibility is critical (eg. highway visibility splays) or to achieve a simple but striking spatial effect. A mown lawn is the ornamental version of a grazed meadow. Its uniformity can be an aesthetic benefit and its durability under pedestrian traffic gives it the important functional role of a circulation surface. A field layer of low shrubs requires carpeting species with similar form and habit to those associated with the tree canopy-field layer structure, but able to able to thrive in conditions of full light where there is no tree or shrub canopy unless they are to be planted in ground which is shaded by buildings or other structures. Examples include *Erica* spp., *Calluna vulgaris*, *Cotoneaster salicifolius* 'Repens', *C. dammeri* and *Hypericum calycinum*.

More intensive maintenance is normally needed if we want to keep low ground cover free from taller shrubs and trees than is necessary to preserve the canopy structure of the other associations. Even the densest of carpeting ground covers such as ivies *(Hedera* spp.) and *Rubus tricolor* will soon become invaded by elder *(Sambucus nigra)*, sycamore *(Acer pseudoplatanus)*, ash *(Fraxinus excelsior)*, birch *(Betula* spp.), goat willow *(Salix caprea)* and other prolific seeding trees and shrubs, and will begin to develop shrub and tree layers.

Horticultural Factors in Plant Associations

The scope of planting design ranges from the creation or management of naturalistic plant communities to small scale gardening with choice and exotic ornamentals. The essence of naturalistic planting design is to employ the species which are best adapted to the prevailing environmental conditions, and to increase species diversity by deliberately increasing the range of microclimatic and soil conditions. On the other hand, traditional amenity horticulture requires the adaptation of the soil and microclimate to suit the needs of plants which would not otherwise thrive. This can result in the gradual transformation of a diversity of soils towards the horticultural ideal of a neutral or slightly acidic, moist but well drained deep loam.

This distinction between choosing the species to fit the site and modifying the site to fit the species is not necessarily the same as the difference between native and exotic planting. Exotic species may be planted or may naturalise in naturalistic planting schemes; for example, larch *(Larix* spp.) and false acacia *(Robinia pseudoacacia)* grow successfully in many naturalistic woodland plantings, and exotic herbaceous species such as winter aconite *(Eranthis hyemalis)* can be encouraged to naturalise in woodland gardens. Conversely, native species may require just as much horticultural care as exotics if they are to be grown in a location with unsuitable soils or microclimate: witness the care lavished on heathers and heaths

(*Calluna vulgaris* and *Erica* spp.) in gardens and parks in all parts of the British Isles, regardless of the soil type.

The key technical consideration for the planting designer is the kind of site preparation and the level of aftercare required in order to sustain the desired plant association. Although it is feasible, given adequate resources and horticultural expertise, to create and sustain almost any combination of plants, in the majority of cases the objective will be to gain the maximum functional and aesthetic benefit for the minimum input of human and material resources. If this is our aim we must select species which will grow and develop together naturally to form an easily sustainable association. Their ability to do this depends on their growth requirements, relative competitiveness, mode of spread, habit and longevity.

Growth Requirements

Each species used in a planting scheme must be well enough suited to the site conditions for it to grow strongly and remain in good health. In some situations it will be an advantage if the plant is able to spread, either by setting and disseminating viable seed or, as is more common, by vegetative means of increase. This would be desirable, for example, where an unregulated mixture of naturalising species is required. In many planting schemes, however, it will be sufficient if the component plants are able to grow strongly and establish quickly in the locations in which they are planted. A species which will have to struggle to survive because it is planted near the limit of its environmental tolerance is wasted in any planting scheme, whether naturalistic or ornamental and regardless of the level of horticultural attention that it will receive. The dictum 'choose the right plant for the place' should never be ignored. There are numerous reference books and catalogues which give the growth requirements of plants, and these should always be consulted when we are choosing species, but we should also take every opportunity to supplement and confirm the advice of others with personal experience and observation.

Relative Competitiveness

Vigorous and healthy growth is important for a robust and attractive scheme but the competitiveness of plants grown in close proximity must be carefully matched if we are to avoid aggressive species overrunning others. A number of trees and shrubs, and particularly certain tall herbs, are capable of very rapid extension of the foliage canopy. In this way they 'forage' for light, searching it out in whatever direction it can be found, shading and suppressing their neighbours in the process. Such species need to be placed with care in plant combinations to ensure that they do not suppress weaker neighbours. Herbaceous plants show particularly rapid growth rates over short periods with canopy extension reaching its peak in May and June. This is possible because of large food reserves collected the previous growing season and stored in perennating organs during the dormant winter period in preparation for the next growing season. Nettles (*Urtica* spp.), *Astrantia major*, *Geranium ibericum* and Japanese knotweed (*Polygonum cuspidatum*) are examples of foraging competitors.

Shrub species which exhibit rapid canopy extension under favourable growing conditions include elder (*Sambucus nigra*), goat willow (*Salix caprea*) and a number of vigorous woody species with a climbing or rambling habit such as *Clematis*, Honeysuckle (*Lonicera* spp.), Russian vine (*Polygonum baldschuanicum*) and *Rubus tricolor*. Such vigorous shade casting shrubs must, like herbaceous competitors, all be carefully located or managed. They must either be associated with species of comparable vigour or planted where there is sufficient free space for their canopy to extend without interfering with adjacent species. The latter option is best achieved by associating them with plants of a higher canopy level.

Although shading is the most important way in which dominance is achieved, competition for water and nutrients can also be significant at the establishment stage. Many grasses, for example, develop extensive root systems which are highly efficient at extracting soil moisture and significantly reduce the water available to other plants which share the same soil volume. The effect of this can be seen in the performance of trees or shrubs planted into a grass sward. Their establishment and growth is significantly reduced by comparison with the same species in mulched or bare ground. It is interesting to note that trials have shown mown grass swards to reduce tree growth to a greater extent than uncut grass.

The growth check experienced by trees and shrubs in grass is considerably reduced once their canopies begin to cast significant shade and shed leaf litter on the grasses below. At this stage the trees start to exert their natural dominance. Mature trees and shrubs suppress the growth of plants below them by shading, leaf litter and by competition for soil moisture and nutrients. Only shrubs and herbs which are adapted to both dry and shady conditions will be able to thrive beneath mature trees, and these tend to be much less competitive than grasses. An extreme example of this dominance effect can be observed along the bottom of hedges composed of nutrient demanding species such as privet (*Ligustrum ovalifolium*) or leyland cypress (x *Cupressocyparis leylandii*), or with surface feeding root systems such as beech (*Fagus sylvatica*).

Mode of Spread

A plant's success in competition with other members of an association will depend not only on the growth rate and ability to exploit soil water and nutrients, but also on its mode of spread. Once established, plants which are well suited to the local environmental conditions will begin to propagate themselves either by seed or vegetative means.

Increase by Seed

Not only native species but also many exotics propagate themselves efficiently by seed. Sycamore (*Acer pseudoplatanus*), Norway maple (*Acer platanoides*), *Rhododendron ponticum*, *Buddleja davidii* and Spanish broom (*Spartium junceum*) are examples of species which naturalise freely by seed under certain conditions. This can be either a benefit or problem depending on the site and the objectives of the planting. Sycamore and rhododendron are often unwelcome colonists due to their prolific spread and tendency to exclude the majority of other species by rapid growth and heavy shading. Self-sown *Buddleja* and Spanish broom, on the other hand, can contribute a great deal by their wildlife value and attractive flowers, and especially by their ability to colonise inhospitable locations such as demolition sites and railway sidings where plant establishment by conventional means is difficult.

Vegetative Increase

In the majority of exotic plantings it is the different modes and rates of vegetative spread that are most likliey to affect the composition of the association. The common methods are by stolons, runners, rhizomes, suckers and rootstocks.

Stolons. Many of the common ground cover plants owe their effectiveness to an ability to spread rapidly and produce a low dense canopy which excludes the majority of weeds. The fastest spreaders include *Rubus tricolor, Hedera* 'Hibernica', *Cotoneaster* 'Skogholm' and *Vinca major,* all of which propagate themselves by sending out vigorous, long shoots which root where they touch the ground. These creeping stems are either true stolons (arching stems which curve down to the ground and root), eg. *Cotoneaster* 'Skogholm' and *Vinca major,* or trailing stems which root at intervals along their length as in the case of *Hedera* .

In both cases, the species has the ability to rapidly and continuously invade new areas of ground. The new roots and shoots are fed in the early stages by the parent plant which allows them to establish quickly, even among competing vegetation. So stoloniferous spreaders are well equipped to invade other field layer vegetation by scrambling and 'leap frogging' over the competition. This may be a great benefit if the object is simply to achieve an impenetrable ground cover, or if an intermingling mixture of plants is desired. If, however, we want to maintain clear and constant boundaries between the territories of different species, such rampant invaders demand regular curtailment to keep them within bounds.

Runners. Species which spread by runners show a similar ability to build up a dense and extensive foliage carpet. Runners are a special form of stolons which consist of an aerial branch or shoot which roots at its end to form a new plant. Their prime function is to propagate the plant rather than to make 'feeding' growth. Runners are only found in herbaceous plants, and examples include strawberry *(Fragaria vesca)* and foam flower *(Tiarella cordifolia).*

Rhizomes. Rhizomes are underground stems which act as both organs of perennation and as a means of increase. Rhizomes are generally horizontal in their growth, and may be short fleshy food stores, as in the common flag iris *(Iris germanica),* which spreads gradually outwards from its original planting position to form broad clumps. Some species of herbaceous plants and shrubs produce much more extensive and vigorous branching rhizomes which enable them to spread rapidly into adjoining ground. These are often mistaken for true roots but can be distinguished by the presence of nodes and internodes. The rhizomes produce branches at the nodes which appear above ground as new shoots and are accompanied by a new root system. Couch grass *(Agropyron repens)* and horsetail *(Equisetum arvense)* are familiar examples that are very difficult weeds to eradicate from ornamental planting because of their far creeping and persistent rhizomes.

A number of shrubby species including rose of sharon *(Hypericum calycinum)* and some bamboos *(Arundinaria pygmea* and *A. anceps)* also send out long rhizomes which produce numerous plantlets. These may arise at some distance from the parent plant. This habit enables them to form a dense mat of ground cover which expands rapidly to exploit new ground. The aggressive habit of rhizomatous spreaders like rose of sharon brings with it similar benefits and similar management problems to those experienced with the vigorous stoloniferous species. But rhizomatous plants can be even more difficult to keep in check because pulling them up normally leaves pieces of the rhizome in place below the ground, each of which will quickly grow into a new individual.

Suckers. An ability to throw up vigorous shoots at some distance from a parent plant is a characteristic of suckering trees and shrubs. Suckers are shoots which arise from adventitious buds on the roots of woody plants. *Prunus* spp., lilac *(Syringa vulgaris*), snowberry (*Symphoricarpos albus*), aspen (*Populus tremula*) and stagshorn sumach (*Rhus typhina*) are well known by gardeners for their persistence in producing suckers, despite considerable efforts to eradicate them. Indeed, any disturbance of the roots whilst removing suckers stimulates further shoots and so can be counter-productive. The more vigorous suckering shrubs such as *Symphoricarpos* can be difficult to contain in most associations, and we may have difficulty if we want to maintain an individual specimen of *Rhus* or *Syringa* free from ancillary stems.

Rootstocks. Rootstocks are common among herbaceous plants. The term decribes a short upright underground stem which gives rise to fresh aerial shoots as it grows. The resulting plant is comparatively slow in its lateral spread and so appears as a compact clump. This habit can be observed in the cranesbills (*Geranium* spp.), *Tellima*, lupins, delphiniums and ice plant (*Sedum spectabile*). Ground cover plants with rootstocks rely on close planting and the vigour of their expanding foliage to suppress weeds in the early years of their establishment before they have spread to occupy the majority of the ground area. Their compactness and contained spread is an asset in many planting schemes where rampant ground cover is not necessary.

Habit

The canopies of trees and shrubs exhibit a great variety of form. We have examined this from an aesthetic point of view, but a plant's habit of growth also affects its ecological compatibility with other members of an association. Canopy habit can be understood most simply as the form in which a plant grows and occupies space. Habit can be classified firstly according to life form; that is trees, shrubs, herbaceous perennials and annuals. The canopies of these different life forms occupy a variety of different levels above the ground surface. This allows coexistence of different life forms within the same ground area. In addition, each life form will include a variety of plants whose habit is of a particular size, shape and density. They may have a compact habit which presents a closely knit surface to the light or they may have an open, even straggly canopy with widely spaced branches leaving large gaps between them. Their form may be narrow and erect, arching, rounded or spreading.

The more open the habit, the more opportunity it offers for close association with other species both because it is likely to cast a lighter shade on lower layers of vegetation, and because it allows more space within the bulk of its canopy for the branches and shoots of other species in the same layer. Open habited species include birch (*Betula* spp.), ash (*Fraxinus* spp.), firethorn (*Pyracantha rogersiana*) and *Caryopteris x clandonensis*.

Compact, dense canopies produced by shrubs like *Viburnum tinus*, *Senecio greyi* and *Calluna vulgaris* are less able to share the space within their canopy boundary with other plants, and will allow only the sparsest of layers below them. For this reason, low and medium height shrubs or herbaceous plants with dense canopies are the most effective at forming ground cover of a single species. They allow very little room for the invasion of weeds.

Longevity and Life Cycles

One of the factors which affects the balance and composition of an association is the life span of the constituent plants. In addition, the vigour, size and form of most plants vary significantly over the different phases of their life cycles. This means that competitiveness, rate of spread and habit will depend on the age of the plant, as well as the species and the environmental conditions.

Plants normally grow with their maximum vigour during the late establishment and semi-mature phases, but how soon this occurs varies, of course, with different species. Many herbaceous plants establish very rapidly, especially shortlived perennials and annuals. This early start of growth can be of great value in a planting scheme, lending vigour, bulk of foliage and an appearance of partial maturity in the earliest years. Ground covers such as *Geranium macrorrhizum*, *Symphytum grandiflorum* and *Lamium maculatum* can form a complete carpet within two growing seasons, while transplanted trees and shrubs may take this length of time to establish their root system properly.

If a field layer which is quick to establish is planted under the canopies of trees and shrubs it will form a vigorous carpet during the early years. But when the roots and crowns of the layers above reach their maximum vigour they will compete strongly for light and moisture, and if the field layer species are not tolerant of this shade and dryness they will begin to die back and would need to be replaced by better adapted ground layer species. A similar cycle can be observed in shrubs planted amongst trees. But if the shrubs are tolerant of both the open sunny conditions they will experience in the early stages, and of shadier, dryer conditions that will prevail later, then replacement or regeneration will only be necessary as they reach over-maturity. This kind of wide ecological amplitude is displayed by many species of *Cotoneaster* and *Berberis,* for example, and is one of the chief reasons for their popularity in public and institutional plantings where management commitments must be kept to a minimum.

It is a useful rule of thumb that the shorter the life span, the earlier is the period of maximum vigour. This applies not only when comparing different life forms of vastly different life expectancies (cf. oaks and annuals), but also among trees and shrubs. Trees which exhibit the fastest growth in their early years are often short lived species such as poplar *(Populus* spp.), willow *(Salix* spp.) and birch *(Betula* spp). Likewise, the fastest growing shrubs are often the most short lived, for example *Senecio,* lavender *(Lavandula* spp.), broom *(Cytisus* spp.) and gorse *(Ulex europaeus).*

The different rates of development must be carefully considered at the design stage to ensure that the plants in an association will be compatible throughout its development. The need to replace or regenerate different parts of the association of different times must be understood and planned for in advance. It is in this area, what might be called the developmental dynamics of planting, that the designer needs to have a particularly sensitive understanding of the growth and management of plant associations.

Plant Knowledge

There are sufficient examples of poor horticultural design to illustrate the problems that arise from lack of knowledge. In many cases, plant assocations only approximate to the designer's intentions, and only achieve this thanks to the frequent and laborious attentions of gardeners. The compatibility of different species can certainly be improved by thinning, pruning and soil amelioration, but it is important to keep the need for this to a minimum. Management resources should be employed creatively and cost effectively in order to gain the maximum benefit from all the elements of a plant association. It is poor design if time is wasted tending struggling plants or restricting the excessive vigour of those which are too aggresive for their neighbours.

If we fully understand the growth requirements, competitiveness, mode of spread, habit and life cycles of the plants with which we design, we can be sure of creating effective, sustainable planting schemes. This is the essence of good horticulture. To gain this degree of knowledge of a wide range of plants inevitably takes considerable time, and cannot be obtained from books or databases alone The designer must work with plants and observe them growing under different conditions and in different associations. It is not possible to be a good planting designer without belng something of a gardener as well.

PART 2

Process

CHAPTER 9

A Method for Planting Design

Good designers have a working method which helps them achieve their aims. It may be unorthodox, even unpredictable at times, but it is still a sound method if it helps them make the best use of their flair and imagination. It can be of particular assistance when the designer feels (as we all do at some time) blocked, frustrated or overawed by the apparent magnitude of their task.

We will experience many different demands and feelings during the creative process. These can range from excitement at glimpsing the potential of a site, through frustration with the problems which obstruct our progress, to delight and satisfaction at seeing our vision become a reality. And throughout we will be conscious of the need to provide a professional service to the client without whom we would not have the opportunity to work on the project.

It is essential to recognise that a good working method is not a straight-jacket imposed on creative thinking. On the contrary, it can greatly aid the imagination by freeing it from the multitude of minor decisions inherent in the process of design. The design process to be described is based on a generally accepted sequence for integrated landscape design. It can be adopted whether we are designing with all the elements of the external environment or concentrating solely on planting. The thought processes and methods of communication are similar in both cases, but the medium is, of course, more restricted for planting design alone.

There are a number of distinct stages in the process. In some projects these need to be followed strictly in sequence, and they usually result in drawings or reports which are formally submitted to the client, planning authority and other professionals. Many of the steps desribed are intended to help the designer arrive at the formal presentation stages, and can be more easily modified to suit the skills and temperament of the individual.

Although the design process is described in a linear sequence it is important to remember that when we are designing we will almost certainly find ourselves leaping forwards, exploring diversions and returning to earlier stages. The process should be imagined not so much as a straight and narrow path but more as a guiding orientation.

The linear nature of the description is necessitated by the verbal mode of communication of a book. It is interesting to compare verbal thinking and expression, which is generally linear and sequential in its nature with graphic thinking and expression, by which we can conceive of numerous elements simultaneously. Whereas the analytic stages of the design process are aided by goal oriented, convergent thinking, the creative, synthesising stages need a playful, exploratory approach. It is the exploration of design possibilities which is most dependent on the graphic mode of thinking.

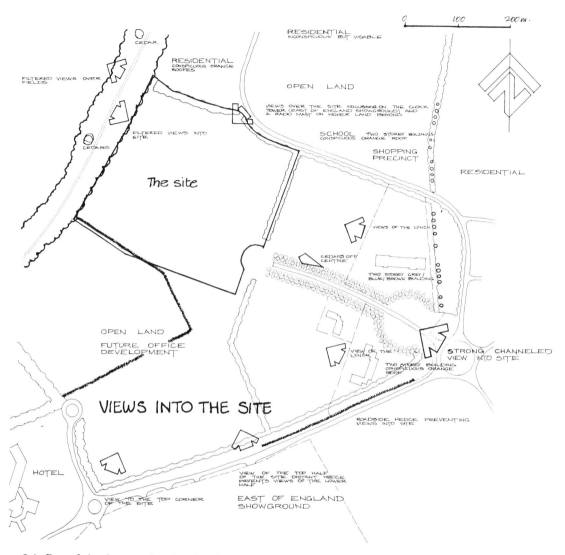

Figure 9.4 Part of visual survey drawing showing major views and describing visual character. (Prof. A.E. Weddle, Landscape Architect)

are those which manage to assess the value of the different aspects of the site without losing sight of the interrelationships between them. Visual quality may be ultimately connected to ecological diversity, the experience of a panoramic vista can be heightened by exposure to the elements at the point of prospect.

Some of the conclusions and recommendations which arise from the analysis will be based firmly on scientific evidence and will be difficult to refute. Others will be the result of judgement which is partly subjective. If these judgements are well informed by our knowledge and experience this should help them to carry sufficient weight with our client and colleagues. Many aspects of landscape design are inaccessible to science because they cannot be quantified. In particular, any attempt to evaluate the aesthetic qualities of a site will inevitably include a measure of subjectivity. Different people's responses to wildness, for example, to enclosure and openness, even to particular plant species, vary considerably. As professional designers we must cultivate a degree of detachment in order to make impartial judgements and to help us understand the true character and spirit of the place, but we should combine this professional distance with an awareness of the personal feelings elicited by the site. These personal responses can give us valuable information, even inspiration, for design ideas.

Opportunities and problems. One of the best ways of coordinating the findings of analysis is to produce a summary of the main opportunities and problems presented by the site and the brief. These may well cross the boundaries of physical, biological, cultural and visual aspects, and so help us towards an integrated assessment of the site. Furthermore, a problem can often be redefined as an opportunity if it is perceived in an open-minded and imaginative way. For instance, a nutrient poor, dry soil, could be a problem for establishing certain kinds of planting, but is an opportunity to encourage a wide diversity of stress tolerant wild flowers in the absence of very competitive coarse weed growth.

Much of the success of planting design depends on the skill with which different functions are integrated. Mediocre design is often the result of narrow thinking and a refusal to see the opportunities to achieve many varied ends at the same time. For example, a screen of leyland cypress is a screen and nothing else; on the other hand, a screen planting could also be attractively diverse and a wildlife habitat whilst requiring only minimal maintenance.

The statement of design objectives and planting functions is valuable information, and should be fully utilised both to communicate our intentions to the design team and the users, and also as a checklist for our own purposes. Frequent referral to this will make sure that no needs are overlooked and no opportunities wasted.

Synthesis – generating and organising ideas.

Planting Policies

Whereas objectives are aims, policies are the intended means of implementing those aims. So with the drawing up of design policies we make our first proposals for the site. Policies are necessarily general in nature, they are statements of intent which will require interpretation and application in order to translate them into concrete design details. Policies should address the opportunities and problems of the site and indicate, for example, how circulation will be articulated by planting or car parking areas could be integrated into existing tree planting.

But how exactly do we arrive at design policies? In some cases it is an obvious step from design functions. For example, if the site includes steep slopes which require protection from erosion and if hard engineering solutions would be too costly, a planting policy of dense vegetation cover can be a reliable alternative. Other policy decisions might require more imaginative insights drawing on experience of a wide range of design solutions. In the grounds of a hospice, for instance, the need for tranquility along with a stimulating and refreshing environment could be met by the extensive and co-ordinated use of water in pools, canals, fountains and cascades.

The presentation of planting policies can form an important consultative stage in larger projects. It is the first opportunity that the client will have to consider the scope, if not the details, of the planting proposals. With planting policies we begin to communicate firm proposals to the client and can gauge their response

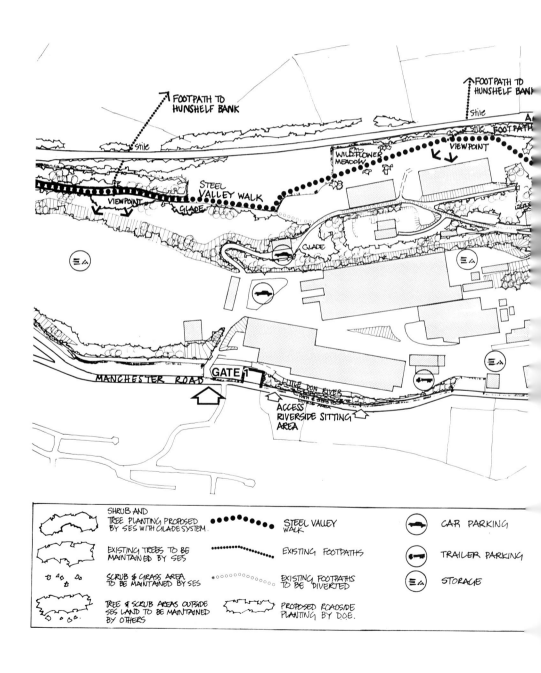

FOOTPATH TO
HUNSHELF BANK

FOOTPATH TO
HUNSHELF BANK

stile

stile

SIDE FOOTPATH

WILDFLOWER
MEADOW

VIEWPOINT

STEEL
VALLEY WALK

VIEWPOINT

GLADE

GLADE

STORAGE

CAR PARKING

MANCHESTER ROAD

GATE 1

LITTLE DON RIVER

PATH & STEPPING

TRAILER PARKING

ACCESS
RIVERSIDE SITTING
AREA

STORAGE

	SHRUB AND TREE PLANTING PROPOSED BY SES WITH GLADE SYSTEM.	••••••••	STEEL VALLEY WALK		CAR PARKING
	EXISTING TREES TO BE MAINTAINED BY SES	••••••••	EXISTING FOOTPATHS		TRAILER PARKING
	SCRUB & GRASS AREA TO BE MAINTAINED BY SES	∘∘∘∘∘∘	EXISTING FOOTPATHS TO BE DIVERTED		STORAGE
	TREE & SCRUB AREAS OUTSIDE SES LAND TO BE MAINTAINED BY OTHERS		PROPOSED ROADSIDE PLANTING BY D.O.E.		

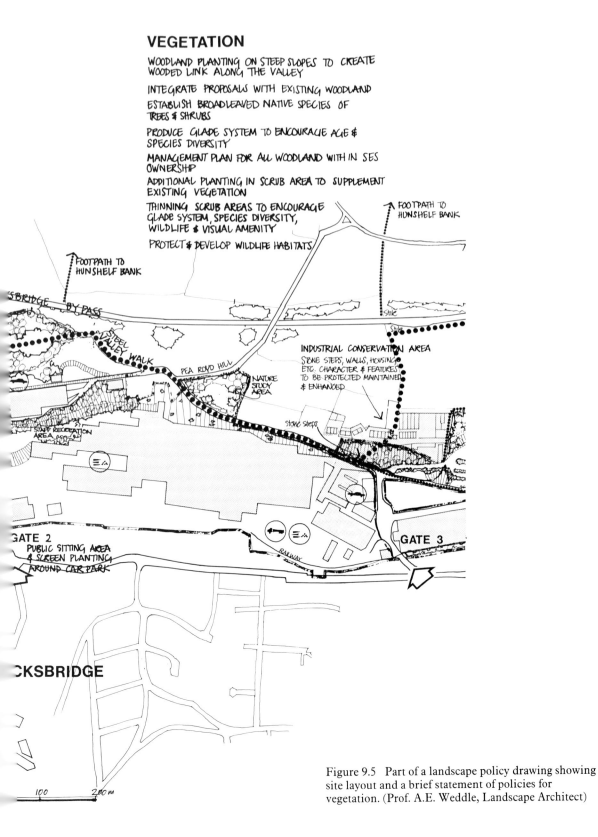

VEGETATION

WOODLAND PLANTING ON STEEP SLOPES TO CREATE WOODED LINK ALONG THE VALLEY

INTEGRATE PROPOSALS WITH EXISTING WOODLAND

ESTABLISH BROADLEAVED NATIVE SPECIES OF TREES & SHRUBS

PRODUCE GLADE SYSTEM TO ENCOURAGE AGE & SPECIES DIVERSITY

MANAGEMENT PLAN FOR ALL WOODLAND WITH IN SES OWNERSHIP

ADDITIONAL PLANTING IN SCRUB AREA TO SUPPLEMENT EXISTING VEGETATION

THINNING SCRUB AREAS TO ENCOURAGE GLADE SYSTEM, SPECIES DIVERSITY, WILDLIFE & VISUAL AMENITY

PROTECT & DEVELOP WILDLIFE HABITATS

FOOTPATH TO HUNSHELF BANK

FOOTPATH TO HUNSHELF BANK

SBRIDGE BY PASS

STEEL VALLEY WALK

PEA ROYD HILL

NATURE STUDY AREA

STAFF RECREATION AREA

Stile

Stile

INDUSTRIAL CONSERVATION AREA
STONE STEPS, WALLS, HOUSING ETC. CHARACTER & FEATURES TO BE PROTECTED MAINTAINED & ENHANCED

Stone steps

GATE 2
PUBLIC SITTING AREA & SCREEN PLANTING AROUND CAR PARK

RAILWAY

GATE 3

CKSBRIDGE

100   200 m

Figure 9.5   Part of a landscape policy drawing showing site layout and a brief statement of policies for vegetation. (Prof. A.E. Weddle, Landscape Architect)

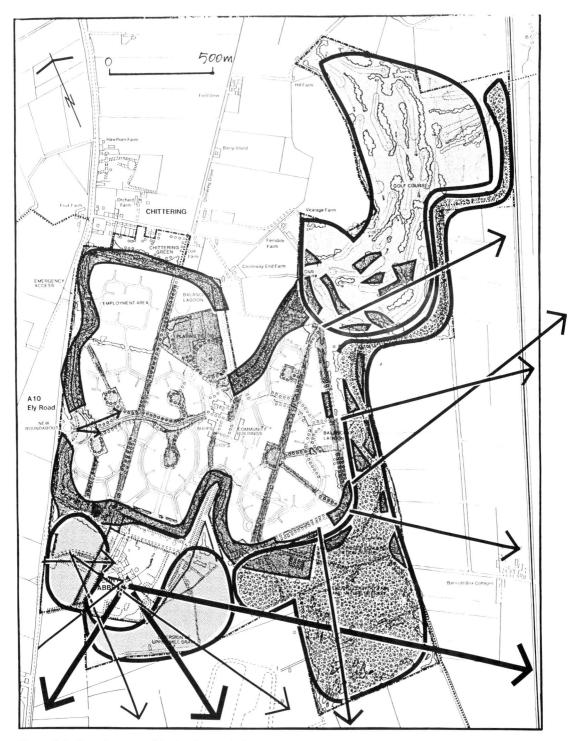

Figure 9.6   Key elements of the landscape design concept for a new settlement, drawn up for presentation. The drawing shows woodland structure, fenland country park and nature reserve, main open space structure, fields managed in accordance with English Heritage requirements, golf course and key views. (Landscape Design Associates)

before we commit ourselves to the development of those ideas. Once policies are agreed with the client we have a sound foundation for the design development stages which follow.

Design concept

A design concept drawing is a graphic interpretation of policies. It allows us to explore the spatial relationships between the various site uses and design functions. This can be expressed most simply in an abstract diagram, often called a bubble diagram, which shows spatial organisation. It explains the sequence, connections and hierarchy of spaces but does not show exact geographical location or scale. It can be a topological map of proposed functions for the site and an interpretation of the original brief. There will almost always be more than one possible design solution to the brief, and bubble diagrams are particularly useful for investigating alternative relationships between functions and help us to explain these quickly and concisely to others.

A design concept provides an overview of how the various elements will fit and function together. It is a conceptual whole, yet it is still largely abstract in nature. It is built of functions and ideas not of bricks and mortar or plants and soil. A high degree of abstraction is necessary at this stage of design because this allows us to handle large amounts of information and complex ideas simultaneously and so facilitate the rapid exploration of different solutions to the brief without the need to laboriously work through the details of layout and materials.

Schematic Planting Design

Once a good fit for the various functions has been discovered we can be more precise about the exact locations of spaces and zones of planting character on the site. In doing this we must maintain the spatial organisation of the concept whilst responding to the physical detail of the site.

In practice the development of the concept and the schematic layout often go hand in hand. Various abstract spatial relationships can be tested out in a schematic way on a base plan of the site area. The proposed design can then be based on the fit of functions to site as well as function to function.

In order to produce a schematic planting layout we must locate the different planting types such as ornamental, naturalistic, shelter, screen and so on. We should also show the positions of the major elements of planting structure such as hedgerows, copses, avenues, etc. A more realistic picture of the site is now beginning to emerge - a schematic planting design will explain the distribution of planting types on the site and define the approximate location and size of the spaces to be created by structure planting. It should be drawn at a scale which is convenient for the size of the site. For a large site this might be 1:1000 or 1:500, for a smaller site, 1:500 or 1:200. In order to avoid too much concern with detail it can be helpful to show schematic proposals at a smaller scale than the master plan or sketch design to follow.

Master Plan

If the site is large (say greater than one hectare), and particularly if it includes a variety of land uses, building structures or distinct vegetation types, it will normally require a landscape master plan. A master plan represents an advance from schematic proposals, but is still at a strategic rather than detailed level of design. It is normally drawn at a scale of 1:500 or 1:1000.

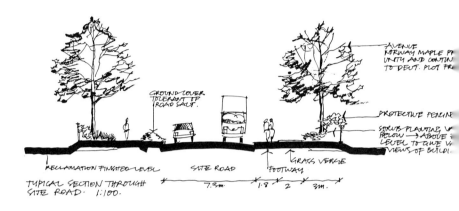

AVENUE
NORWAY MAPLE P?
UNITY AND CONTIN
TO DEVT. PLOT FR?

GROUND COVER
TOLERANT OF
ROAD SALT.

PROTECTIVE FENCIN

SHRUB PLANTING V
BELOW → ABOVE
LEVEL TO GIVE V
VIEWS OF BUILDI

RECLAMATION FINISHED LEVEL   SITE ROAD   GRASS VERGE
FOOTWAY

TYPICAL SECTION THROUGH
SITE ROAD. 1:100.

7.3m   1.8 2 3m.

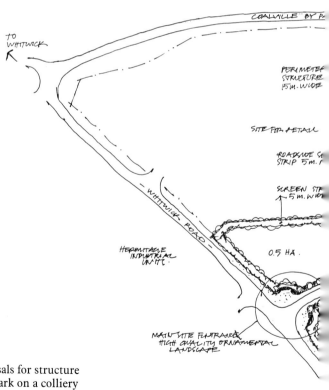

COALVILLE BY P?

TO
WHITWICK

PERIMETER
STRUCTURE
15m. WIDE

SITE FOR RETAIL

ROADSIDE S?
STRIP 5m. ?

SCREEN STR?
5 m. WID?

WHITWICK ROAD

HERMITAGE
INDUSTRIAL
UNITS.

0.5 HA.

MAIN SITE ENTRANCE
HIGH QUALITY ORNAMENTAL
LANDSCAPE

Figure 9.7   Schematic proposals for structure
planting for a new business park on a colliery
reclamation site. (Robinson Burrows,
Landscape Architects)

AL SITE ROAD LANDSCAPE : SKETCH VIEW OF ACCESS TO DEVT. PLOT.

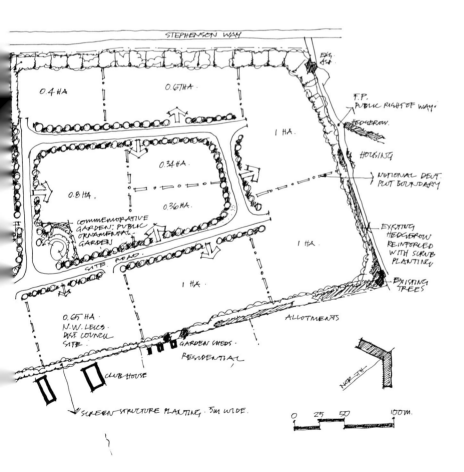

STEPHENSON WAY

0.4 HA

0.67HA

EXG 4x4

1 HA.

F.P.
PUBLIC RIGHT OF WAY.

HEDGEROW.

HOUSING

0.34 HA.

0.8 HA.

0.36 HA.

NOTIONAL DEVT.
PLOT BOUNDARY

COMMEMORATIVE
GARDEN: PUBLIC
ORNAMENTAL
GARDEN

EXISTING
HEDGEROW
REINFORCED
WITH SCRUB
PLANTING

1 HA.

EXISTING
TREES

SITE ROAD.

1 HA.

0.65 HA.
N.W. LEICS.
DIST. COUNCIL
SITE.

ALLOTMENTS

GARDEN SHEDS.
RESIDENTIAL

NORTH

CLUB HOUSE

SCREEN STRUCTURE PLANTING. 5M WIDE.

0   25   50   100 M.

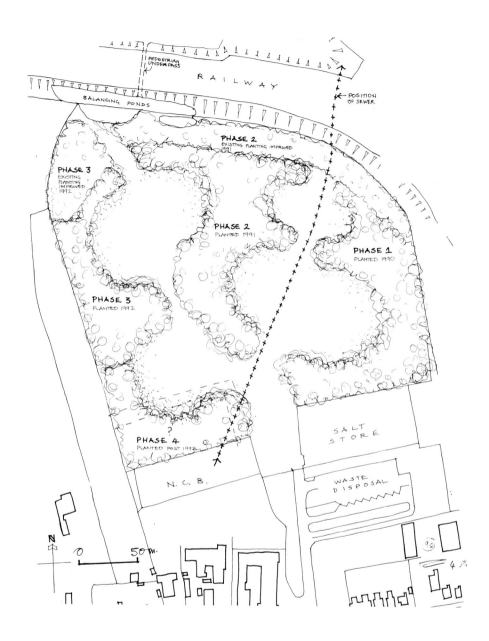

Figure 9.8   Schematic planting structure for a new woodland park on a landfill site. Likely phasing of planting areas is shown. (Environmental Consultancy, University of Sheffield)

railway sidings

balancing pond

boardwalk to proposed tunnel

car park

Key

EXISTING TREES TO BE RETAINED

PROPOSED TREES

STRUCTURE PLANTING

ORNAMENTAL PLANTING

MOWN GRASS

LONG GRASS

GRAVEL PATH

SEATING

FENCING

PROPOSED CONTOUR

0   40m

Figure 9.9   Master plan for new woodland park on landfill site. (Environmental Consultancy, University of Sheffield)

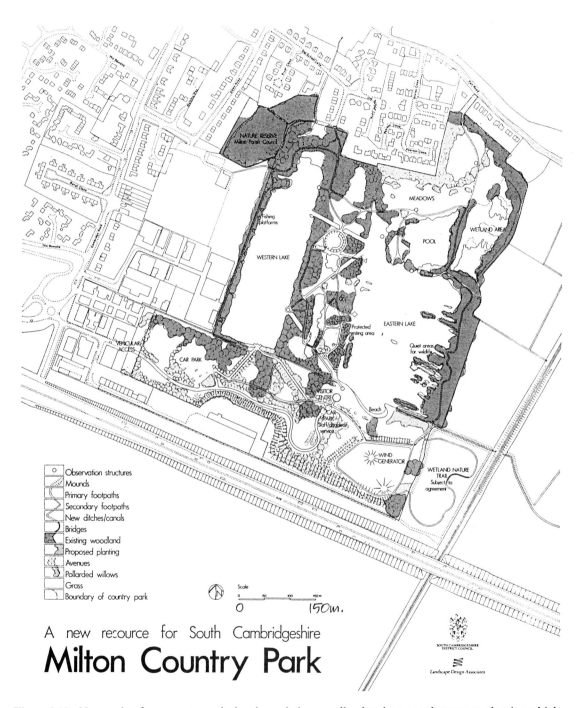

Legend:
- ○ Observation structures
- Mounds
- Primary footpaths
- Secondary footpaths
- New ditches/canals
- Bridges
- Existing woodland
- Proposed planting
- Avenues
- Pollarded willows
- Grass
- Boundary of country park

Scale
0   50   100   150 m

0   150m.

A new resource for South Cambridgeshire
Milton Country Park

SOUTH CAMBRIDGESHIRE
DISTRICT COUNCIL

Landscape Design Associates

Figure 9.10   Master plan for a country park showing existing woodland and proposed structure planting which will form a strong nature-like structure for recreation and conservation. (Landscape Design Associates)

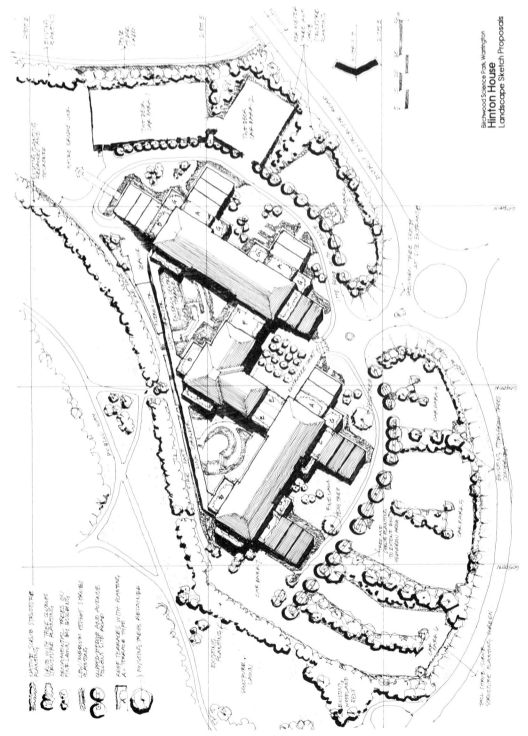

Figure 9.11 Master plan for an office development showing generous woodland belts enclosing the site and car parks, and areas of ornamental planting in the building curtilage and courtyards. (Prof. A.E. Weddle, Landscape Architect; drawn by Nick Robinson)

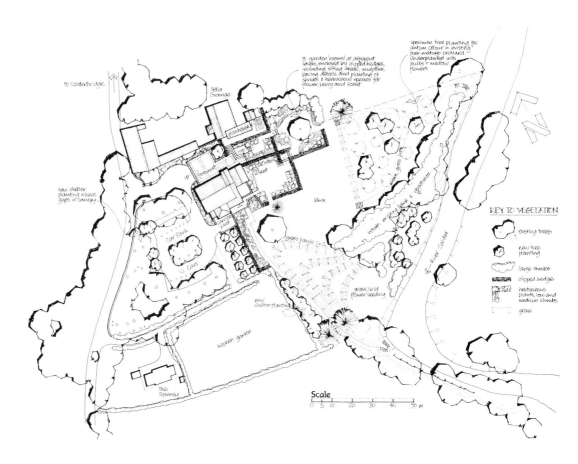

Figure 9.12   Master plan for grounds of a Jacobean house to be converted into an hotel. Grounds will include car parking and service areas in addition to gardeners' and riverside walk. (Prof. A.E. Weddle, Landscape Architect; drawn by Nick Robinson.)

The main difference between schematic design and master plan is that the latter commits us with more precision to the layout of planting. The detail and refinement that can be shown is limited by the scale of the drawing. Structure planting, avenues and specimen trees can be positioned with a fair degree of accuracy, but the layout of ornamental planting can only be shown in a notional way, even at 1:500 scale. These limitations are in fact a very useful restraint on the designer, forcing them to work out the spatial structure of the landscape before elaborating the furnishing and decoration of those spaces.

The master plan is, as its name implies, an authoritative design document. It should always be discussed and agreed with the client and design team, and it is often submitted for approval by the local planning authority. This formal procedure of approval can be a major benefit for the designer. It allows us to establish definitive patterns of use and planting at a comparatively early stage of design, and in doing so we gain agreement for the extent and location of at least the major planting areas.

Sketch Planting Proposals

Sketch proposals are drawn up at a larger scale (commonly 1:500 for structure planting, 1:200 for general amenity planting, and 1:100 or 1:50 for detailed ornamental planting), and this allows us to concentrate on the composition and character of the spaces which were outlined at the previous stage. To work at this larger scale we may need to consider one part of the site at a time. If we do have to fragment the site it is important to choose reasonably self-contained sections, and it is essential to work strictly within the integral framework of function and character established in our design policies and master plan. If we do not do this, much of our earlier efforts will be wasted.

Sketch proposals allow us to explore the detailed composition and furnishing of spaces, that is the degree of enclosure, shape and proportion, the geometry and patterns within them and the location of focal elements. It is also the stage at which we can most easily begin to envisage the aesthetic character and pattern-form of the planting. For example, an enclosure of given proportions could be laid out with rectilinear or curvilinear patterns of hard and soft surfaces; the planting within it could be dense and jungly, loose and cottage or simple and formal.

In order to define the three dimensional structure of the space we must decide on the height and habit of planting within reasonable working limits. Shrub planting should therefore be distinguished according to whether it will grow above eye level to give physical and visual enclosure, or below eye level to provide some spatial definition but no visual enclosure. Depending on the scale of the sketch design plan and the amount of detail that can be shown, planting below eye level can be further subdivided into 'medium shrubs' which will grow above knee level and low planting which will remain below. This is a useful distinction, because medium height planting above knee level controls movement and separates areas much more firmly than low ground cover, which merely carpets or edges the floor of a space. We should also distinguish dense, impenetrable thickets from open shrubbery which allows a degree of visual penetration, and indicate if herbaceous plants are to form a significant proportion of low or medium planting, because this will affect both the seasonal character of the vegetation and the level of management that will be required.

The heights and form of trees should also be shown. Useful categories are tall 'forest' trees (approximately 20 metres or more high when mature), which require considerable room if they are to develop naturally and will become major structural elements in any landscape; medium height trees (approximately 10-20 metres tall), which are more easily accommodated in the urban landscape but are nonetheless of comparable scale to many buildings and other structures; and small trees (approximately 5-10 metres tall), which can play an important decorative and structural role within smaller spaces such as gardens and courtyards, but are generally subordinate to the built structures of the urban environment.

A list of the main height categories is summarised below. We can, of course, choose from these or refine them further if necessary, but all areas of planting shown on the sketch plan should be identified as belonging to one category or to a combination:

Tall trees (20m+)
Medium trees (10-20m)
Small trees (5-l0m)
Tall shrubs (1.6m+)
Medium shrubs (0.5-1.6m)
Low shrubs and ground cover (-0.5m)

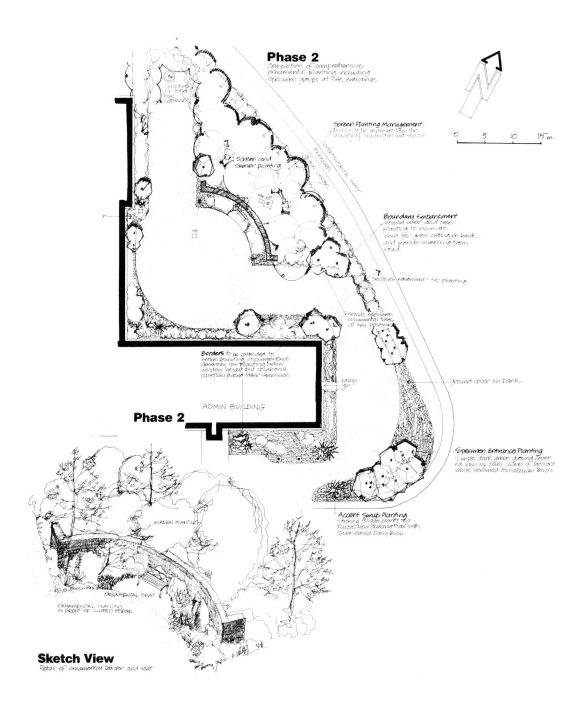

Figure 9.13   Part of a planting sketch design for an office building. Graphics and notes indicate character and purpose rather than planting detail. Species mentioned are illustrative only. (Environmental Consultancy, University of Sheffield; drawn by Nick Robinson.)

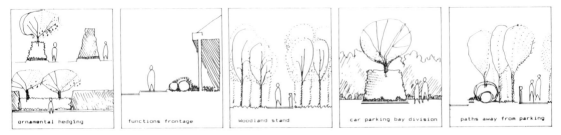

Figure 9.14 Sketch illustrations of planting proposals for an hotel development showing the structural role of planting. (Landcare)

Although we should keep them in mind, it is usually advisable not to define the precise heights of proposed trees in metres because of the difficulty of predicting them with accuracy, and because different elements in the scheme will reach maturity at different times. It is helpful, however, to draw the plan and accompanying sketches as the planting is imagined to look a given number of years after planting. Ten or 15 years is a good period because this is usually within the forseeable future for the client.

Massed plantations should be distinguished from individual or grouped specimens and avenues. This is important for a number of reasons. Firstly, the mode of planting will help to express its function, for example, mass planting will be most effective where screen and shelter are needed, small groups or individual specimens where the decorative function is paramount. Secondly, it will affect the growth habit and appearance of the individual plant and of the whole plant association. For example, mass shrub thicket planting produces rapid growth, but later results in drawn plants with less foliage at lower levels of their canopy and in the interior of the association. Lastly, the cost of establishing a tree or shrub is likely to be considerably greater if it is planted as a specimen than as part of a plantation because of the size and quality of nursery stock and the intensity of aftercare required.

The management of trees will also affect their role in spatial composition, and so it should be clear whether they are to be pruned to produce a clean bole with raised crown, if they are to be pleached or trained, pollarded or coppiced, or allowed to spread naturally.

It further helps to articulate the design intentions if accent plantings or focal groups of trees, shrubs or herbaceous plants and areas of bulbs are located and larger areas of the most ornamental planting are distinguished from others of similar height range. Thus, some features might be labelled as follows:

Specimen tree(s),
Specimen shrub(s),
Focal plant group,
Ornamental shrub and herbaceous planting,
etc.

Much of this information can be communicated graphically on plan and in elevations, but explanatory notes will always be helpful. We should use rapid freehand graphics in pencil or sketching pen because this will encourage us to try

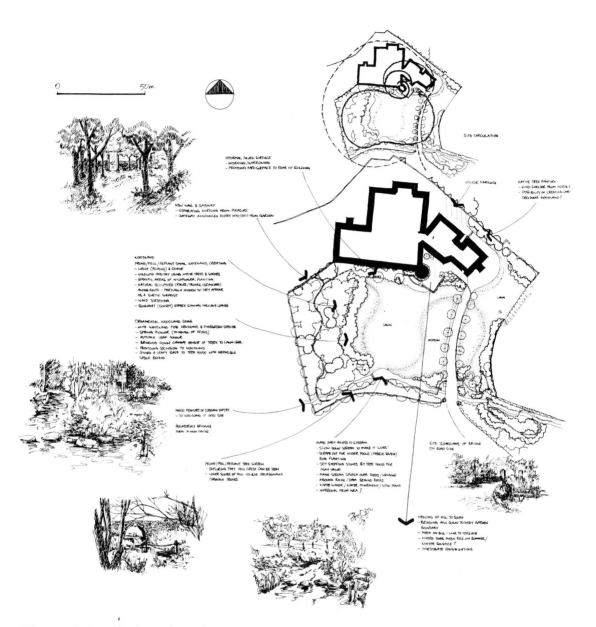

Figure 9.15   Part of a sketch design for a private garden. Good use is made of sketch views to show the character of the proposals. (Landcare, Landscape Architects)

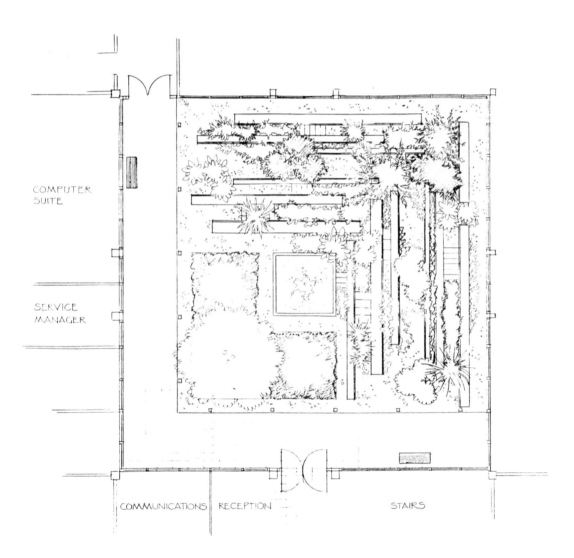

COMPUTER
SUITE

SERVICE
MANAGER

COMMUNICATIONS | RECEPTION   STAIRS

Figure 9.16   Sketch proposals plan for layout and planting of courtyard. The contrast between geometric and organic form is an important element of the design proposals. (Landscape Design Associates)

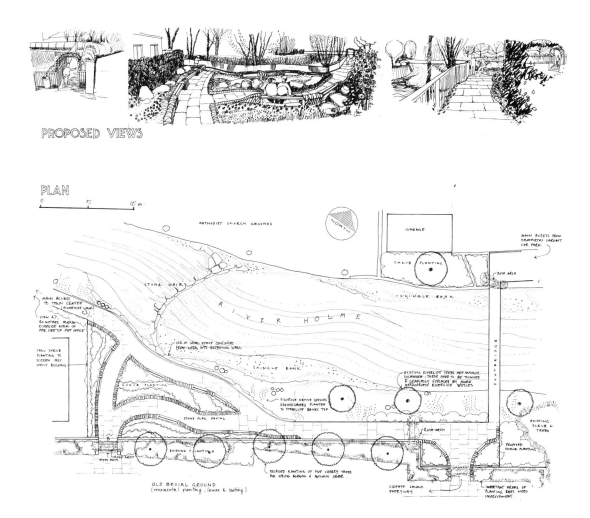

Figure 9.17   Sketch proposals for a riverside seating area. The character and purpose of planting is explained by notes on the plan and sketch views. (Landcare)

as many alternatives as possible. Three dimensional sketches, elevations, sections and plans will all help us to visualise different kinds of enclosure planting, different layout patterns, and different planting styles.

Note that all the essential qualities of planting structure and character can be decided upon without choosing particular species, and sketch planting proposals are often presented without naming any species, but plans should be generously illustrated with vivid sketches of important views and typical planting character.

We may, however, have certain plants or broad associations in mind from an early stage. These choices are often based on the existing vegetation of the site or surroundings or inspired by associations we have seen elsewhere. In the sketch design it can be informative to name some of the key species which we hope to include, particularly those with a major structural role such as avenue trees, important specimens or the dominant components of woodland associations. This will give a more vivid impression of our proposals, and help to convince our client that we understand what kind of plant material will be suited to their site. But it is wise to strictly limit the number of species named at this stage, otherwise there is the risk of 'not seeing the wood for the trees'. Furthermore choosing the right species is a time consuming task and most of it is best left until the layout, structure and general character of the planting has been agreed.

Detailed Planting Design

Once our sketch proposals have been approved we can move on to systematically consider the choice and arrangement of species for the whole site. To do this imaginatively and thoroughly is a lengthy task which is best dealt with in a series of steps.

Choice of scale. Detailed planting design must be done at a sufficiently large scale. For woodland and outfield planting this is normally 1:500 or 1:250, for general amenity planting 1:250 or 1:200 and, for detailed ornamental planting, 1:100 or 1:50. This may be the same scale as the sketch proposals, but it should be the scale at which final construction drawings will be produced. The correct choice of scale will allow us to plan the positioning of plants in the finest detail appropriate to the type of planting.

Height structure. The next step is to confirm, or if necessary alter, the height categories set out in the sketch proposals. Some refinement of these will almost certainly be necessary if we are working at a larger scale. We should clearly mark on a working rough the precise layout of grassland and planting beds and, within these, the extent of areas, groups, drifts and specimens of each height category.

Planting character or theme. We should now also confirm or develop our ideas about the character of planting for different parts of the site. This will depend on the use and character of the setting. We should decide whether we want the planting to be, for example, colourful and dramatic, subdued and restful, or mysterious and exotic, and clarify whether the plants need to be robust and resilient or can be more delicate and horticulturally demanding.

It is maybe helpful to go further and choose a specific planting theme. This could be based on aesthetic characteristics such as colour or scent, or seasonal interest such as autumn foliage or winter colour, or on a function such as wildlife conservation.

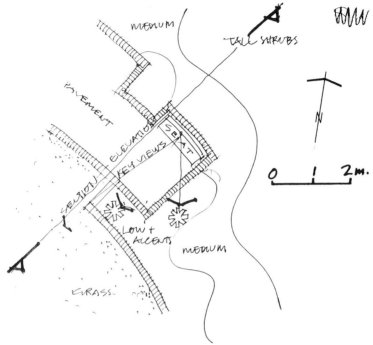

1. Height categories and locations of
   key accents in plan.

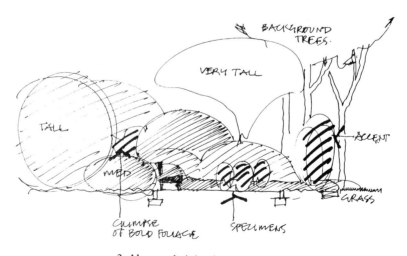

2. Abstract height, form and texture
   study in elevation.

Figure 9.18   An example of planting composition studies:

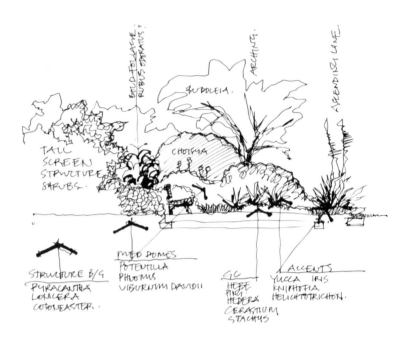

TALL
SCREEN
STRUCTURE
SHRUBS.

STRUCTURE B/G
PYRACANTHA
LONICERA
COTONEASTER.

MED DOMES
POTENTILLA
PHLOMIS
VIBURNUM DAVIDII

GC
HEBE
PING
HEDERA
CERASTIUM
STACHYS

ACCENTS
YUCCA IRIS
KNIPHOFIA
HELICHTOTRICHON.

COLOURS:
SUBDUED — (FORM DOMINANT)
GREY GREEN FOLIAGE.
PASTEL FLOWERS : YELLOW/SILVER/WHITE CREAM (BLUE)

3. Representative composition study
   in elevation with possible species
   annotated.

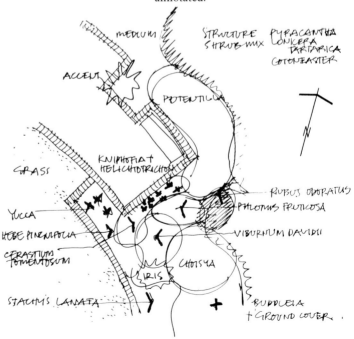

MEDIUM

STRUCTURE
SHRUB MIX

PYRACANTHA
LONICERA
TARTARICA
COTONEASTER

ACCENT

POTENTILLA

KNIPHOFIA +
HELICHTOTRICHON

GRASS

RUBUS ODORATUS
PHLOMIS FRUTICOSA

YUCCA

HEBE PINENIFOLIA

VIBURNUM DAVIDII

CERASTIUM
TOMENTOSUM

CHOISYA

IRIS

STACHYS LANATA

BUDDLEIA
+ GROUND COVER.

4. Species areas shown on plan.

indispensible design tool for the most important and the most visible associations.

Choosing species: Whilst we are sketching suitable species from the select lists may come to mind and can be labelled on the drawing. However, for a designer without an extensive plant knowledge it is better not to encumber the explorations of visual composition with the need to identify all species at the same time as drawing. It is usually easier to choose plants from our palette once we are happy with the arrangement we have sketched. This sequence also allows us to refine the composition by thinking through the effects of alternative plants from the palette and we can go back and redraw our sketches to suggest the appearance of alternative plants before finally committing ourselves to a particular species.

Not all species can be identified and located with precision on an elevation or section. Full plant selection can only be done with the aid of a scale plan, and a plan is certainly essential for the accurate communication of the detailed planting design and the instruction of the landscaper who will implement the scheme. Only in plan can the whole site be seen at once, so the composition studies should be transposed back into plan. This will allow us to confirm plant positions in the horizontal plane and to complete the selection of species for the remaining areas.

Some designers prefer to work in plan from the beginning of detailed design, perhaps because this appears to save time. However, this method requires experience and an excellent ability to visualise in three dimensions, so it is advisable to draw elevations or perspectives of the most important planting associations at some stage before the species are confirmed on plan.

Seasonal tables: Composition studies help us to design in three dimensions with confidence, but we must also remember the time dimension. The appearance of plants will change through the seasons with some species only looking their best at certain times of the year. For example, the leaves of many coloured foliage plants such as golden sycamore (*Acer psuedoplatanus* 'Worleei') and *Robinia pseudoacaia* 'Frisia' have faded to an undistinguished green by midsummer.

We must plan the periods of main interest of the plants in order to achieve both attractive simultaneous combinations and a succession of display. The most reliable way of doing this is to list the species for a proposed association in a table such as the one below which shows periods of flowering, fruiting, autumn leaf colour, spring foliage colour and winter stem colour.

Species	Periods of main interest											
	J	F	M	A	M	J	J	A	S	O	N	D
Cornus 'Elegantissima'	...........—stems ....x................foliage...............................x-autumn colour-											
Pyracantha 'Mojave'	........-berries-			-flower-				..........................berries.........			
Betula pendula	....................bark ....autumn colour-											
Vinca minor	...flower.....................................flower											
Buddleja davidii	.......flower.......											

By looking down the the columns of such a table we can see what is happening in any month of the year and check that there are no extensive periods with little interest.

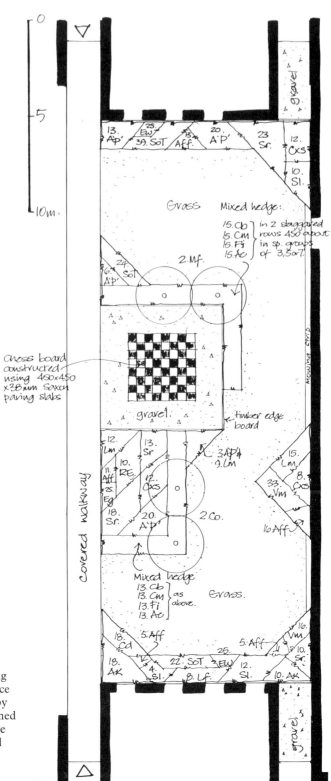

Figure 9.22 Construction drawing for ornamental planting in an office courtyard. Species are identified by key letters which would be explained in a schedule on the drawing. Note that the first letters of a genus and species are used to aid quick identification. (Appleton Deeley Partnership)

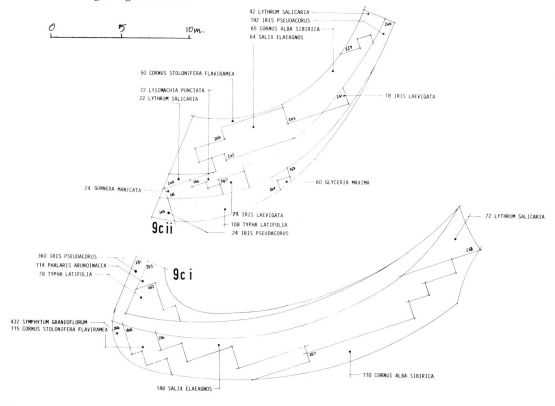

Figure 9.23 Part of construction drawing for ornamental planting in a garden festival site, including marginal aquatics. The beds shown are keyed into a location plan. Note the rectilinear shape of drifts which assists the calculation of plant numbers and setting out. The angular shapes will be less noticeable on the ground and will soon disappear as plants establish. (Ian White Associates, Landscape Architects)

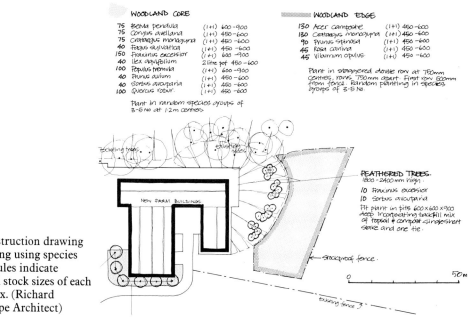

Figure 9.24 Construction drawing for outfield planting using species mixes. The schedules indicate numbers, age, and stock sizes of each species in each mix. (Richard Sneesby, Landscape Architect)

The three methods outlined above give us all the flexibility we need to achieve any arrangement of plants. There are ways of introducing considerable sophistication into the description of planting mixes and we will examine these in part three in the context of woodland and outfield planting.

Ornamental planting: For ornamental planting it is common to employ mainly methods 1 and 2 with occasional use of 3 when plant mixes are too extensive to be described by a combination of drifts overlaid with spot locations. The most detailed ornamental planting such as found in gardens and courtyards may require a plan scale of 1:50; other ornamental plantings can be adequately shown at 1:100.

Outfield planting: Outfield planting of woodlands, hedgerows, shelter belts, copses and screen belts is of a larger scale and so is normally detailed on smaller scaleplans, commonly 1:500 or occasionally 1:1000. This is quite adequate because the exact location of the majority of the individual trees or shrubs or even of groups of the same species, is not critical for the function and composition of the association. For reasons of economy of time and paper, much more use is made of mixes for outfield planting. The make-up of these can be described in notes on the plan or by drawing a planting unit which is then repeated over large areas. This repetition of a standard pattern is sometimes called a planting matrix.

In woodland, hedgerow, shelter belt and other outfield structure planting much of the design skill is in the composition of these mixes or matrices. Different mixes will be needed to suit different ground and microclimatic conditions and to achieve different functional and aesthetic effects. In addition, we can achieve a little more sophistication and control by showing single specimen trees or strategic clumps in spot locations, and delineated areas within or adjacent to the mix. The design and description of planting mixes will be examined in detail in the Chapter 10.

Urban amenity planting: It is helpful to distinguish a type of planting which is intermediate in scale and character between the more highly ornamental planting and outfield structure planting. This is found in streets, squares, parks and institution grounds commonly with a high proportion of exotic species, and is often called urban amenity planting. It can usually be adequately detailed on plans at 1:250 or 1:200 scale, and using graphic techniques similar to ornamental planting but often with more reliance on shrub mixes. If the planting covers larger areas, these mixes are an economical and appropriate way of introducing variety in extensive planting where there is not the need for constant control of detailed composition.

Specifications

In the majority of projects planting plans are supported by detailed written specifications which define the quality of plants and other horticultural materials, and the operations of ground preparation and planting. These specifications form part of a planting contract with a private landscape contractor, or can constitute instructions to a direct labour force. The detailed horticultural knowledge required for writing specifications and drawing up contracts is beyond the scope of the present book. We shall take a brief overview of this part of the process, and look in a little more detail at how, in certain contracts and implementation arrangements, design refinements and modifications can be made during planting and management.

Realisation – implementing and refining the design proposals.

Turning proposals into reality requires the services of a specialist landscape contracting firm or other landscape unit such as the direct labour organisation (DLO) of a local authority, or the in-house landscape team of a large private

Figure 9.25   An example of a repeating unit for woodland planting. The setting out of units would be shown on a separate plan. (Ian White Associates, Landscape Architects)

Figure 9.26   Construction drawing for urban amenity planting to light industrial units. Note: full name, numbers and spacings are annotated on the plan. Plants are arranged in spot locations, drifts of single species and mixes. (Environmental Consultancy, University of Sheffield)

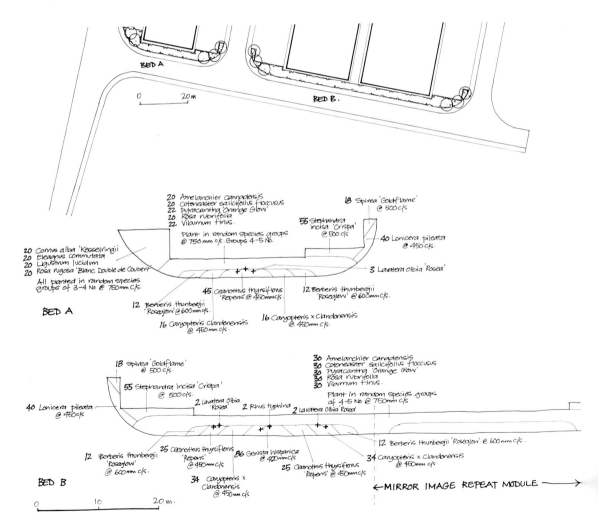

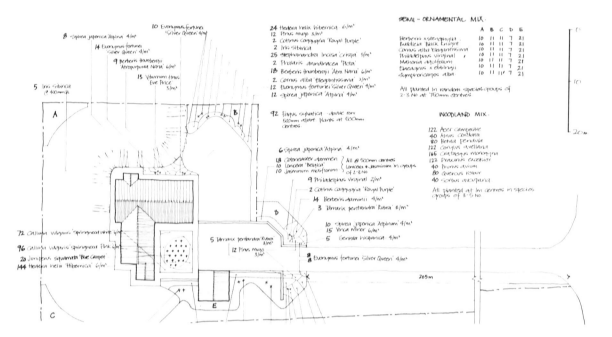

Figure 9.27 Part of drawing showing ornamental planting and woodland edge planting linked by a 'semi-ornamental' shrub structure planting mix. The proposals are for a private garden. (Richard Sneesby, Landscape Architect)

company. If the work is to be implemented by contract the landscape architect will normally have full responsibility for supervising the planting operations, and will be in a good position to ensure that the construction drawings are correctly interpreted on the ground. Contractual relationships and responsibilities can be complex, and for comprehensive guidance to landscape contracts the reader is referred to Hugh Clamp's *Landscape Professional Practice* (1989). If the planting is carried out by DLO the landscape architect's relationship with the person on the ground will be less formally defined than for a contract drawn up with standard conditions, but the designer will still retain a degree of control over the implementation of the proposals.

Because planting is a craft as well as an art, designers should be familiar with the techniques of establishing plants and tending plants. Only then will they understand the needs of the landscaper, whether private contractor or DLO, and be able to solve the practical problems that arise during implementation and management. This practical knowledge also gives designers the opportunity to work more closely with the landscaper and, if the conditions of contract or the DLO working relationship allow, to refine and develop aspects of the design during implementation.

Planting

The planting operations are likely to take place over a period of months during the autumn to spring planting season. Subsequent phases of planting may be implemented during following seasons if the project is large, or if parts of the site are unavailable at the early stages.

During the implementation numerous decisions need to be made by the designer in order to interpret details of the design proposals and to solve the unforeseen problems that frequently arise during operations on site. The implementation phase may also be an opportunity to refine and, in some cases, to modify the design. There are strong arguments in favour of adhering strictly to the construction drawings for reasons of economy and simplicity, but in most cases the designer can, if they wish, instruct variations and thereby modify the arrangement of plants on the ground. In fact, it is accepted practice to omit the positioning of certain plants from the construction drawings and instead to specify that these will be set out on site by the landscape architect. This kind of flexibility is needed most when there are significant aspects of the site or hard construction layout which are unknown at the detailed design stage. For example, the exact position of an underground service run may need to be determined on site during the planting operations, and only then can trees be confidently located at a suitable distance.

Design refinement can also be made for purely aesthetic reasons. We may wish to set out an important group of specimen trees or shrubs ourselves if their exact positions are critical for the composition. Avenues and other formal plantings are good examples of plant groupings whose positioning must be at least carefully checked on site if they are not set out by the designer in person.

Establishment

The implementation of any planting scheme will normally include an establishment phase following the actual planting. This lasts for a period of either one, two or three years, during which the contractor will ensure that the scheme does not succumb to weed competition, drought or other problems during this vulnerable phase of its life cycle. In a landscape contract the establishment phase is made up of two elements; the contractor's liablity for plant failures (usually called the Defects Liability Period) and paid aftercare work (usually called Aftercare or Maintenance Works).

During the Defects Liability Period (DLP) all plants and other materials and workmanship which are found to be defective are rectified by the contractor at no additional cost. This will include the replacement of plant losses ('beating up') after each growing season in the DLP. In effect the contractor is required to guarantee a full complement of healthy plants at the end of the Defects Liability Period subject to specified exclusions such as vandalism damage.

The Aftercare Works comprise routine maintenance tasks such as weed control, watering, pruning, hedge clipping, grass cutting and litter collection. All these are essential for successfill establishment, and without them it would be unreasonable to expect the contractor to guarantee the planting.

The chief object of the establishment phase is to achieve a closed canopy or ground cover of vigorous, healthy plants. But the establishment period is also an excellent time for the designer to take stock of the success of the scheme. Any need for additional planting to strengthen the initial groupings should then become apparent. What is required may be no more than half a dozen transplants on a corner or another drift of bulbs beneath a grove of trees, yet it can make a significant difference to the immediate impact of the scheme.

On some sites there may be a degree of uncertainty about which species will establish most successfully. If this is the case, it is only sensible to wait for one or two seasons to see which are the best adapted and then to use these species to beat up or thicken up the plantations or beds. The best way to give ourselves the flexibility to modify and add to the planting during both installation and aftercare is to set aside a sum of money in the budget to cover additional planting, and to make it clear to the client and the landscaper that these operations are a necessary and anticipated part of the operations. No designer can be expected to forsee all eventualities or to get the design exactly right on the drawing board.

Management

The full effect of mature planting which is envisaged by the designer on the drawing board will only be achieved during the period of landscape management, and so its success depends on the interpretation of the designer's intentions by the landscape manager.

The management period of a planting scheme can be regarded as starting at the end of the establishment period and continuing for as long as vegetation exists on the site. It includes maintenance, that is, the regular tasks required to keep the site clean and tidy, weed and pest free, and the seasonal work of grass cutting, pruning and replacing occasional losses.

But management is also an important design tool. Indeed, many of the best loved qualities of richly planted parks and gardens are as much the result of continuing creative management as they are the product of the original design. By pruning, thinning, replanting and allowing selected plants, even 'weeds', to naturalise and spread, landscape management shapes and controls the development of the plant association which was initiated during implementation. With pruning we can encourage the most attractive aspects of plant habit or restrict some plants in favour of others. By thinning we can remove some plants altogether to make way for others, or we can radically change the structure and spatial characteristics of woodland or tall shrub planting by opening up glades within it or reducing its density.

With the exceptions of the longer lived trees, all planting will need some kind of regeneration within the foreseeable period of landscape management. This can be allowed to happen spontaneously by providing the right conditions or we can control the process more closely by coppicing, pollarding or replanting chosen species. At relatively short intervals of five to ten years herbaceous plants and the shorter lived shrubs will need dividing or replanting. Longer lived shrubs and trees will not necessarily need attention in the short term, but it is wise to begin to develop a varied age structure at an early stage in the life of the planting scheme in order to prevent wholesale senescence at a later date. Finally, some of the most delightful effects are achieved by the spontaneous spread of both planted and 'weed' species, and it is sensitive management that will allow and encourage just the right balance.

The scope within landscape management for creative intervention and what is, in effect, periodic redesign should be clear. A designer's sensitivity, if not a full design training, is an invaluable asset for a landscape manager. Indeed, this is often essential if the designer's full intentions are to be realised. It is an unfortunate fact that too many planting schemes degenerate rapidly after the end of the establishment period for want of proper understanding and care.

There are a number of ways we can, as designers, be involved in landscape management. The greatest control is achieved if we draw up a management contract which specifies the detail of the operations to be carried out as well as the objectives of the design. These operations are supervised by the designer on site, giving us the opportunity to make the necessary decisions ourselves about pruning, thinning, restocking, weed control and to instruct the contractor accordingly. Management contracts are normally term contracts, renewable after a period of between three and five years. This time scale will allow us to see at least the shrub and herbaceous planting achieve maturity before the end of the second management contract. By this stage the tree planting will also be well on its way towards an effective role in the planting composition, even though it may not reach full maturity until 50 to 100 years after planting. After one or two periods of a management contract we can clearly demonstrate to the client and landscape management staff what we are trying to achieve and hand over responsibility, if necessary, with reasonable confidence that our design intentions are understood.

If we do not have the opportunity to supervise a management contract we may be able to draw up a management plan which includes a specification and an outline work programme for use by the landscape manager. This should include a full explanation of the intended form and character of the planting as well as the main operations that will be required. It is a great help if we can arrange for regular meetings with the landscape manager to oversee the general direction of the management work and help make key decisions.

If no continuing involvement is possible the very least we can do to safeguard the investment of time and money in a planting scheme is to make sure that the landscape manager or maintenance staff are thoroughly briefed when the site is handed over to the client at the end of the establishment period. This briefing should take the form of a well illustrated management report, a discussion at which the management staff have the opportunity to quiz the designer on all aspects of the design, and visits to or, at the very least, a slide show of mature sites of a similar character.

Learning Through the Design Process

We have now seen the design process through the phases of inception, analysis synthesis and finally realisation. The realisation of our vision can be the most satisfying part of the work; it should certainly be the most edifying. When we see our design on the ground and growing towards maturity we have an invaluable opportunity to learn from both our successes and our mistakes. There is no other way to be really sure to what extent we have solved the problems and achieved our design objectives than to assess the finished product.

So design does not end with realisation. We should feed the lessons from each completed scheme into the process of the next project. In this sense we can see design as a cycle. Observation and evaluation of one design can inspire and generate ideas for the next.

This creative cycle can be seen to operate not only from one design project to the next, but also within the stages of the design process. It is the means by which we generate ideas and select from alternative options. For example, the observation of a variety of different approaches to planting a road verge would allow us to judge the advantages of each and also help us to see the possibilities for a different approach for our own situation. We should then observe and evaluate in turn the success of our own proposals once they have been implemented.

Both analysis and synthesis play a part in this cycle. Indeed Lasceau (1989) regards these reductive and expansive types of thinking as overlapping through the design process: 'while the ... design process involves decision making aimed at the reduction of alternatives in search of a final solution, it also involves elaboration aimed at expanding the range of possibilities.' Decision making requires a focussed, single mindedness, whereas elaboration grows from the attitude of exploring for its own sake, for the fun of it. Perhaps it is the ability to integrate these complementary frames of mind that is the key to creativity. If we can allow them to co-exist, to support and cross fertilise each other, then problem solving will become an adventure and playful exploration will lead us to the answers.

PART 3

Practice

CHAPTER 10

Structure Planting

Introduction

The third and final part of this book will examine the practice of detailed planting design. Our intention here is not to explain the horticultural techniques which would be defined in the planting specification document, nor is it to identify the role of planting in any specific land use such as housing, industry or recreation. Rather, we shall address the questions of design technique: what range of plants is appropriate, and how can they be used effectively and imaginatively?

Our aim is to establish a basic repertoire of design techniques. We can then select from these and adapt them as necessary to meet the needs of the majority of sites we are likely to encounter in mainstream landscape practice.

Structure planting and ornamental planting deserve separate treatment because the plant species and design idiom are usually quite distinct. However, there are significant areas of overlap between structural and decorative functions, so we should not forget the principles of visual composition when we are detailing structure planting, nor the space forming qualities of an ornamental association.

Woodland

Moore Mitchell and Turnbull in *The Poetics of Gardens* (1988) suggest that 'planting a new tree is one of the noblest acts of optimism'. As landscape architects we have many opportunities to establish trees by the thousand in new woodlands. From a long term, environmental perspective this might be regarded as the most valuable part of our work, especially in a country such as England, where the natural vegetation is deciduous woodland, but which suffers from the lowest proportion of land area (approximately 10%) occupied by forest in Europe. These new woodlands can range in scale from a small copse to continuous forest of many hectares and locations can be rural, urban fringe or, increasingly, within urban areas.

In rural areas landscape architects now play a significant role in the design of many commercial forestry plantations. Their contribution includes advice on the location and shapes of plantations, on the conservation of valuable existing vegetation, and on the planting of indigenous broadleaf fringes to crop species. An excellent treatment of landscape design for forestry can be found in Sylvia Crowe's *Forestry in the Landscape* (1972). Amenity, wildlife and commercial functions are increasingly being integrated in forest design, often with the help of landscape architects.

New woodlands which have public amenity or wildlife conservation as a chief objective are normally on a smaller scale than commercial forestry but can,

Plate 119 Ash *(Fraxinus excelsior)* and sycamore *(Acer pseudoplatanus)* woodland has colonised and established itself in an abandoned chalk quarry. Note the rich shrub and herb growth beneath the trees.

nonetheless contribute a great deal to the visual and ecological qualities of the rural landscape. In rural and urban fringe locations they are most commonly associated with development of some kind. Recreational developments such as country parks or visitor facilities in national parks and other areas of scenic beauty are often accompanied by extensive new woodland or the regeneration of existing woodland. New industrial development in rural areas sometimes gives the opportunity for substantial woodland planting, and a very significant contribution to tomorrow's woodlands is provided by plantations on reclaimed industrial land such as colliery spoil and old quarry workings. In some cases the land purchase necessary for new road building can leave sufficient area not only for highway verge planting, but also for larger adjacent blocks of woodland. A further opportunity is provided by recent changes in agricultural policy which encourage the establishment of lowland forestry of various scales on less productive farmland.

In urban areas the opportunities for establishing new woodland are, at first sight, more restricted due to two major ractors. Firstly, high land values maintain constant pressure for land use which offers a substantial financial return and, secondly, public perception of urban woodland has long been rather negative, seeing it more as cover for attackers, rubbish tippers and other urban undesirables, than as a habitat for non-human wildlife. However, these perceptions are changing with the growth of the urban wildlife movement and environmental consciousness in general, and with the successful establishment of multiple use urban woods. Urban tree planting of all scales and styles is now being recognised as essential strands of the 'urban forest' - a fabric of trees and small woodlands which are interwoven with buildings, roads and open areas.

When designing woodlands there are a number of essential questions we must ask. The answers to these will be the main determinants of the species we use and how we arrange them.

What functions will the woodland perform?

We shall not deal here with commercial forestry functions. For further information on planting and managing woodlands for economic production, J.D. Matthews, *Sylvicultural Systems* (1989) and J. Evans *Sylviculture of*

Broadleaved Woodlands (1984) are recommended. In woodlands designed by landscape architects, functions such as shelter, screening, visual amenity, recreational activities and wildlife conservation are commonly the most important and will be major factors in determining what canopy structure and which species will be appropriate.

What canopy structure is ultimately required?

We saw in Part 1 that the number of vegetation canopy layers (strata) and the density of these layers give the woodland its spatial qualities, and that this spatial structure in turn influences the use of woodlands and adjacent land. Although these layers only develop fully over many years we must, at the outset, choose the correct balance of species and distribute them in such a way that will ultimately create the required canopy structure, and so satisfy the functional requirements of the woodland planting.

What are the soil and climatic conditions?

The growth conditions on the site and the species which are known to grow successfullly in similar conditions in the locality are further guides to species selection.

What woodland species grow successfully in the locality?

If site conditions are similar to those on nearby land and if we want to reflect and maintain the existing character of the area, it is wise to rely chiefly on locally proven species. We should broaden this palette only for a specific purpose, and with restraint and sensitivity. Woodland plantations are not the place for collections of unusual trees and shrubs. We may need to establish woodland on a site with unusual soil conditions such as derelict land, or there may simply be no existing woodland in the vicinity, perhaps because our site is to be a green island in an urban area, or because the tree cover of the surrounding countryside has long been denuded. In these circumstances we must study the vegetation of comparable sites elsewhere and look for recommendations in the technical literature on our particular landscape problems.

How will the woodland be perpetuated?

The level of future management likely to be available is a further consideration. If we suspect that little or no thinning and restocking will be carried out then we should anticipate this at the design stage, and we may need to sacrifice some short term advantages in order to provide a woodland that would be able to survive and regenerate itself in the absence of management. On the other hand, an assured management programme carried out by skilled staff would allow us to achieve rapid establishment and a quick design impact, as well as a diverse and sustainable woodland in the long term.

Once these questions have been answered we are in a position to draw up a plant palette for the woodland. There are strong reasons for us to confine this largely to native and long naturalised species. Woodland is one of the largest scale elements in the landscape, and so it has a powerful effect on the character and qualities of both the rural and the urban scene. Large tracts of exotic species tend to be conspicuous and appear foreign to the surrounding landscape, especially in rural settings. Even more important than these visual reasons is the urgent need to protect and extend the habitats available for wild plants and animals at every opportunity. By planting woodland we can help increase both the amount and diversity of wildlife.

Native trees and shrubs are the most valuable for creating wildlife habitats, and reflect the indigenous character of our landscape most strongly. But many species which are not native to the British Isles are nonetheless familiar in the countryside, even in the wilder parts of Britain. These have been introduced from other regions of the world, some from Europe, others from more distant lands which have a similar climate to that in Britain. Many are so well suited to the conditions in Britain that they have naturalised and begun to spread in competition with indigenous species; for example, Spanish chestnut *(Castanea sativa)*, Turkey oak *(Quercus cerris)* and Norway maple *(Acer platanoides)* in South East England. Some, however, have colonised with such great vigour that they spread at the expense of native plants, and so tend to reduce species diversity; for example, sycamore *(Acer pseudoplatanus)* and *Rhododendron ponticum.* Great care should be taken before contributing to the even wider spread of such species.

Athough they rarely support as many species of insect as native trees and shrubs, many introduced species do provide food and shelter for wildlife, and so can be valuable for conservation in amenity woodland alongside true natives. In particularly difficult soil and climatic conditions some exotic species may be more suitable than natives. For example, *Acer pseudoplatanus* and *Larix decidua* are fequently planted for shelter and in the most exposed upland locations.

Until recent decades the techniques of establishing woodland were largely based on well proven methods from commercial forestry combined, in some cases, with a more horticultural approach of the kind employed by the larger estates. The inclusion of short term, nurse trees (mostly very hardy natural pioneers with rapid growth) to shelter longer lived but initially slower growing species, the use of one to three year old transplants and regular spacing in rows, were standard practice in landscape plantations in the UK until the late 1960s and early 1970s, but at this time techniques of ecological design and establishment were first tried out on a significant scale, mainly in new towns such as Warrington and Milton Keynes. Ecological, or

Plate 120   In this high canopy oak woodland *(Quercus robur)* a cross section of three layered woodland structure has been revealed by felling in preparation for road construction. An understorey of shrubs including elder *(Sambucus nigra)* and hazel *(Corylus avellana)* is well developed and clearly distinguishable below the oak canopy. Beneath the shrubs a field layer of bramble *(Rubus fruticosus)*, honeysuckle *(Lonicera periclymenum)* and shade tolerant herb species can be found, although its density is limited by the shade cast by the two strata above it.

Plate 121   This high canopy oak *(Quercus robur)* wood, which is located in a country park, demonstrates a two layer structure. The understorey is largely absent, but a field layer of grasses and other herbs is well developed. The spatial qualities are quite different to those in a three layer wood, and the openness beneath the tree canopy is well suited to informal recreation use by comparatively large numbers of people.

naturalistic planting as it is often called, has since been developed and refined with some considerable success and the design of woody plantations has, as a result, become much more sophisticated.

Because the primary aim of commercial forestry is the production of good quality, saleable timber in the shortest practicable time, commercial plantations are designed to produce rapid, even growth of trees with straight unbranched trunks which provide the best possible financial return on the investment in land, labour and materials. Commercial plantations are also characterised by clear felling of large areas, and this can be ugly. Although timber plantations can, on occasions, also create attractive and multi-purpose woodland, many of the characteristics of the woodland structure and the individual trees in commercial forests are poorly suited to landscape woodland because its objectives are different.

On occasion we may want woodland to consist of a monoculture such as a grove of Scots pine or a beech hanger on the crest of a hill. At other times we will want diversity of appearance, structure and wildlife habitats. This diversity is achieved by the use of different canopy layers and different species within each layer. The basic unit of woodland design is the species mix comprising a range of trees and shrubs which will occupy different niches in the developing plantation.

Many new woodlands require more than one species mix Indeed, a plantation may consist of a mosaic of different mixes in different areas, the constituents of each having been carefully selected to suit the ground and microclimatic conditions, and to provide the desired canopy structure. From a design point of view, it is most useful to categorise woodland mixes by canopy structure in the first place and then according to different environmental conditions.

High Canopy Woodland (High Forest)

A high canopy woodland mix, which ultimately provides the innerstand of mature wood or forest is often called a woodland core mix. This can contain, at time of planting, the species which will eventually form either one, two or three canopy layers.

It may include dominant high canopy species; in the UK these would be chosen from oaks *(Quercis robur* and *Q. petraea)*, ash *(Fraxinus excelsior)*, beech *(Fagus sylvatica)*, Scots pine *(Pinus sylvestris)*, hornbeam *(Carpinus betulus)*, Spanish chestnut *(Castanea sativa)* or limes *(Tilia platyphyllos* and *T. cordata)*.

Trees which do not attain the full height of the high forest dominants can also be included in order to give variation in the ultimate height of woodland canopy. These species, which are sometimes refered to as sub-dominants, include rowan *(Sorbus aucuparia)*, field maple *(Acer campestre)*, gean *(Prunus avium)*, birches *(Betula pendula* and *B. pubescens)* and wild service tree *(Sorbus torminalis)*. In the innerstand of a wood they are most commonly found where gaps in the dominant canopy allow sufficient light for them to flourish. Some species, however, such as rowan, field maple and wild service tree, are moderately shade-tolerant, and so are sometimes found just below the canopy of the dominant trees where this is not too dense. Mature dominant and sub-dominant trees are often referred to as the 'overstorey' of a woodland, because together they form a more or less continuous storey above the shrubs and saplings which grow in glades and in the shade below the tree canopy.

The shrub layer or understorey will comprise large shrub and small tree species tolerant of moderate to heavy shade. These include hazel *(Corylus avellana)*, holly *(Ilex aquifolium)*, box *(Buxus sempervirens)*, wild privet *(Ligustrum vulgare)*, elder *(Sambucus nigra)*, midland thorn *(Crataegus oxycantha)* and, to a lesser extent, common hawthorn *(C. monogyna)*. In an established woodland the understorey may also include large numbers of tree saplings, especially the more shade-tolerant species such as beech *(Fagus sylvatica)* and sycamore *(Acer psuedoplatanus)*. More light demanding shrubs and tree saplings will be found in clearings within the innerstand and at the margins.

The third stratum which is useful for the designer to recognise is the field layer. In established woods this normally includes a high proportion of herbaceous species but shade-tolerant, low shrubs may also form a significant part. Field layer shrubs can be included at the planting stage, but only under certain conditions of aftercare and management. These will be discussed later in the present chapter. Suitable species can include bramble *(Rubus fruticosus)*, ivy *(Hedera helix)*, honeysuckle *(Lonicera periclymenum)* spurge laurel *(Daphne laureola)* and, on acid soils, bilberry *(Vaccinium myrtillis)*. Herbaceous field layer species cannot be successfully established until the woodland structure is well developed and the conditions of shade and exposure at ground level are suitable.

Arguments have been put forward for excluding the future dominant high canopy trees from the initial planting, especially the slower growing species such as oak, beech and hornbeam. Baines (1986), for example, believes that:

> We should allow for much more natural colonisation. Instead of attempting to produce native woodland in one stage I am convinced results would be far better if initially we established dense scrub, and so created a sheltered woodland environment at ground level. There is hardly a site in Britain that would not naturally acquire climax species, such as oak.

This approach is ecological in as much as it follows the natural sequence of spontaneous regeneration and succession that can be observed in certain circumstances. It is also true that the majority of dominant high canopy trees and shade-tolerant understorey species establish most successfully after a pioneer community has first colonised the ground. This is particularly noticeable on the more inhospitable sites where the shelter, shade and improved soil that pioneers can provide are especially valuable.

One problem with this approach is the time required before high canopy woodland trees start to colonise. Even if the pioneers are planted and managed to encourage the most rapid establishment possible it may be between 10 and 50 years before conditions are right for colonisation by the desired species. As Baines points out, this delay 'hardly matters if we are realistic about the time scale of oak woodland.' However, we may wish to speed up the process if we cannot be sure that the developing woodland will get the right kind of management in the future, or if it is important to be seen to be re-establishing a woodland of similar composition to one which may have been lost due to development.

It is quite feasible to establish species such as oak, beech, ash or lime at the outset if the soil and microclimatic conditions are suitable. Oak, in fact, is not only a high forest dominant but also a woodland pioneer, especially in grasslands where its large seeds provide the foodstore necessary to grow above competing meadow herbs. Oak and other high forest trees can be established in a pioneer plantation either, as Baines suggests, by direct seeding at the earliest opportunity after the establishment of the planted species or by including a proportion of young transplants in the plantation mix. Most high canopy dominants are slower in their initial establishment than pioneer species, so if they are included in a plantation mix they should be arranged so that the faster growing trees and shrubs aid rather than interfere with their growth in the early years.

In commercial forestry and traditional landscape practice it is common to include both nurse trees and longer lived species. Suitable nurse trees include birches *(Betula pendula* and *B. pubescens)*, alders *(Alnus glutinosa, A. incana* and *A. cordata)*, larches

(*Larix kaempferi, L. decidua* and *L. x eurolepis*), willows (*Salix* spp.) and poplars (especially *P. tremula*). These are normally planted with the intention of removal after 7 to 20 years to allow the long term dominants to flourish. In commercial forestry the nurse crop may also be a source of early financial return. In landscape plantations they can be valuable if height and bulk of planting is needed quickly, for example, where screening or shelter is a priority. Although fast growing nurse and pioneer trees are planted mainly for their early impact, selected groups of these species are often retained during thinning operations in order to add to the diversity of the mature woodland. A grove of birch or willow amongst stands of oak or ash can provide a welcome surprise, increasing both the habitat diversity and the visual interest of the wood.

The close association of nurse with long term species can, however, pose a number of difficulties. Firstly, at the common landscape spacings of between 1 and 2 metre centres, nurse species will soon begin to suppress slower growing trees and shrubs by their vigorous spread and dense foliage unless frequent attention is given to thinning and cutting back so as to provide sufficient light for the less competitive trees. Although trees such as birch (*Betula* spp.) and aspen (*Populus tremula*) are pioneers which naturally give way to oak, beech and other climax species in many successions, this second wave of colonisers normally establishes below gaps in the canopy. In small glades, perhaps formed by the loss of a mature birch or poplar, the conditions near ground level are light enough for seedlings of many of the climax species, but still too shady to allow the widespread regeneration of the more light demanding pioneers.

Secondly, vigorous, well established nurse species are not always easy to eliminate. All the nurse species mentioned above, with the exception of larch, regenerate freely from cut stumps, and the resulting regrowth is bulky and rapid. Unless this 'coppice' is cut regularly it will continue to be highly competitive and will ultimately form large, multistemmed trees. The stumps of felled trees can be killed with herbicides such as 'Amcide', but the large scale use of these powerful chemicals is discouraged due to the danger to other plants and wildlife. Mechanical stump removal by grubbing out or grinding is difficult in the confined space of the plantation. In addition, simply felling nurse trees which are likely to be, at that stage, the largest in the plantation, can be difficult without causing unacceptable damage to other trees and shrubs.

In order to avoid these difficulties it is often advisable to omit the vigorous nurse species from the woodland core altogether and rely on shrubs and trees of moderate growth rate to give early visual effect and shelter. Ash (*Fraxinus excelsior*), gean (*Prunus avium*), rowan (*Sorbus aucuparia*), elder (*Sambucus nigra*) and hawthorn (*Crataegus monogyna*), for example, all make good growth in the early years provided that exposure is not too harsh, and will offer significant protection for species such as oak (*Quercus robur*), beech (*Fagus sylvatica*) and limes (*Tilia cordata* and *T. platyphyllos*).

Alternatively the nurse species can be segregated from the long term components of the mix to avoid excessive competition and allow easier management. This principle is employed in forestry, where the nurse and main crops are planted in separate rows so that at the first thinning the nurse trees can be easily felled and removed to leave space for the spread of the main crop. The appearance and spatial qualities of such a regular planting grid would be quite out of character for many landscape plantations, and so more sophisticated irregular distributions are often used. Nurse species can be grouped in variable blocks or bands to allow easier thinning, and to maintain gaps between their massed canopies. These gaps become glades where the slower growing species can thrive in the comparatively light and sheltered microclimate.

Developing a Planting Mix

Let us now look at some examples of woodland core mixes which include several canopy layers and a variety of species in each. We shall use a high forest core mix to demonstrate a method of deciding on the proportions, grouping and spacing of the constituent species. It should be stressed that all the mixes suggested are intended primarily to illustrate the method of design and should not be taken as standard mixes for the soil type and locality. Every site is different and every woodland plantation must be designed afresh with full knowledge of all the constraints of the site.

For the sake of illustration we will assume a planting site in lowland southern Britain, reasonably sheltered and with a moist clay or loam soil. This is the kind of land which under natural conditions would support mixed pedunculate oak woodland. It would be almost impossible, and certainly unnecessary, to attempt to install all the components of the natural climax vegetation at the outset. There is no value in attempting to slavishly imitate natural communities which arose under different conditions and over a very long period of time. But by studying the indigenous vegetation we can be confident about the suitability of species for the environmental conditions and their compatibility with one another. Many successful woodland mixes are based on indigenous associations modified to accommodate the particular constraints of design, plant availability and implementation methods which obtain on the project.

Constituents of the Mix

The dominant high canopy could consist of pedunculate oak *(Quercus petraea)* mixed with smaller numbers of co-dominants such as hornbeam *(Carpinus betulus)* in the South and East. Sub-dominants associated with oak are field maple *(Acer campestre)* and gean *(Prunus avium)*, and sometimes rowan *(Sorbus aucuparia)* or crab apple *(Malus slyvestris)*, and some of these could be included if required.

Understorey planting might consist of hazel *(Corylus avellana)*, holly *(Ilex aquifolium)*, hawthorn *(Crataegus monogyna)*, and midland thorn *(Crataegus oxycantha)* all of which are common in the interior of oak woods. Midland thorn, however, is difficult to obtain in its typical form in the nursery trade, but elder could be substituted if it is necessary to maintain a high level of diversity in this layer.

The field layer of an established oak woodland would be likely to include bramble *(Rubus fruticosus)*, honeysuckle *(Lonicera periclymenum)* and ivy *(Hedera helix)*, in addition to numerous herbaceous species. Because of chemical weed control techniques used in young plantations, and because of their rampant scrambling habits, it is not always easy to successfully establish field layer shrubs from the outset. However, if more labour intensive management can be provided during the establishment phase this would allow the extra care necessary to avoid herbicide damage and regular cutting back to ensure that bramble and honeysuckle do not smother adjacent trees and shrubs before they are strong enough to outgrow the scramblers. We should also note that bramble is rarely available from nurseries, and so if required is best transplanted in small quantities as stolons from a suitable, agreed local source. Ivy is rarely suitable for plantations because its low spreading evergreen foliage makes it particularly susceptability to herbicide damage. The herb species which are typical of the wood floor cannot be established until the plantation has reached a stage of early maturity and conditions are suitably shady. At this stage they might be introduced by seeding or planting pot grown material if they do not colonise spontaneously from local sources. The herbs which would succeed in the soil and light conditions of the establishment period of the plantation are likely to be coarse and highly competitive species such as grasses, docks and nettles, and would constitute serious competition for the woody transplants. Herbaceous species are therefore more likely to require control than encouragement during the establishment phase of a plantation.

Our high forest core mix might thus comprise the following:

Overstorey:	Dominant trees:	*Quercus robur* (pedunculate oak)
		Carpinus betulus (hornbeam)
	Sub-dominants:	*Acer campestre* (field maple)
		Prunus avium (gean)
Understorey:		*Corylus avellana* (hazel)
		Ilex aquifolium (holly)
		Crataegus monogyna (hawthorn)
		Sambucus nigra (elder)
Field layer:		*Rubus fruticosus* (bramble)
(subject to management)		*Lonicera periclymenum* (honey-suckle)

In this mix *Prunus avium, Sambucus nigra* and, to a lesser extent, *Acer campestre* are the fastest growing species. *Sambucus* can act as a nurse in the early years, although their maximum height is normally 6-7 metres. Because of its early vigour, *Sambucus* can inhibit the establishment of trees such as *Quercus* and *Carpinus*, and so regular coppicing will probably be needed.

If a more simple canopy structure is wanted the understorey may be omitted from the planting mix. The remaining strata could also be simplified by reducing the number of species present. A plantation of, say, two species could eventually provide a woodland of memorable character by virtue of its simplicity. Beech and birch are species which often provide examples of attractive woodland mono-cultures. However, if we are going to rely on just one or two species we must be absolutely confident of their success on the site. In many cases it may be wiser to include a range of species both for visual and habitat diversity, and as an insurance against poor establishment by some members of the mix.

An example of a high forest core mix without the understorey would be (site conditions as before):

Overstorey:	Dominant trees	*Quercus robur*
		Fraxinus excelsior (ash)
	Sub-dominants:	*Prunus avium*
		Acer campestre
Field layer		*Rubus fruticosus*
(subject to management)		*Lonicera periclymenum*

Such an association if correctly managed would eventually form a canopy above and an open space below punctuated only by the columns of the tree trunks. Honeysuckle and bramble would scramble on the ground, and honeysuckle would occasionally clamber up a well lit trunk, supporting itself on spurs and twigs, to clothe the column with sprays of foliage. This 'woodland room' type of structure would be ideal if, for example, views were required through the woodland, or if free circulation was needed beneath the canopy.

A further variation in woodland structure might consist of a more abrupt distinction between high canopy and dense shrub understorey. This would be achieved by omitting the sub-dominant trees which can bridge the gap between shrubs such as *Sambucus* and *Corylus* and trees such as *Quercus* and *Fraxinus*. In addition, the shrub layer could be regularly coppiced to promote dense, bushy growth and prevent the shrubs from being drawn into tall spindly specimens. Shrubs which coppice well include *Corylus, Sambucus, Cornus sanguinea* and guelder rose *(Viburnum opulus)*, but almost all deciduous shrubs can be safely cut down to near ground level. Not only shrubs but also trees such as *Fraxinus, Carpinus* and Spanish chestnut *(Castanea sativa)* respond well to cutting back, and so might be included to form part of the coppiced layer. Traditional standard and coppice woodland was managed for the production of timber and underwood from cutting the coppice and from the less frequent felling of mature standards. If the high canopy is not too dense, such a structure is very beneficial for wildlife due to the diversity of light and shade and of clearing and thicket which is produced by the rotational cutting of sections of the shrub layer.

A high canopy-shrub layer amenity mix for a similar site to our pedunculate oak woodland, but suitable for coppicing would be:

Overstorey:	*Quercus robur*
	Fraxinus excelsior
Coppice shrub layer:	*Corylus avellana*
	Sambucus nigra
	Cornus sanguinea
	Viburnum opulus
	Prunus spinosa

Blackthorn *(Prunus spinosa)*, although intolerant of dense shade, could be included if the tree canopy is to be sufficiently open to allow high light levels in some areas. It is a valuable component of dense understorey because it forms spreading thickets and provides excellent nesting cover.

If coppice trees are to be included in the understorey the mix could be modified as follows:

Overstorey:	*Quercus robur*
	Fraxinus excelsior
Coppice layer:	*Crataegus monogyna*
	Corylus avellana
	Carpinus betulus
	Fraxinus excelsior

Plate 122   This wood is being managed as coppice and standard. It can be seen from the age of the standard oak that it is still in its early years. The coppice layer consists mainly of Spanish chestnut *(Castanea sativa)* and rowan *(Sorbus aucuparia)*. The birch *(Betula pendula)* in the foreground has also been cut back and is re-growing strongly.

The four mixes above indicate how species selection for planting can help achieve a variety of different woodland structures. Note that the number of species in each varies from six to ten. This may seem a small number if the mix is to cover a large area, but the plantation as a whole may consist of several mixes, and so the total number of species may be up to two or three times that in the core mix alone.

The role of management is crucial in controlling the structural development of woodland, but at the time of planting our main task is to provide a selection of species which can be easily managed to produce the desired woodland association and structure. The relative proportions and arrangement of these species will also have an influence on the management required and the ultimate form of the wood.

Mix proportions

Because of their eventual size the high forest trees can form a dominant canopy from a relatively small number of plants. In traditional coppice and standard woodland the number of mature standards could be as low as 12 per acre, that is, 30 per hectare (Tansley, 1939). This density produced a very open canopy which ensured that the underwood would flourish. A denser high canopy of, say, 45 trees per hectare could be achieved if the dominant species formed 10% of the original planting at 1.5 metre centres, and we assume that approximately one in ten will grow to maturity. Thus we could plant groups of nine or ten oak and nine or ten hornbeam at intervals across the plantation core, and aim to manage these so that at least one tree of each group grows to maturity. This would give mature dominants at approximately 15 metre spacing.

Of course, we are not necessarily aiming for regular spacing, nor for an exact density of mature trees. Quite the opposite, we may well want to encourage considerable variation in plant distribution. These figures are intended only as an explanation of initial proportions and spacing. They demonstrate that 10% can be an adequate starting proportion for the largest, dominant tree species. If we wished to favour oak over hornbeam we might give them 7.5% and 2.5%, respectively.

Holly, being slow growing and comparatively expensive, is best kept to a low proportion, say 5%. The ground layer brambles and honeysuckle should also be small in numbers due to their propensity to compete with the other trees and shrubs in the early stages. A total for these of 5% is quite adequate to innoculate the plantation and ensure that, if conditions are favourable later, they will spread to occupy their natural niche.

This leaves us with 80% to distribute between the remaining shrubs and smaller trees which, being quicker to establish, will make up the bulk of the woodland in its early stages. A total of 20% for the smaller overstorey trees would be sufficient to introduce significant diversity into this stratum when it begins to differentiate from the shrub layer. The understorey shrubs are now left with 20% of the mix each.

The proportions of the mix would be as follows:

Overstorey:	Dominants trees:	*Quercus robur*	7.5%
		Carpinus betulus	2.5%
	Sub-dominants:	*Acer campestre*	10%
		Prunus avium	10%
Understorey:		*Corylus avellana*	20%
		Crataegus monogyna	20%
		Ilex aquifolium	5%
		Sambucus nigra	20%

Field layer:		*Lonicera periclymenum*	2.5%
		Rubus fruticosus	2.5%
			———
			100%

Spacing and Grouping

A glance into a woodland glade with regenerating oak or at drifts of birch colonising open ground will quickly demonstrate the prodigious abundance of seed and seedlings that nature provides. Multistemmed saplings resulting from several seeds germinating in one location, and single seedlings at spacings from only a few centimetres upwards are common. This apparently extravagant provision not only acts as an insurance against losses but also helps give the young trees an advantage over competing herb and woody species. Even comparatively light foliaged trees such as birch will, in close knit young clumps, soon cast enough shade to suppress plants which cannot match their extension rate. In addition, there will be competition for light between the seedlings themselves, and this may draw them up at faster growth rates than they would achieve in open ground. This mutual competition may also result in self-thinning, that is, the success of the most vigorous genotypes at the expense of the weaker individuals which cannot obtain enough light to survive in good health.

When establishing new woodland the closest we can come to imitating spontaneous regeneration is by the technique of direct seeding of tree and shrub seed. But if we use the more traditional method of planting nursery grown transplants the principles of 'over provision' and competition still apply. If initial spacing of transplants is sufficiently close, the young trees and shrubs will quickly reach the size at which they form a near continuous canopy capable of suppressing weed competition and accelerating the growth of the planted stock. In practice, the choice of spacing is determined by the need to find the right balance between the costs of labour and materials at planting and the cost of establishment and management work which follow. Dense initial planting will rapidly give a closed canopy of trees and shrubs which reduces the need for weed control and beating up but will, on the other hand, require earlier thinning in order to avoid drawn and whippy plants. Wider spacing of trees and shrubs at planting will postpone the need for thinning, but will also extend the vulnerable period during which establishment work is required and before an equivalent visual impact is achieved.

Practice suggests that spacings of between 1 and 2 metres will give a reasonably quick establishment without incurring excessive management costs. Under favourable growing conditions planting centres of 1 metre are likely to give a more or less closed canopy after three growing seasons, and 2 metre centres would probably extend this to five seasons. These establishment periods are greatly influenced by soils, microclimate and variations in weather conditions, especially rainfall. Under average conditions spacings of 1.5 metres are a good compromise. If very rapid impact is needed, or if the growth environment is particularly harsh, these might be reduced to 1 metre or, in extremes, to 0.75 metres. If the implementation budget is low and there is no urgency for a visual effect, 2 metre centres could be adequate.

The simplest approach to setting out would be to intimately mingle all species in their given proportions and to plant the resulting mix randomly at constant spacing across the plantation area. For this approach the schedule to be shown on the planting plan should appear as follows with the percentage column simply translated into the total number of each species in the core mix area. If we assume an area of 1 hectare (l0,000m^2) and a spacing of 1.5 metres (equivalent to 0.45 plants/m^2) it would read as follows:

	Total No.
Quercus robur	340
Carpinus betulus	115
Acer campestre	450
Prunus avium	450
Corylus avellana	900
Crataegus monogyna	900
Ilex aquifolium	225
Sambucus nigra	900
Lonicera periclymenum	115
Rubus fruticosus	115
	4510

All plants shall be randomly mixed and planted at 1.5 m c/s throughout the mix area.

(Note that quantities are rounded up to the nearest 5.)

This method of random distribution has in practice been shown to result in a number of problems. Chief amongst these is the tendency for the most vigorous species to dominate the entire area from a very early stage because they are more or less evenly mixed with the slower growing trees and shrubs. This necessitates constant attention to thinning or coppicing in order to avoid suppression and loss of the long term species. In addition, random distribution does not allow us to vary the spacing of plants to take account of the growth rates and habits of different species. The management responsibilities for this kind of planting are onerous and therefore are often not properly attended to. This results in a *laissez faire* woodland in which only the most aggressive species succeed.

To overcome this problem one common practice is to group each species in drifts or clumps. Between five and 50 plants of the same species are often planted in each group. Grouping also has advantages in appearance as well as culture. In nature species commonly grow in dense stands, and these bold masses have an immediate, strong visual impact. This arrangement allows us to specify different spacings for different species, and even to vary the spacings used for any particular species. Slower growing, less competitive trees are best placed in medium sized groups of between 10 and 20. This will establish an area free from immediate competition which is between 10m^2 and 50m^2 in area, large enough to ensure good light conditions for at least a proportion of the group, and yet small enough to benefit from the shelter of surrounding species. At least one of each group can then be expected to grow to maturity.

The faster growing trees and shrubs, or those chosen specifically as a short term nurse can be treated in a number of ways. If they have reasonably compatible growth rates such as larch and birch, they can be intimately mixed, or they might be segregated from one another into drifts for aesthetic reasons. Thus, groups of fast growers could form extensive bands weaving through the plantation and protecting pockets of the less competitive species, either in single species drifts of between 30 and 50 or in larger mixed groups. Alternatively, the fast growing trees might be spread in smaller pockets of 10 to 20 through a mass of competitive but lower growing shade-tolerant shrub species.

Figure 10.1 Part of a drawing showing woodland planting on a power station pulverised fuel ash reclamation site. Note the use of tables to show plant numbers in each plantation area in an economical way. Species are to be randomly mixed within each mix area. (Prof. A.E. Weddle, Landscape Architect)

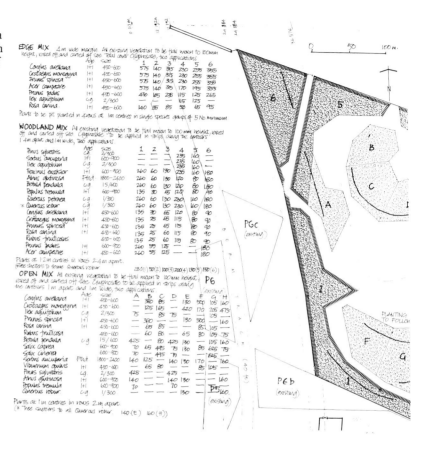

Species included in very small proportions are usually best planted in occasional small groups. For example, holly or hornbeam might be grouped in fives or tens, but because of their slow growth care should be taken to locate the groups amongst other slower growing species such as oak rather than allow them to be smothered by, say, poplar or willow. Holly, however, is tolerant of comparatively low light levels and so would suffer less than most species from overtopping.

Group sizes can be included in the mix schedule with spacing remaining uniform as follows:

Group	Total size	Total No.
Quercus robur	10	340
Carpinus betulus	10	120
Acer campestre	15	445
Prunus avium	15	445
Corylus avellana	20	900
Crataegus monogyna	30	900
Ilex aquifolium	5	225
Sambucus nigra	30	900
Lonicera periclymenum	3	111
Rubus fruticosus	3	111

All plants shall be planted at 1.5 m c/s in single species groups of the size shown. Groups shall be evenly distributed across the mix area except where otherwise shown on the drawing.

(Note that number totals are adjusted to be divisible by the group size.)

Further sophistication and a more nature-like appearance can be achieved by varying the spacing of species. For example, whereas most of the hazel can be safely planted in groups of between 10 and 30 at 1.5 metre centres, some could be packed densely into bunches of say 10 or 15 at 300mm centres if notch planted, or all in one large hole if to be pit planted. This would simulate multiple shoots from coppice stumps (and perhaps confuse the landscape archeologists of the future!). Birch is commonly found in a multi-stemmed form in nature, and this can best be produced in planting by inserting three or five birch transplants in one large pit. Ash can be treated in a similar fashion, indeed, as can many other trees and shrubs. For some species, variety could be introduced by giving a range of acceptable centres, say 0.5 to 2.0 metres, rather than defining a constant spacing.

There is ample scope for experimentation of this kind provided that any instructions given to the landscape contractor are clear and not too onerous, but it is safer if new and experimental techniques are at least demonstrated on site by the designer if not carried out by them in person. Many of these imaginative touches have been tried out with some success in Warrington New Town (Tregay, 1983) where they even break the rules of most standard specifications by planting some transplants at odd angles rather than upright in order to produce mature specimens of more varied and interesting form.

Spacings for each species in the mix might be shown as follows:

	Group size (No.)	Spacing within group (m c/s)	Note
Quercus robur	10	1.5	
Carpinus betulus	10	1.5	
Carpinus betulus	50	2.0	(1 group = 5 clumps of 10 @ 0.3m c/s)
Acer campestre	15	1.5	
Prunus avium	15	1.5	
Corylus avellana	20	1.5	
Corylus avellana	50	2.0	(1 group =5 clumps of 10 @ 0.3m c/s)
Crataegus monogyna	30	1.0-1.5	
Ilex aquifolium	5	1.0	
Sambucus nigra	30	2.0	
Lonicera periclymenum	3	1.5	
Rubus fruticosus	3	1.5	

All that then remains to fully specify the composition and setting out of this more complex mix is to calculate the total quantities of each species required. Because we are using different spacings it is simplest to apportion species by the area we wish them to occupy rather than by number. So if *Quercus* is to occupy 7.5% of the mix area we can calculate the total number of square metres to be planted with *Quercus*

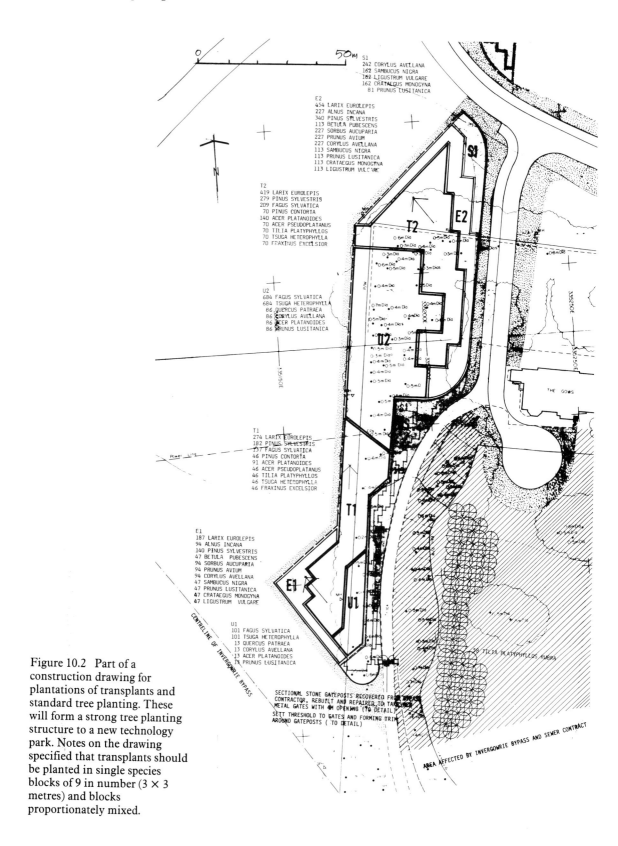

Figure 10.2 Part of a construction drawing for plantations of transplants and standard tree planting. These will form a strong tree planting structure to a new technology park. Notes on the drawing specified that transplants should be planted in single species blocks of 9 in number (3 × 3 metres) and blocks proportionately mixed.

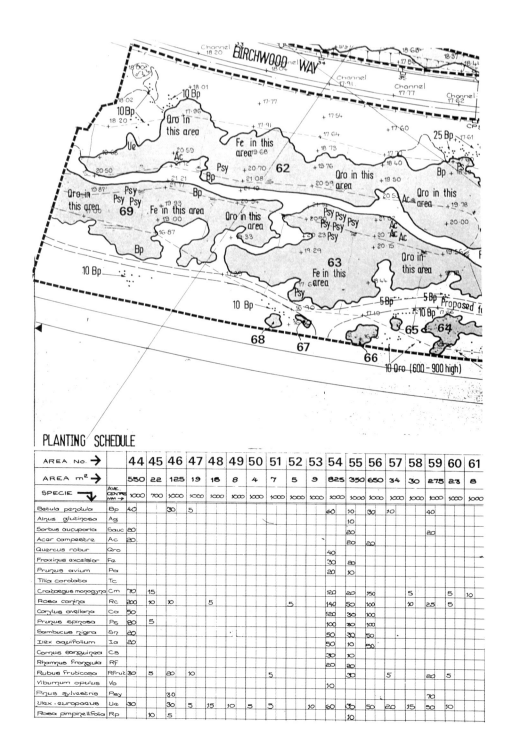

PLANTING SCHEDULE

SPECIE		AVE. CENTRE MM →	44	45	46	47	48	49	50	51	52	53	54	55	56	57	58	59	60	61
AREA No. →			44	45	46	47	48	49	50	51	52	53	54	55	56	57	58	59	60	61
AREA m² →			550	22	125	19	18	8	4	7	5	9	825	350	650	34	30	275	23	8
			1000	700	1000	1000	1000	1000	1000	1000	1000	1000	1000	1000	1000	1000	1000	1000	1000	1000
Betula pendula	Bp	40			30	5							60	10	30	10		40		
Alnus glutinosa	Ag													10						
Sorbus aucuparia	Sauc	20												20				20		
Acer campestre	Ac	20											20	20						
Quercus robur	Qro												40							
Fraxinus excelsior	Fe												30	20						
Prunus avium	Pa												20	10						
Tilia cordata	Tc																			
Crataegus monogyna	Cm	70		15									120	20	150		5		5	10
Rosa canina	Rc	200		10	10		5				5		140	50	100		10	25	5	
Corylus avellana	Ca	50											120	30	100					
Prunus spinosa	Ps	80		5									100	30	100					
Sambucus nigra	Sn	20											50	30	50					
Ilex aquifolium	Ia	20											50	10	50					
Cornus sanguinea	Cs												30	10						
Rhamnus frangula	Rf												20	20						
Rubus fruticosa	Rfrut	30		5	80	10					5				30		5	20	5	
Viburnum opulus	Vo												10							
Pinus sylvestris	Psy				30													70		
Ulex europaeus	Ue	30			30	5	15	10	5	5		10	60	35	50	20	15	50	10	
Rosa pimpinellifolia	Rp			10	5								10							

Figure 10.3   Part of a construction drawing showing nature-like woodland and scrub planting. Note the complex edge to planting areas and the concentration of certain species in selected areas. (Robert Tregay, Landscape Architect, Warrington and Runcorn Development Corporation)

and then multiply by the planting density to arrive at the total number of that species. For example, if the mix occupies 1 hectare (10,000m^2):

	Area	Group Size	Spacing	Density	Total area	Total plants
Quercus robur	7.5%	10	1.5m	0.45/m^2	750m^2	340

The same calculation is performed for each component of the mix. The schedule of species shown on the planting plan need not include the columns for percentage, density or total area and so would appear as follows (woodland core mix, total area 10,000m^2):

	Group size	Spacing within group (m c/s)	Total plants	Note
Quercus robur	10	1.5	340	
Carpinus betulus	10	1.5	90	
Carpinus betulus	5 ×10	2.0	100	(1 group = 5 clumps of 10 @ 300mm c/s)
Acer campestre	15	1.5	450	
Prunus avium	15	1.5	450	
Corylus avellana	20	1.5	860	
Corylus avellana	5 ×10	2.0	250	(1 group = 5 clumps of 10 @ 300mm c/s)
Crataegus monogyna	30	1.0-1.5	1280	(ave. density 1/m^2)
Ilex aquifolium	5	1.0	250	
Sambucus nigra	30	2.0	500	
Lonicera periclymenum	3	1.5	111	
Rubus fruticosus	3	1.5	111	

Once again, the species totals have been rounded up so that they are divisible by the group size, thus avoiding sub-division of groups.

The more complex elements of setting out such as coppice imitation and continuously variable centres are best illustrated with sample plan or section details as many landscaper contractors will be unfamiliar with this approach. Otherwise, a schedule such as that above need only be identified with the mix area on the plan which it applies to, either by code (a letter, number, colour or tone) or arrow.

Subsidiary Mixes

Any major variations in soil or microclimate which are noticeable before planting could be exploited by planting a range of trees and shrubs which are specifically adapted to those conditions. In long established spontaneous woodland such specific communities arise naturally, and are called 'societies' to distinguish them from the main associations. For example, ash and alder societies form on wet ground in oak woods. Ash and alder are the dominant canopy trees of the society but the shrub and field layers are also different from those in the adjacent oak woodland. Subsidiary mixes might be drawn up for noticeably wet hollows, for very exposed ridges or for steep slopes where the soil is likely to be thin and dry.

An example of a wet woodland mix would be:

Tree layer:	*Alnus glutinosa*	20%
	Betulus pubescens	20%
	Salix alba	10%
Shrub layer:	*Frangula alnus*	20%
	Salix cinerea	10%
	Viburnum opulus	20%

We can also respond to variations in site conditions by identifying the most successful species in different parts of the site after, say, five years, and promoting

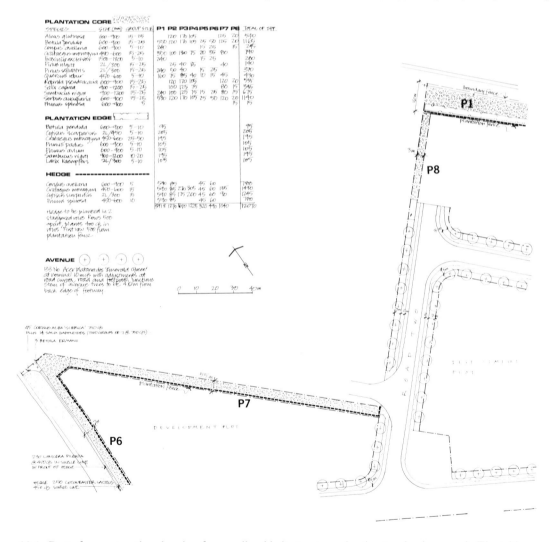

Figure 10.4   Part of a construction drawing for woodland belt structure planting to a business park. The table shows number of each species in each mix area, size of groups of each species and nursery stock size. Woodland core, woodland edge and perimeter hedge mixes are all represented. The setting out of mixes areas and plant spacing is shown in the cross-section in Figure 10.5. (Robinson Burrows, Landscape Architects)

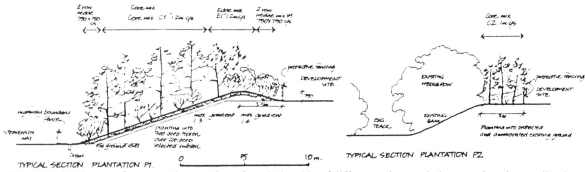

Figure 10.5   The use of cross-sections to show the relationship of different mixes and plant spacings in woodland belts around a business park. (Robinson Burrows, Landscape Architects)

Plate 123   The pioneer species birch *(Betula pendula)* and goat willow *(Salix caprea)* have colonised open land to form an extensive stand of low woodland. Note the high canopy woodland developing in the background.

Plate 124   A mosaic of young birch *(Betula pendula)* and oak *(Quercus petraea)* woodland and open land where space and vegetation interweave. (Photo: Owen Manning)

Plate 125   A plantation containing a woodland scrub mix of shrub transplants and scattered groups of staked ash whips *(Fraxinus excelsior)* immediately after planting. Note that the plantation incorporates and protects a remnant of an old hedgerow.

these with management. Indeed, the more subtle variations in soil and drainage can sometimes only be identified by noting variations in species performance.

Low Canopy Woodland

A different approach to establishing woodland is to concentrate exclusively on early stages of succession. As we have noted, the final dominants may arrive spontaneously or may, if required, be deliberately introduced at a later stage. On the other hand, the long term development and composition of the wood may not be a practical concern of the designer or, more positively, pioneer or transitional woodland may be characteristic of the locality. In these circumstances we can design planting mixes which exclude high canopy dominants such as oak and beech and rely on medium sized trees such as rowan, birch, aspen and alder. Ash might also be included, being an early coloniser, especially in secondary succession. These fast growing trees could be associated with light demanding shrubs which would survive in areas of open tree canopy, and shade-tolerant shrubs could be included to form an understorey below the trees.

Let us imagine a free draining, mildly acidic soil, in the moister areas of Norlh or West Britain. The indigenous low canopy woodlands are likely to be dominated by birch (*Betula pubescens* or *B. pendula*) associated with rowan (*Sorbus aucuparia*), goat willow (*Salix caprea*) and bird cherry (*Prunus padus*), with a shrub layer of hazel (*Corylus avellana*) and occasionally guelder rose (*Viburnum opulus*), in the shade of the tree canopy, and gorse (*Ulex europaeus*) and broom (*Cytisus scorparius*) present in glades and areas of open woodland. Thus a possible low canopy woodland planting mix would be:

Overstorey:	Tree layer:	*Betula pendula*	10%
		Betula pubescens	10%
		Sorbus aucuparia	20%
		Prunus padus	5%
		Salix caprea	5%
Understorey:	Shrub layer:	*Corylus avellana*	20%
		Viburnum opulus	20%
Glades:	Shrub layer:	*Ulex europaeus*	5%
		Cytisus scorparius	5%

If wind exposure is severe on the site we would be wise to increase the proportion of the most wind hardy plants, *Ulex*, *Cytisus*, *Betula* and *Sorbus*. Under reasonably sheltered conditions the most competitive species in the early years would be *Salix caprea*. This should be either kept to a low proportion as shown above or, if required in larger numbers for quick effect or a nurse, it should be segregated into large drifts or groups. Note that, overall, 50% of the mix consists of tree species. This proportion will ensure that the planting will develop a strong woodland character with a more or less closed canopy, but including some more open stands and occasional glades.

Woodland Scrub

Woodland scrub represents a transition state in the succession from scrub, which is dominated by shrub species, to mature woodland. It would contain a similar range of pioneers and small trees to that found in low canopy woodland, and it may also include young trees of high forest dominants, but all these trees would form only a scattered, open canopy allowing a thicket of light demanding shrubs and sapling trees to thrive below.

This kind of canopy structure could be created from the low canopy woodland mix by thinning and coppicing to maintain large glades and an open canopy. However, if woodland scrub is our objective at the design stage, we can anticipate by including a higher proportion of light demanding shrubs and species which flower and fruit better in the light. These would be accommodated by reducing the proportion of tree species at planting. Our low canopy woodland mix for a mildly acidic soil could thus be modified to a scrub woodland mix as follows:

Emergent trees:	*Betula pendula*	10%
	Sorbus aucuparia	10%
Shrub layer:	*Ulex europaeus*	15%
	Cytisus scorparius	15%
	Viburnum opulus	15%
	Craraegus monogyna	20%

Thicket Scrub

Thicket scrub was identified in the early years of descriptive ecology by Salisbury (1918) as a subseral or, rarely, climax community characterised by dense stands of shrub species almost entirely devoid of trees. Because these are often the result of grazing they are dominated by thorny species such as hawthorns (*Crataegus monogyna* and *C. oxycantha*), gorse (*Ulex europaeus*), blackthorn (*Prunus spinosa*), wild roses (*Rosa* spp.) and brambles (*Rubus fruticosus, sensu lato*) which give protection to small numbers of unarmed shrubs, including hazel (*Corylus avellana*) and dogwood (*Cornus sanguinea*). Bramble and field rose (*Rosa arvensis*) would scramble among and into the taller growing shrubs.

In fenced plantations a thicket scrub community will eventually progress to woodland if tree species are allowed to colonise and establish in the protected environment between shrubs. In the most vigorous stage of a thicket scrub plantation, however, the dense canopy close to ground level would prevent the establishment of any field layer, including tree seedlings. The thicket scrub thus becomes a single layer association if planted at high densities. A more open and varied plantation, however, would allow the development of a field layer as well as an earlier succession to woodland.

A possible thicket scrub mix for a well drained calcareous soil would indude:

Tall shrubs:	*Crataegus monogyna*	20%
	Prunus spinosa	20%
	Rosa canina	10%
	Cornus sanguinea	10%
	Ligustrum vulgare	10%
	Corylus avellana	10%
	Rhamnus catharticus	10%
Low - medium shrubs:	*Rubus fruticosus*	5%
	Rosa arvensis	5%

If these were spaced at 1 or 1.5 metre centres they would rapidly form a close knit low canopy providing visual screening and good cover for nesting birds and other shy wildlife. If the spacing is varied in different parts of the plantation from, say, 1 to 3 metre centres more diversity in ground conditions would develop, and hence the scrub should be attractive to a wider range of fauna and flora. Alternatively, areas could simply be left unplanted to become glades.

High Scrub

In the case of both woodland scrub and woodland thicket we could modify the eventual structure to include free space below the canopy by exduding the lower growing, spreading species and planting chiefly taller shrubs which grow to a small tree like form. *Crataegus, Sambucus niara* and *Salix caprea* all grow to between six and ten metres under favourable conditions and, especially when planted *en masse*, will develop a raised tree-like canopy above head height. This structure is called low woodland by Gustavsson (1983), which is fitting because it resembles a scaled down version of high woodland and can include additional layers below the dominant canopy. Clearly, the categorisation of anything as variable as plant communities is liable to be imprecise, and there is bound to be some measure of overlap between categories. However, it is valuable to retain the term 'scrub' to describe associations dominated by shrub species and 'woodland' to indicate the presence of a significant proportion of trees.

Edges

The edges of plantations are also of great importance for a number of reasons. From outside the plantation they are the most visible element, and at close quarters play a key role in the structural character of the woodland or scrub as a whole.

Edges could be open allowing views beneath the canopy and between the tree trunks into the core and giving free access from adjacent land. They could be closed with dense shrub growth forming a barrier to access and vision and giving more shelter within the core of the woodland.

The edges of both woodland and scrub offer rather different environmental conditions to the innerstand. They are lighter, normally experiencing only periodic or light shade and may, depending on aspect, experience greater wind exposure. If a more or less closed edge is desired we have the opportunity to design specific mixes to take advantage of the higher light levels and to provide maximum shelter.

The marginal vegetation of established woods is characterised by dense shrub growth and small, light demanding tree species. The shrubs may include shade bearing species, but growing with greater vigour to a fuller canopy and flowering and fruiting with greater profusion than in the shade. *Crataegus, Sambucus, Lonicera periclymenum* and *Rubus fruticosus* are all examples of shrubs which, although they are common in the shrub and field layers of innerstands, produce flower and fruit more profusely at the wood edge. This is attractive to people and to wildlife.

Shrubs and trees with a requirement for high light levels will be restricted in the long term to the edge and glades of woodland. These include gorse (*Ulex europaeus*), broom (*Cytisus scorparius*), roses (*Rosa* spp.), wayfaring tree (*Viburnum lantana*), dogwood (*Cornus sanguinea*), blackthorn (*Prunus spinosa*), crab apple (*Malus sylvestris*), birches (*Betula* spp.) and wild cherries (*Prunus* spp.). Many of these are also common in scrub associations, indeed, woodland edges can be regarded as narrow bands of scrub restricted by the shade of the innerstand on one side and by a different land use or landscape management regime on the other.

The edges of established woodland frequently display a gradient in height from small trees and tall shrubs, which are tucked under the outer line of the high canopy, down to low shrubs and herbs at the border of the meadow, path or other surface

Plate 126   Scattered planting of low thicket scrub transplants protected by tree shelters in an exposed coastal location. Species include burnet rose *(Rosa pimpinellifolia)*, gorse *(Ulex europaeus)* goat willow *(Salix caprea)* and sea buckthorn *(Hippophae rhamnoides)*. (Photo: Prof. A.E. Weddle, Landscape Architect)

Plate 127   Low scrub, including gorse *(Ulex* spp.) and dwarf willow *(Salix* spp.), is now well established on a South facing slope at the wildlife garden site, planted for the 1984 Liverpool International Garden Festival.

Plate 128   High canopy woodland in an urban park with an open edge which allows free access between the open space, the path which follows the edge, and the interior of the wood.

which bounds the woodland. Tall scrub will often show a similar but more restricted gradient. This gradient or ecotone represents a transition between the communities of the woodland core or tall scrub and the adjacent land. In proportion to the area it occupies it offers a relatively high visual and habitat diversity.

In plantations we can best imitate the marginal ecotone if we design a low edge mix for the outer perimeter and a tall edge mix to be planted between this and a woodland core mix. In order for it to establish successfully and to really contribute to the ecotone the optimum width for an edge mix is about five metres and a minimum width of 2 metres is essential. The width of the edge mix planting areas need not, of course, remain constant, and greater visual interest and habitat diversity is achieved if there is enough space for them to vary considerably in width, broadening out in places into patches of scrub on the woodland margins and disappearing altogether in others.

We can achieve a doser match to microclimatic conditions as well as introduce further diversity if we vary the constituents of the mixes according to aspect. South facing edges will be warm and sheltered, and they will receive prolonged direct sunlight and allow filtered sunlight further into the woodland core. This can be reflected in a wide edge and a high proportion of light demanding and attractive flowering species such as *Viburnum lantana* and *Rosa* spp. North facing edges, although considerably less shaded than the plantation interior, will receive only short periods of direct sunlight and will bear the brunt of cold winter winds. Thus hardier, more shade-tolerant species will be suitable here, for example *Sambucus nigra* and *Prunus spinosa*. In Britain, West facing edges suffer the strongest and most prolonged winds, and East edges are prone to cold drying easterly winds which can be damaging in spring. Species should be chosen accordingly, avoiding evergreens on East edges due to their vulnerability to physiological drought, and including the most wind firm species on west edges.

Tall Edge

Suitable species will include many that would be selected for high scrub and woodland scrub. A tall edge mix for the oak woodland core mix described earlier could include some innerstand tree layer sub-dominants and shrub layer species which would benefit from the more open conditions. It should also include specifically light demanding trees and shrubs in order to provide greater species diversity. Trees should be of small or medium stature and confined to a low proportion to avoid excessive shading of shrubs as they mature. Shrubs should be chosen from the taller species capable of reaching 3 metres or more in height. A possible mix would be:

Medium/small trees:	*Acer campestre*	5%
	Prunus avium	5%
	Malus sylvestris	5%
Tall shrubs:	*Crataegus monogyna*	25%
	Ligustrum vulgare	20%
	Rosa canina	20%
	Viburnum opulus	15%
	Salix caprea	5%

Note that *Salix caprea* is restricted to 5% due to its vigour and rapid canopy spread.

Low Edge

Many of the low and medium height British native shrubs are characteristic of the more extreme soil or climatic conditions. For example *Ulex*, *Calluna*, *Erica* and *Cytisus* on exposed acidic sites, and *Erica tetralix* and *Myrica gale* on permanently damp soils. A small number, however, would be suitable for a low edge mix around woodland on neutral loam or clay. In time tall herb species could be permitted to colonise the plantation edge and supplement the low shrubs, but in the early stages of establishment these would be highly competitive with the shrub transplants and should be controlled.

A possible low edge shrub mix for neutral soil would be:

Cornus sanguinea	30%
Prunus spinosa	35%
Rosa arvensis	30%
Rubus fruticosus	5%

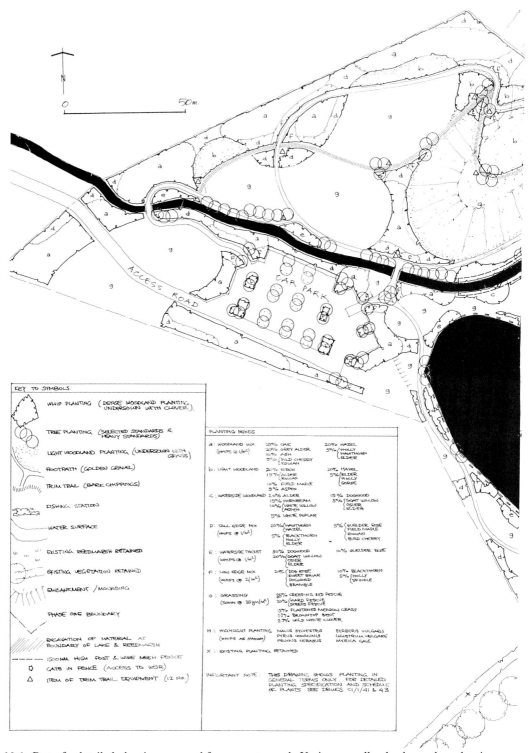

Figure 10.6 Part of a detailed planting proposal for a country park. Various woodland, edge and scrub mixes are proposed to suit environmental conditions and achieve structural and habitat diversity. (Martin Popplewell, Landscape Architect)

Plate 129   Gorse (*Ulex europaeus*) and wild roses (*Rosa arvensis* and *Rosa canina*) form a low edge to roadside woodland planting in Milton Keynes.

Plate 130   A clipped hawthorn (*Crataegus monogyna*) hedge forms a neat dense edge to this roadside plantation.

Plate 131   Outlying groups of self-sown birch (*Betula pendula*) add to the spatial intricacy and microclimatic diversity on the edge of this wood.

Rubus fruticosus is included in only small proportion because of its rampant growth and tendency to scramble over and smother small shrubs, and because it is difficult to obtain in large quantities in the nursery trade and may have to be transplanted as stolons from local sources.

Plant spacing for low edge mixes should normally be closer than for core mixes and tall edge mixes because of the slower spread of many of the species. If the core and tall edge spacing is 1.5 metres then 1.0 metre would be suitable for many low edge species, or if a more rapid establishment is desired 0.75 metre centres could be used.

Perimeter Hedging

In some instances we may require a very rapid closing of the plantation edge and a neat, well tended appearance. This can be provided by a perimeter hedge of two or three rows of closely spaced transplants trimmed once or twice each year. The narrow width may be particularly advantageous if space is too limited for full development of a tall and low edge structure. A perimeter hedge could have the character of a rural hedge or hedgerow, or it might be more formal with connotations of parkland or urban landscape. The choice will depend on the setting and function of the plantation. The design of plantation hedges is very similar to that of 'free standing' hedges and the reader is referred to the section on hedges and hedgerows.

Outlying Groups

Established woodlands and scrub which are bounded by cultivated or otherwise intensively managed land will possess a sharply defined edge beyond which no spread of trees or shrubs is possible. Where the adjacent land is unmanaged the woodland or scrub will, sooner or later, colonise, beginning the process of succession towards climax woodland. Various stages of this colonisation can be observed on abandoned pasture, around unmanaged scrub, along roadside and railway verges and other 'disused' land. The sight of this spontaneous process underway without interference from people can be particularly satisfying, giving a real sense of nature in the landscape.

We can encourage or imitate marginal colonisation around the edges of plantations, if space allows. It will, of course, happen naturally under the right conditions of management, but only after the plantation trees and shrubs had reached the reproductive stage, or if there are other parent trees to provide seed. For an earlier effect we can plant small groups of various shapes and sizes, and occasional individual trees or shrubs in grassland adjacent to the plantation. Suitable species would include those already present in the woodland edge mixes and light demanding scrub and pioneer trees. These outlying groups are thus rather like pieces of the edge or scrub mix broken off and scattered beyond the main body of the plantation.

The intricacy and variety of the plantation margins will be further enhanced if the edge of the main plantation is irregular in its outline, creating bays and spurs which interlock with surrounding grassland. Not only does this fragmented edge give a more natural appearance, but its greater length and the numerous small scale variations in light and shade and shelter and openness further diversify the habitats available for wildlife.

It should be noted that this approach to the layout of plantation edges would require any fence line to be beyond the undulating edge and outlying groups where it can retain a simple and economical alignment. This would restrict public access to the plantation edge, and the management of grassland or bare soil between the planted promontories and outlying groups may be less efficient. These considerations make complex edge design most suitable for plantations which do not need stock proof or rabbit fencing to protect them.

Woodland Belts

Woodland belts are narrow strips of woodland which are too wide to be called a hedgerow but too narrow to allow the full development of both edge structure and innerstand. They consist of linear plantations between approximately 3 and 15 metres in width, and are much used in the layout of major landscape projects because of their ability to provide a firm vegetation structure which separates and encloses different land use or character zones. They are economic in the ground area which they occupy, often smoothing out irregularities in the shape of site boundaries and leaving conveniently shaped plots within the site for developement and other activities. They can also be important in providing shelter and a generally improved microclimate within these landscape compartments, but we should note that at widths of less than 10 metres woodland belts will not be able to provide the best shelter possible. For a full treatment of the theory and practice of shelter belt planting the reader is referred to Caborn (1975) and Ministry of Agriculture, Fisheries and Food (1968).

Although woodland belts are an important and often essential element in the structure of the landscape, they bring certain management problems which should be understood by the designer. They are one of the most difficult types of planting to perpetuate without large scale and often unacceptable intervention. The felling which would be necessary in preparation for successful replanting in, say, 50 to 80 years would leave comparitively large and noticable gaps and would greatly reduce the screening and sheltering functions of the belt for many years to come. If the width of the belt is less than the mature height of the trees, say 15 to 25 metres, the necessary felling would result in the complete removal of sections of the belt. This apparently drastic action is needed because replanting or spontaneus regeneration of an established woodland requires glades of a diameter between one and two times the dominant canopy height if they are to provide enough light to produce strong, well grown mature trees in the future.

Thus woodland belts of less than about about 25 metres in width have a finite lifespan as a screen or shelterbelt, and at the end of it large scale clearance is required if they are to be regenerated. The most vulnerable woodland belts are those which consist of dense stands of fast and evenly growing, shortlived trees of the kind that are often planted to provide quick screens around intrusive developments. These may be highly successful in their early years, providing rapid impact and so pleasing both the client and the planning authority, but future generations will be left with the difficult decision whether to clear fell or to regenerate in compartments. Neither of these alternatives are likely to be popular at the time, and so the management of woodland belts is often neglected and the result is their gradual decline over a long period.

If we wish to provide for the perpetuity of a woodland belt we should design it to have a more varied and open canopy structure which includes glades and areas of scrub which can be planted with forest trees in the future without the need to remove major sections of an established, uniform stand. With this approach the overall structure of the belt would be maintained even though individual trees and groups of trees come and go.

The choice and arrangement of species for woodland belts can be approached in exactly the same way as for larger plantations. The desired canopy structure must be decided upon according to the height and the degree of visual and physical enclosure that is required and the future management considerations. On many sites we will wish to achieve the best screening and sheltering that is possible. If a plantation width of 25 to 30 metres is available, we can achieve both a dense screen and shelter and allow for future regeneration. However, we frequently find it difficult to persuade the client to allow more than a 5 to 10 metres width for planting, and so we may need to accept that our screen or shelter belt will be a temporary feature and make the best use of the limited width available.

The maximum bulk and density of vegetation in a woodland belt could be achieved with a high or low woodland innerstand including a dense shrub understorey and an edge mix along at least one margin, preferably the edge which faces the prevailing wind. Impenetrability will not necessarily be the objective, however. We may want more openness and visibility as the plantation matures, in which case we might plant only a high canopy tree mix so that the end result is tall trees supporting their canopy on clear boles with open space below. Many examples of woodland belts of this structure can be seen in the earlier British new towns. These were often planted as standard trees *en masse* in mown grass, but more recent experience has shown that we can achieve the same results more quickly and more

Plate 132 A woodland belt of ten metres width forms part of the landscape structure of Birchwood Science Park. Low edge species include *Rosa* spp. and snowberry (*Symphoricarpos* spp.).

Plate 133 This belt of woodland scrub is no more than four metres wide, but provides an excellent screen to extensive car parks. The photograph was taken ten years after planting. In the future, selected coppicing of shrubs and thinning of trees will be necessary in order to maintain the visual density of the belt throughout its height.

cheaply if we adopt a woodland planting and management approach staning with transplants at close centres.

For a woodland belt plantation to include an innerstand and an edge along both margins we would need a minimum of two mixes, a core mix and an edge mix. If the plantation were wide enough, say 15 metres, we could introduce more variety with low and tall edge mixes on different sides or, if the belt ran roughly east-west, the south margin could support a more light demanding edge mix than the north margin. This would give us a maximum of five primary mixes. If ground conditions vary significantly within the plantation we may need to reflect this in subsidiary mixes. A final level of subtlety can be introduced by inserting clumps or even single specimens into the mixes near or just beyond the edge of the plantation in key positions such as entrances. These would stand out from the backcloth of foliage and act as eye-catchers or accents.

Although such subtle variations may be necessary to meet the functional requirements of the planting, to make maximum use of the habitat potential and to introduce visual richness we should not forget that it is often the most simple effects that are the most memorable. Generous belts of one or two well chosen tree species, such as the shelter belts of Scots pine in Breckland, Norfolk, can imbue the landscape with a strong character and become landmarks in their own right.

Clumps and Copses

Whereas woodland belts are narrow extended strips of woodland, clumps and copses are compact, contained patches. The words do have slightly different connotations. Copse derives from coppice and so suggests a small wood which, if not actually managed as coppice, does include a shrub understorey. Tree clumps on the other hand make us think of small stands of trees in parkland which are often open below the canopy or contain only a sparse understorey.

Clumps and copses, although isolated elements, are of sufficient scale to contribute structure to the largest outdoor spaces. They do not provide continuous endosure, but a number of them will create a fluid space which opens and closes as we move around and between them. A single clump or copse can be a focus or landmark in parkland or the wider landscape. Their structural role is similar to that of single trees but on a larger scale.

The canopy structure of a tree clump can best be achieved by a woodland design approach but using a simple mix including only trees. Single species clumps are often the most successful because of their boldness and uniformity of appearance. We could use a single species at planting or, if the chosen tree needs shelter to establish well, we could add nurse species to the mix which would all be removed once the long term trees had become strongly established.

A copse, on the other hand, would require a more varied innerstand mix including shrub as well as tree species, and could be further diversified by the use of edge mixes. In order to fully develop both edge and innerstand structure the diameter of the plantation should be at least 15 metres, and preferably 20 metres. If less than 15 metres a simpler structure would be advisable; for example, a single edge mix could follow only part of the perimeter, or a single woodland mix could be used which includes shrub species and small trees that will adapt to both the shade in the interior of the copse and the partial shade at its margins.

Hedges and Hedgerows

A hedge is most easily defined by its function. Hedges originated in agriculture as stock barriers and, even in their ornamental and symbolic roles, the barrier function remains essential. Thus a succinct definition would be a line of woody plants managed to form a barrier. A distinction between hedge and hedgerow is helpful for the designer. We shall use 'hedge' to describe a linear planting which is either regularly trimmed to keep it compact and impenetrable, or it consists of naturally compact shrubs which require no more than occasional clipping to maintain a continuous barrier. The hedge itself would not include trees growing in their natural tree form habit. It is common for tree species to seed into rural hedges, but these are trimmed along with the shrubs and become an integral part of the hedge tapestry. A hedge is thus a compact living wall akin to a simple free standing masonry wall.

We shall use 'hedgerow' to describe both hedges which have become overgrown and include shrub and tree species at various stages of development, and hedges in which trees have been deliberately planted or carefully selected during management to grow to maturity above the hedge. A hedgerow thus contains either trees or tall shrubs in their natural habit, and is rather looser and more varied in form than a hedge. If it has developed from an unmanaged hedge, it may have lost its original barrier function.

Hedges and hedgerows are familiar and characteristic features of large parts of the agricultural landscape in lowland Britain. They are a delightful example of integrated functions; a balanced co-existence of human activity and nature conservation. Although when originally planted they were probably never intended to be anything other than the most economic means of sub-dividing land and facilitating efficient farming, they have since become havens for wildlife. Hedged fields in livestock farming areas are of a moderate, human scale and the hedges give a sense of enclosure and protection which is not common in intensive agricultural landscapes in the industrialised world. From a more distant viewpoint they can be seen to weave the fields, woods, tracks, roads and other elements of the rural scene into a single green tapestry. Rural hedges and hedgerows give an effective and attractive landscape structure which helps to integrate the economic, wildlife and visual functions of the countryside.

Hedges are also long established as essential elements of park and garden design.

Here their primary roles have been to give structural definition and enclosure, to express sculptural form and decorative pattern and to provide a backcloth to ornamental displays and focal elements such as sculpture.

Thanks to the long tradition of hedge planting and management in agriculture and horticulure, there are well established techniques for the establishment of hedges. We shall describe the methods which are most useful for general landscape practice.

The primary function of a hedge, whether it is in the rural or urban landscape and whether it encloses a farmer's field or gardener's display, is to provide a dense barrier within a narrow strip of ground. The technical objective of hedge planting is therefore to establish an impenetrable canopy of foliage, and usually as quickly as possible. We can achieve this by choosing species with a dense growth habit and by regular trimming to promote this habit and keep the hedge within the desired dimensions.

Rural Hedges

The scale of rural hedging is usually much greater than in urban or garden settings. Good species for rural hedging will thus need to be inexpensive, because of the quantity required. Growth habit is also important, dense twiggy growth to near ground level is essential. The best hedging plants respond well to regular trimming or laying, producing compact side shoot growth rather than vigorous extension shoots. In addition, it is important that the species chosen fit well with the character of the local vegetation, as in most cases we will want to blend and harmonise with the existing hedges, woods and scrub.

With age, rural hedges and hedgerows can gain a considerable diversity of woody and herb species. The majority of these colonise by seed or vegetative means from local sources, and so the hedge comes to reflect the flora of the surrounding landscape. From an ecological viewpoint hedges could be regarded as narrow strips of scrub in which the succession to climax woodland is prevented by management and hedgerows, including trees, might be regarded as strips of woodland scrub or woodland edge, and indeed they show much of the species richness of marginal communities. Rural hedges may have originated in several different ways - as woodland relics which have survived clearance; from spontaneous scrub colonisation of unmanaged field boundaries; from hedge planting of mixed species, or from hedge planting of a single species (Pollard *et al*, 1975). Many parts of Britain are characterised by particular hedge species, for example, hazel in Monmouthshire, elm in Somerset and *Pittosporum crassifolium* enclosing the bulb fields of the Scilly Isles. But some of the typical plants in old established hedges may not be the best in terms of growth habit and so, when planting new hedges, we need to decide whether our first priority is the local character or the effectiveness of the hedge as a barrier.

Species for Rural Hedging

The most commonly planted hedging species since the enclosures of the 18th and 19th centuries has been hawthorn *(Crataegus monogyna)*. It is ideally suited to large scale work because it is economical to propogate in quantity and establishes quickly in a wide range of soils and climates to form an impenetrable, thorny barrier. Local names for hawthorn include quickthorn and quickset which reflect its rapid establishment. Other species which have been planted to form rural hedges include hazel *(Corylus avellana)*, especially in Wales, holly *(Ilex aquifolium)* in Staffordshire, blackthorn *(Prunus spinosa)* and elm *(Ulmus* spp.) in various parts of Britain, beech

(*Fagus sylvatica*) on the margins of Exmoor, and fuchsia (*Fuchsia magellanica*) in the west of Ireland. All these have been used in single species hedges because of their growth habit is so well adapted to hedge management.

Many other shrubs and trees have been planted in mixed hedges in the past because of their availability as young seedlings in local woods and scrub and, more recently, by conservationists and landscape designers wishing to achieve diversity in new hedges and hedgerows. They could also be used to create an unusual single species hedge under the right conditions. These secondary species include field maple (*Acer campestre*) which is an excellent hedging plant and much used in France for this purpose, hornbeam (*Carpinus betulus*) which, like beech, is rather slow and more common in parks and gardens, wild privet (*Ligustrum vulgare*), cherry plum (*Prunus cerasifera*) which is not a British native but fits well in the rural landscape in its green leafed forms, dogwood (*Cornus sanguinea*), guelder rose (*Viburnum opulus*), wayfaring tree (*Viburnum lantana*) and the oaks (*Quercus robur* and *Q. petraea*) which, although they may become rather open at the base, respond well to regular trimming by retaining their brown leaves in winter like beech and hornbeam.

All the above species could be used in the rural landscape provided that careful attention is paid to local character and vegetation. Many of them are likely to have colonised existing hedges if they were not part of the original planting.

It should be mentioned that there are a number of species which are planted for hedges in rural areas, some of them recent introductions, which are difficult to harmonise with the British landscape. The commonest is leyland cypress (x *Cupressocyparis leylandii*) which is now one of the most popular hedging plants on account of its extraordinary growth rate. An annual height increment of 1 metre is common. It is used in gardens, parks, estates, industrial screenings and windbreaks by fruit growers and market gardeners. In its form and in its various foliage colours it is unlike any other native or naturalised vegetation in our countryside and so can be conspicuous and intrusive in the rural landscape. This effect is exacerbated by individual trees and hedges of leyland cypress growing to great size. Once above about 4 metres hedges are difficult and expensive to trim on top. Leyland cypress hedgerows of 10 to 15 metres tall are now common, and these dimensions will continue to increase. Perhaps this view could be considered rather conservative, and some would argue that, whatever its aesthetic merits, leyland cypress is irreplaceable as a near instant hedge or screen.

There are also some native species which should be avoided if an even, dense hedge is required. Elder (*Sambucus nigra*), the larger willows (*Salix* spp.), and poplars (*Populus* spp.) all grow so rapidly that they dominate and suppress other species, and will result in a hedge of very uneven height within a month or two of trimming. In addition, they have a leggy habit and leave large gaps near the ground, even when regularly cut. These vigorous species could, however, be included in hedgerows where a more variable and informal character is desired.

There is a good range of reliable hedging plants to choose from even without exotic species and the more vigorous natives. Our selection must, of course, take into account the local conditions of soil and exposure. Some species are highly adaptable, hawthorn and blackthorn, for example, whereas others are best suited to specific conditions, such as wayfaring tree to calcareous soils and guelder rose to moist ground. Another important factor for large scale hedging is cost. Close spacing is required for a quick dense hedge, and so large quantities of plants are needed. Prices vary greatly; the cheapest species is usually hawthorn, whilst holly can be ten times as expensive due to the propagation techniques employed, its slower growth and the need for container grown or rootballed stock.

Hedge Mixes

Let us assume we require a quick growing hedge for a site with an average loam or clay loam soil in a reasonably sheltered midland site. If we wished to keep the costs of implementation down the chief constituent of the mix might be hawthorn. Other species could be drawn from the characteristic local hedge and scrub flora. A total of five or six species would be adequate to provide an attractive diversity, but there is no hard and fast rule about this, and many factors such as local character, food and shelter for wildlife and availability will affect the range to be used.

A possible mix would be:

Crataegus monogyna	50%
Prunus spinosa	15%
Corylus avellana	15%
Acer campestre	15%
Cornus sanguinea	5%

This selection would be likely to form a hedge resembling many established rural hedges in the locality. If winter foliage is important and the rate of establishment less critical, an alternative mix would be:

Ilex aquifolium	30%
Fagus sylvatica	30%
Crataegus monogyna	10%
Acer campestre	15%
Prunus spinosa	15%

The evergreen foliage of *Ilex* and the retention of leaves through the winter on *Fagus* would make this a colourful and varied hedge throughout the year. These species are slower growing than the remainder of the mix, but the more vigorous components, although included in smaller numbers at planting, will ultimately form a comparatively large proportion of the established hedge.

Setting Out and Spacing

In order to create dense even growth from near ground level upwards, hedges are traditionally planted as small stock at close spacings. For example, it is common to use two year old hawthorn transplants which can be any height between 30cm to 60cm. Occasionally, seedlings between 20cm and 40cm tall are transplanted to their final positions after just one season's growth in the nursery. Spacing can be varied according to the budget available, but 30cm is common for the smaller transplants. Occasionally, three year old transplants of between 60cm and 90cm tall are used. These and the larger two year plants can be set 45cm apart.

It is comparatively rare to use larger plants, especially for long hedges in rural locations, but occasionally there may be the need for a strong visual impact immediately after planting. This could be achieved by using plants 90cm-1.2m tall at, say, 45cm or 50cm centres. The larger stock sizes are, of course, more costly, and it may be more difficult to get dense branching near ground level because these plants are likely to have been shaded and drawn up in the nursery rows. If larger stock is cut back to one third of its height, this will promote good bushy growth from low down and produce better hedging plants. From a cultural point of view this hard pruning is preferable to the short term gain in height achieved by not pruning.

The densest barrier will be produced by planting two staggered rows 30cm or 45cm apart. With this method the longitudinal distance between plants will be halved when the hedge is viewed at right angles, and the additional row will help to reduce the risk of gaps at the base. Three rows may be justified if a broad hedge is wanted and they should again be staggered for maximum overlap. Single row hedges are sometimes planted in rural locations, but are more common in gardens and urban sites where space is strictly limited and they are most successful if the densest growing species are used.

For single species hedges the setting out can often be described on the planting plan in words, although a small sample detail of the dimensions within and between rows and to adjacent plants or edges can be helpful. For mixed hedges, particularly with more than two species, not only dimensions but also the relative positioning of different species should be drawn. This can be done most economically by designing a hedge unit, perhaps between 5 and 15 metres long, which is to be repeated along the entire length of the hedge. This technique is similar to the repeating unit matrix which can be used to detail large scale plantation mixes.

Hedgerows

In hedgerows the barrier function is less important, and trees or large shrubs can be allowed to grow to maturity above the smaller species. The lower layer may either be trimmed to maintain its compactness or it can simply be allowed to develop its natural form.

If the hedgerow is to include fully grown trees these should be carefully positioned at the desired intervals and, if it is to be trimmed in its early years, these

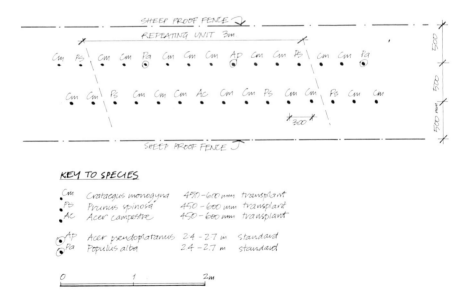

Figure 10.7 Part of a drawing showing a repeating unit for hedgerow planting on a reclamation site. Note close spacing for quick establishment of a stock proof barrier and standard trees confined to one row for ease of hedge maintenance. (Redrawn from Prof. A.E. Weddle, Landscape Architect)

trees should be planted as staked feathered trees or standards rather than as transplants to distinguish them from the shrub species. If this is not done we run the risk of the trees being cut along with the shrubs.

Because a hedgerow is rather like a narrow strip of tall woodland edge or woodland scrub we can approach the choice and arrangement of species in a similar way. The main differences will be the scale of grouping of different species and the advantages of planting in parallel rows rather than randomly. Species groups should be smaller in hedgerows than in woodland or scrub because of their narrow width. Groups sizes from 5 to 15 would give a good balance of diversity and there is less risk of vigorous species completely suppressing their neighbours because the slower growing canopies can spread laterally into the space beside the hedgerow. Hedgerows are best planted in parallel rows because their precise alignment is likely to be important, and because aftercare and establishment work in a narrow strip is made easier by regular spacing.

We need not confine hedges and hedgerows of traditional rural character to rural locations. They can be ideal barriers and boundaries in housing developments, in the grounds of industry and other institutions, in the larger town parks and in urban wildlife parks. Indeed, a design precedent for this has been set by the conservation of existing hedges and hedgerows and their retention within new developments. However, hedges in gardens, town parks and urban areas have traditionally had a more formal or exotic character, and the next section will discuss the design of traditional urban and garden hedges.

Urban and Garden Hedges

Hedges are among the most important structural elements in the layout of gardens and urban landscape. For example, the expertly tended formal hedges at Hidcote in Gloucestershire and Newby Hall in North Yorkshire are crucial to the spatial composition and the experience of these gardens. Formal, clipped hedges would be far more common as enclosure, screens and shelter planting in the urban landscape were it not for the regular and rather laborious attention that they demand. Despite the cost of maintaining clipped hedges they have seen something of a revival in recent years, especially in prestige landscape schemes such as business parks and company headquarters. Here they form distinctive and efficient enclosure for car parks, sitting areas and ornamental planting, and are also employed in the traditional role of boundary definition. In addition to these structural roles, the even colour and texture and the crisp line of a well maintained formal hedge can act as a delightful complement to flowers and foliage in decorative planting.

If a less maintenance intensive or a more informal green barrier is required there are many shrubs such as *Escallonia* and *Rosa rugosa* which, if planted closely enough, will form a compact dense hedge which needs only an occasional light trim. Such informal, low maintenance hedges have become common in recent decades due to the need to keep the labour costs of landscape management as low as possible, but they also have many aesthetic qualities which justify their use. They offer a more gentle enclosure than the sharp outline of clipped yew or box and, because pruning is minimal, many species used for informal hedging offer the bonus of abundant flower and fruit in addition to the qualities of their foliage.

Species for Formal Hedging

In Britain and many other parts of northern Europe the classic hedging plants are yew *(Taxus baccata)*, box *(Buxus sempervirens)* and beech *(Fagus sylvatica)*. All of these look good throughout the year as yew and box are evergreen and beech retains golden brown winter foliage when clipped, and all respond to regular trimming by producing dense twiggy growth down to near ground level. This compact habit, however, is a consequence of their naturally slow growth rate and so we cannot be impatient for such a fine hedge. Yew and box will take approximately ten years to form a full hedge to 2 metres in height, and beech takes seven or eight years to achieve the same.

These three species are all British natives. However, because formal hedges are usually in an urban environment, it is quite appropriate to make use of a wide range of exotics. This gives us a good choice, in particular of evergreen and faster growing species, and with the comparatively generous and attentive care they are likely to receive they should be capable of making hedges of comparable quality to yew, box and beech.

Other species, both native and exotic, which are valuable for clipped hedges are hornbeam *(Carpinus betulus)*, which is very similar to beech in foliage but a little faster growing in good soils, western red cedar *(Thuja plicata)* and white cedar *(Thuja occidentalis)*, which both have emerald green foliage, holly *(Ilex aquifolium)* with its shiny dark blue green leaves, holm oak *(Quercus ilex)*, which is a similar colour to holly but with a matt surface, myrobalan plum *(Prunus cerasifera)*, cherry laurel *(Prunus laurocerasus)* with large shiny bright green leaves, and field maple *(Acer campestre)*, which is more common in continental Europe than Britain. These are faster growing than yew and box, and so are good alternatives where an early impact is needed but need more frequent clipping to maintain the same degree of formality.

Two shrubs which are extensively seen as clipped hedges are garden privet *(Ligustrum ovalifolium)* and *Lonicera nitida*. These are very popular because of their very rapid growth and low cost, and they make good solid hedges. However, they need clipping at least three times each season to keep them shapely and compact. This may be too onerous a maintenance task to impose on the majority of clients.

The choice of species will depend on many criteria. Growth requirements are paramount, of course, but growth rate, cost and aesthetic qualities will also be important. With the exception of cherry laurel, all the species quoted possess fine or

Plate 134 This broad, medium height hedge of box *(Buxus sempervirens)* provides low level enclosure for bays of colourful bedding. A weaving hedge such as this is an excellent means of structuring a linear planting area and creating well proportioned compartments for planting display. (Photo: Owen Manning)

Plate 135 Boundary definition is an important function of hedges in urban as well as rural areas. Yew is a good formal hedging plant for urban locations if we are not impatient for results (Hampstead Garden Suburb.) (Photo: Owen Manning)

medium textured foliage. (This is no coincidence. Small leaves and twigs allow clipping without unsightly foliage damage; also, compact growth with fine twigs and leaves is a characteristic of many slow growing compact plants.) If the hedge is to form a backdrop or we want it to be visually recessive for other reasons, then fine texture is an advantage. Dark colour and matt surface provide an excellent background to brilliant flower and illuminated foliage.

Some shrubs will flower and fruit even when regularly trimmed, provided this is done at the right time of year. For example, *Berberis darwini* produces an attractive quantity of its rich orange flowers even as a clipped hedge. Because it flowers in spring along much of the length of the previous year's shoots, it can be clipped after flowering and again, lightly, in autumn and, unless too much of the summer's growth is removed, will go on to produce a display the following April. *Pyracantha* spp., especially the more compact cultivars, and *Cotoneaster lacteus* can be treated in a similar fashion, and have the added benefit of richly coloured berries in late summer which last well through the winter.

There are numerous additional species which, although not often seen as such, will make attractive and effective hedges. Rosemary *(Rosmarinus officinalis)* can be clipped to form a low aromatic hedge, *Viburnum rhytidophyllum* makes an imposing if sombre edifice, and many species of Berberis including *B. thunbergii* and *B. sargentiana* are highly effective barriers. Indeed, it is worth trying any shrub which has a compact growth habit and we may discover an unusual and attractive hedging plant.

Mixed hedges can be effective in formal, urban or garden planting just as in rural locations. The intermingling of different foliage textures and colours can be very pleasing. The colour variations of green and copper beech, and of beech and holly in winter, or the textural contrast of cherry laurel and field maple, can be quite dramatic. One particularly memorable combination seen by the author was a clipped hedge of *Senecio greyi* and *Berberis thunbergii* 'Atropurpurea' about 1 metre tall, planted as an edging to a car park. The contrast of grey and plum foliage colours was the more enjoyable for the harmony of texture and the consistency of shape and outline.

For successful establishment and ease of maintenance of mixed hedges it is important to choose species with well matched growth rates. If one species is a little more vigorous it can still be included provided that its proportion in the mix is reduced accordingly. For example, 15% of *Pyracantha* in a beech hedge would add winter foliage variety and the attraction of autumn fruits without dominating the slower growing beech.

Species for Informal Hedging

The criterion for successful informal hedging shrubs is a natural compactness of habit and a canopy well furnished to the ground. Their form may vary from rounded dome shaped shrubs like *Viburnum tinus*, *Griselinia littoralis* and *Escallonia* to upright growers such as *Berberis gagnepainii* and *Arundinaria murieliae*, but all these species make a dense barrier to their mature height if planted sufficiently close.

One of the great advantages of informal hedges is that flower and fruit are not inhibited by trimming. Some of the most popular species are chosen for their flower display in addition to their compact habit. Many roses, for example, make effective and showy informal hedges, especially *Rosa rugosa* cultivars, hybrid musk roses and a number of species roses and hybrids such as *R. rubiginosa*, *R.* 'Canary Bird' and *R. pimpinellifolia*. For lower growing, informal hedges species include lavender (*Lavandula spica* and cultivars), *Berberis thunbergii* 'Atropurpurea Nana', *Potentilla* spp., the smaller shrubby veronicas (*Hebe* spp.) and rosemary (*Rosmarinus officinalis*). Many species can be planted as an informal hedge. The most important thing to avoid is, in the case of taller shrubs, a leggy or open habit and, for low hedges, sprawling or excessively spreading growth.

Setting Out and Spacing

For both formal and informal hedges the principles of setting out and spacing are similar to those which apply to rural hedges containing mainly native species. Under most conditions it is best to plant small stock as close together as possible. If the plants are available as field grown transplants the smallest size available should be specified and planted at 35-45cm centres for tall and medium hedges, or 25-35cm centres for low hedges, in two staggered rows 30-40cm apart. If a narrow hedge is required a single row is usually sufficient but the spacing in the row should then be towards the low end of the ranges quoted. For example, bare root *Rosa rugosa*, 45-60cm tall could be cut back to 20cm and planted in a single row 30cm apart.

Many species used in urban and garden hedges are only available as container grown stock and may be difficult to obtain as small 'liners'. They will also be considerably more costly than bare root, field grown transplants. Container grown plants should thus be used more sparingly. For example *Pyracantha* in a 2 litre pot and 45-6cm tall, could be confidently planted in a single row at 50cm apart.

In the case of most species planted as larger stock sizes it is important to prune them after planting by one third to two thirds of their height to promote bushy side branching. There are exceptions to this, however; the leading shoot of yew should not be pruned until it has reached its final height because to do so is unnecessary, and will only slow down the vertical growth of the hedge. The leaders of beech, hornbeam and holly can also be safely left for a number of years after planting unless, for some reason, the hedge is composed of particularly straggly specimens.

The location and alignment of urban and garden hedges is often critical, and small errors or deviations can have a proponionately large effect on the appearance, especially of formal hedges. Because of the precision needed in setting out, considerable care must be taken in the detailing of hedges on planting plans. Dimensions from plant rows to nearby features should be shown, and the relative position of plants in the rows clarified. Unlike the mass planting of a plantation mix or an area of ground cover, the positions of individual plants or at least rows of plants should be shown for hedges.

Trees in Hedges

The aesthetic merits of spreading tree canopies and sturdy trunks above a neat green wall of foliage are very attractive. This collonade-like form can be seen in formal parks and gardens, but it can be difficult to establish and maintain. In the first place, cutting of the hedge is made more laborious by the need to work around the stems of trees. Hand work would be essential to achieve a tidy finish and avoid the risk of damage to the trees. In addition, once the tree canopy begins to thicken and spread the shade it casts suppresses the hedge immediately below it, and tends to produce uneven growth which, in a formal hedge, can be conspicuous and unacceptable. The problem of shade can be reduced by raising the crowns of the trees to allow more light in under their canopies, but it is advisable to avoid planting trees directly in the hedge line if an alternative can be found. A similar structure could be created by setting the trees back approximately 2 metres from the hedge. This distance is enough to reduce root and canopy competition with the hedge plants for many years, and any shade that is cast by the trees will be more evenly distributed along the face of the hedge. Setting trees back also allows easy access to all faces of the hedge for maintenance.

Avenues

For our purposes an avenue will include any regular linear planting of trees in which each tree is identifiable as an individual. They will be taken to include single lines and parallel rows which can be straight or curved, and may follow a single direction, defining a linear space, or can form squares or circles to form a static space. The visual qualities and detailed design of avenues is quite distinct from mass structure planting, but they can be equally dominant elements in the structure of the landscape, defining spaces and boundaries just as effectively but in a more formal manner.

Avenues are traditionally associated with fine buildings, monuments and important routeways. The vista created by a linear avenue is often focussed on the facade of a building or a monument for which it creates an impressive approach. Avenues are also planted to give character and distinction to vehicle or pedestrian routes.

Because of their linear nature, avenues are an effective and economical means of defining territorial and spatial boundaries, and of articulating circulation. Their scale and proportion can vary from an intimate passage beneath small flowering cherries to a grand parade flanked by stately limes or plane trees. The degree of enclosure can also be controlled. Although lines of mature trees alone cannot give complete separation at lower levels, the choice of species and their spacing allows us to create, at one extreme, a continuous green arcade with a roof of foliage or, at the other, the mere suggestion of a boundary line between widely spaced but carefully aligned specimens.

The detailed design of avenues is chiefly a matter of selecting the right species and spacing for the required function and appearance, but this is by no means as straightforward as it might at first seem.

Avenue Species

A formal avenue should be consistent in form and foliage. This uniformity requires a single species of tree which must be absolutely reliable in the location. It should not show undue response to variations in soil and microclimate on site; it should not be over-susceptible to diseases and disorders, and it should not require frequent tree surgery to maintain a safe and well shaped crown. It is a further advantage if the species is available in a cultivar which, having been propagated by cuttings or grafting, will be genetically consistent. Trees propagated by seed may show too much variation in growth rate and habit to make a good formal avenue.

Trees which have been traditionally used for tall avenues in Britain are limes (*Tilia* spp.), planes (*Platanus* spp.), Norway maple (*Acer platanoides*), elms (especially *Ulmus glabra*), horse chestnut (*Aesculus hippocastanum*), Spanish chestnut (*Castanea sativa*), beech (*Fagus sylvatica*) and the more regular species of poplar (eg. *Populus robusta*). For urban areas avenue trees should not cast excessive shade, should be tolerant of the more difficult soil conditions and airborne pollution, and be reasonably free from the more troublesome pests, especially aphids. Norway maple, *Tillia euchlora*, *T. petiolaris* and *Platanus x hispanica* are the most suitable in this regard. Two trees which have recently come into favour for urban planting and should make good tall avenue trees are Turkish hazel (*Corylus colurna*) with its regular conical form, and raoul (*Nothofagus procera*) which is a fast grower and shows signs of being a valuable tree for urban planting where space allows. There are a number of other

Plate 136   An urban hedgerow of Norway maple *(Acer platanoides)* planted in a hedge of *Cotoneaster lacteus.* The restricted width available for planting made this a suitable means of integrating the decked car park within the planting structure of the office development site. (Photo: Prof. A.E. Weddle, Landscape Architect)

Plate 137   Hedge clipping is easier if trees are planted next to rather than within a hedge.

Plate 138   An impressive single line avenue of chestnuts *(Aesculus).* (Photo: Owen Manning)

species which might well produce good tall avenues in suitable conditions, although they are less commonly seen as such in Britain. For urban areas these include Turkey oak *(Quercus cerris)*, which is not the most stately of trees but is fast growing to a broad spreading crown and tolerates air pollution well, and sycamore *(Acer psuedoplatanus)* which grows into grand specimens when given sufficient room to spread. In parkland, estates and rural areas it would also be well worth trying larch *(Larix* spp.), black pine *(Pinus nigra nigra)*, which makes a stately mature tree, hornbeam *(Carpinus betulus)*, Hungarian oak *(Quercus frainetto)*, chestnut leaved oak *(Quercus castaneifolia)* and sessile oak *(Q. petraea)*. The last three species are faster growing oaks than the pendunculate oak, and form a straighter bole and more regular crown.

For an avenue of medium height, that is approximately 10 to 18 metres at maturity, the following species provide a range of reliable trees with consistent habit. Many *Sorbus*, especially *S. ana* and cultivars, *S. intermedia*, *S. x thuringiaca* which has an upright form, *S. aucuparia* cultivars *S.* 'Sheerwater Seedling'; some of the flowering crab apples (especially *Malus tschonoskii* with its compact columnar form), the double flowered gean (*Prunus avium* 'Plena'), the mop head false acacia (*Robinia pseudoacacia* 'Bessoniana'), the compact cultivar of hornbeam (*Carpinus betulus* 'Fastigiata'), the spineless honey locust (*Gleditsia triacanthos* 'Inermis'), manna ash (*Fraxinus ornus*), which is smaller and more compact than mature specimens of *F. excelsior*, Italian alder (*Alnus cordata*) which has attractive glossy foliage and a neat conical crown, and maidenhair tree (*Ginko biloba*), which is a common street tree in Japan and the USA where its naturally fastigiate form is a great advantage.

If consistency of appearance and regulariy of form is less important the choice of avenue trees broadens to include virtually any species that is suited to the local conditions. If pedestrian or vehicular circulation is required beneath the avenue we should choose trees which can be pruned to give a raised crown above head height and are not prone to dropping branches or wind damage. In these circumstances trees such as the type *Robinia pseudoacacia*, which leaves a litter of spiney twigs after strong winds, would not be a good choice.

Small avenues of less than 10 metres mature height tend to be more informal in character unless regular trimming or training is carried out. This is because at this more intimate scale the precision and uniformiy needed to achieve a sense of formal control is considerably greater than at the scale of parkland or boulevard. Small avenues can, nonetheless, be effective and attractive structural elements in the human scale landscape of courtyards and gardens. Good trees for this purpose include flowering cherries and plums (especially *Prunus* 'Accolade', *P.* 'Kursar', *P. padus* 'Watereri', *P. sargentii*, *P.* 'Shirotae', *P.* 'Tai Haku' and *P. cerasifera*), flowering crab apples (especially *Malus floribunda* and *M. hupehensis*), the largest cotoneasters (*Cotoneaster frigidus*, *C. x watereri* and *C.* 'Cornubia'), willow leaved pear (*Pyrus salicifolia* 'Pendula'), the ornamental thorns (especially *Crataegus x lavallei*, *C. crus-galli* and *C. prunifolia*), and the smaller cultivars and species of *Sorbus* (such as *S.* 'Joseph Rock', *S.* 'Embley', *S. hupehensis*, *S. cashmiriana* and *S. vilmorinii*).

Setting Out and Spacing

The spatial arrangement that we have in mind for the avenue will influence our choice of species. We will be looking for a tree with the right spread, height and form. The regularity of geometry and spatial form that can be created with avenue plantings lends itself especially well to architectural metaphor. A single line of closely spaced trees with clear boles and linking canopies becomes a green colonade. Two lines whose canopies also meet overhead can be regarded as an arcade of trees, and if returned around a square become like a cloister enclosing a court. The ascending trunks and branches of large trees can create an outdoor room with the inspiring atmosphere of a cathedral nave. More widely separated trees take on the processional character of rows of columns or statues flanking a ceremonial path.

The spacing of avenues is clearly crucial to the spatial qualities to be achieved. It will also be influenced by the techniques of establishment, and the speed with which the design objective must be achieved.

For avenues of large trees which are to form fully developed specimens at maturity with canopies which spread close to one another, but are not continuous, spacings of 20 to 25 metres are ideal. At this distance the largest species such as lime, plane, horse chestnut and sweet chestnut will be able to develop into fine, broad parkland specimens, but for the full effect we may have to wait up to 100 years. In order to achieve visual impact in a time scale which is acceptable for most landscape sites we can plant two or three times the number and remove alternate trees or two out of every three when the canopies begin to interfere with the growth of their neighbours. The initial spacing would then be between 6 and 12 metres which will give a good sense of continuity and spatial definition by about 15 years after

Plate 139   Limes (*Tilia* spp.) are traditional avenue trees. This lime avenue is reaching early maturity and its spacing of approximately 8 × 8 metres is now sufficient to give a pleasing sense of enclosure.

Plate 140   Poplars (*Populus* spp.) are a suitable avenue tree provided they are not close to buildings or underground services, and are well suited to planting near to water. (Photo: Owen Manning)

Plate 141   These closely planted double avenues of *Fagus sylvatica* are part of the great Renaissance park at Het Loo in the Netherlands. The impression is of great green arcades lifted high on sturdy pillars of the beech trunks. (Photo: Owen Manning)

Plate 142   Small trees such as (*Robinia pseudoacacia* 'Bessoniana') form intimate, human scale avenues and are particularly successful when found within larger enclosures such as urban squares or streets (Vision Park, Cambridge).

planting. The only problem with this method of doubling or tripling up is that when the time for thinning arrives it can be very difficult to find the courage to fell what may be fine young trees, and even more difficult to persuade the public or the client that it is necessary. One way of clarifying the management intentions from the beginning is to choose a faster growing, shorter lived species for the temporary tree. Thus, poplar or Italian alder (*Alnus cordata*) might be interplanted with the long term avenue species and felled without too much contention after 15 to 20 years.

The distance between rows should be of the same order as spacing within them, although it will be partly determined by the width of any road or path that is contained by the avenue. If the lateral spacing of an avenue is less than its longitudinal spacing it will give the impression of passing through a series of arches, and will tend to reduce the strength of enclosure in the longitudinal direction. At this large scale double avenues, with two rows on either side of the axis, or even triple avenues can endow the space with an impressive grandeur. If a multiple avenue is planted the distance between the two inner rows should be greater than between those beyond in order to avoid ambiguity about the location of the main axis.

A linked avenue, where the tree canopies meet to form parallel collonades or an arcade roofed with foliage, will require spacings of significantly less than the mature spread of the tree. Large trees such as lime, plane and chestnut would need to be no more than 15 metres apart at maturity, but are best planted at about 10 metre spacings to achieve this effect more rapidly. As we use increasingly close spacings we will create a greater degree of enclosure, and the avenue will become less like a series of related individuals and more like a continuous form in which only the boles of the trees have any real separate identity. At very close spacings for large trees, say 4 or 5 metres, there is the risk that some individuals which are slightly more vigorous, either by constitution or thanks to better ground conditions, will extend their competitive advantage by shading and suppressing the weaker trees. Differential growth rates can be moderated by judicious pruning, but as the trees become larger this becomes an increasingly time consuming and expensive operation. However, if we are prepared to accept less uniformity, there is no technical reason why we should not plant as close as 2 or 3 metres in the rows. This would certainly create a dramatic effect.

The smaller the spread of the mature canopy the closer we will need to plant if we are to achieve the same degree of continuity. Medium sized avenue trees such as *Sorbus aria* or *Robinia pseudoacacia* 'Bessoniana' would never give an integral appearance at spacing much greater than 9 metres and, for a continuous canopy, 5 or 6 metre centres is recommended. For quick establishment we could need to reduce this dimension to about 4 metres. Trees with a narrow crown such as *Malus tschonoskii* or *Gingko biloba* should be placed correspondingly closer and, although an ascending habit will not be suited to the arcade or colonnade form of linked avenue, spacings of 5 to 7 metres will achieve a strong, integrated appearance. The smallest trees such as *Sorbus vilmorinii* and *Pyrus salicifolia* 'Pendula' are best planted at no more than 5 metre centres.

For regular avenue planting of two or more rows we have the choice of a rectilinear grid or a staggered arrangement. In the former, trees either side of the main axis are opposite one another and this gives a rather more formal appearance. A staggered planting with the lateral alignment at 45 degrees to the main axis gives a less imposing and rather lighter visual rhythm, and when viewed from the side the density of the avenue as a whole will appear greater.

In practice the exact location of trees is likely to be affected by numerous constraints on site such as road junctions, side paths, the windows and entrances of buildings and services, both overhead and underground, so it is rare to be able to maintain identical spacings and relationships between rows throughout the length of an avenue. Fortunately, this is not of great consequence except in the most formal and grandest of designs. On most sites occasional breaks in the avenue and irregularities in spacing look quite acceptable as long as the reason for them can be seen and understood. It is more important to try to overcome the restrictions imposed by invisible constraints such as underground services, and this is best done by anticipating these problems and dealing with them at the site planning stage of the project.

Trained Trees

Pleached limes and laburnum tunnels are traditional examples of the use of trained tree form to achieve a very precise green architecture with strong enclosure and close control over form. In terms of function, trained tree form such as this is similar to closely planted avenues, but the management commitment is, of course, greater and much of the work requires hand labour. Despite these considerations these traditions have seen something of a resurgence in popularity in recent years and designers are beginning to make use of the exciting possibilities they offer for outdoor spaces. Green walls can be raised on pillar-like trunks, arches can be formed over gateways and dark, narrow tunnels can be created to contrast dramatically with the openness and lightness of most outdoor spaces. A further advantage of trained tree forms is that, because clipping or training is accepted as part of the management, trees of this form can be brought much closer to buildings without the fear of them outgrowing the space available, and in the knowledge that not only crown but also root spread

Plate 143   Pleached limes (*Tilia* spp.) separate the building from the bicycle park.

Plate 144   A laburnum tunnel, such as this famous one at Bodnant in North Wales, can excite not only with its spectacular flower display in May but also with its dynamic spatial qualities.

Plate 145   Pleached hornbeam (*Carpinus betulus*), clipped beach (*Fagus sylvatica*) hedges and mown lawns create strong geometric rhythms at Hidcote, Gloucestershire.

Plate 146   Some fruit trees are traditionally trained on frameworks of various kinds. Here apple trees form a shady tunnel at Norton Priory, Runcorn.

will be contained. Pleached limes could be planted within 2 or 3 metres of a building, whereas a free growing tree of this size would normally be located many times this distance away to avoid problems of shading, branch shedding and root damage.

The choice of species for training and pleaching is more limited than for general avenue planting because the trees must produce growth which can be trained along wires or bars, or must respond to clipping with dense side shoots like that produced by good hedging plants. Indeed, many of the tree species used for hedging are also suitable for pleaching. The most reliable are hornbeam *(Carpinus betulus)*, beech *(Fagus sylvatica)*, limes *(Tilia* spp.), holly *(Ilex aquifolium)*, cypress *(Cupressus)* and yew *(Taxus baccata)*. These not only produce dense foliage when trained and pruned, but can also be kept reasonably free from shoots from the bole once this has been cleared to the desired height. Common spacings for pleached trees are between 2 and 4 metres. This ensures a quick establishment of a common canopy of even density.

Training trees over a framework of steel and wires to create a tunnel has been practiced with laburnum *(Laburnum* spp. especially *L. x vossii)* and *Wisteria*, and as a means of cultivating fruiting apples with the objective of a startling display of their pendulous flowers in late spring. Laburnum tunnels can be rather gloomy during summer, but this is because as the foliage is dull and uninteresting, and because the tunnel is often dauntingly long and not properly conceived as part of a varied spatial sequence. A more permanent contribution to a planting scheme could be created by deliberate use of the confinement of the tunnel to contrast with bright, expansive spaces at the ends and by choosing species which have attractive foliage and winter canopy in addition to flowers. Species and cultivars of *Wisteria* are excellent for this purpose in addition to many other climbing shrubs.

CHAPTER 11

Ornamental Planting

Ornamental planting can be regarded as the furnishing and decorating of landscape spaces. This is carried out after the basic proportions have been formed by structure planting, landform or built elements. We should, not however, regard this distinction as a rigid one, because structure planting frequently has many detailed and decorative qualities, and ornamental planting can contribute to the definition and sub-division of a space, rather like the furniture in a room. It is really a matter of functional priorities. The main purposes of structure planting include spatial definition, visual and physical enclosure and climatic amelioration, whereas the prime functions of ornamental planting are decoration and the articulation of detailed use and enjoyment of the space.

The difference between structural and ornamental functions is also, to some extent, a question of scale. In small gardens, courtyards and single beds ornamental planting alone may create small scale spaces. For example, a seat may be tucked into the sheltered niche between two spreading shrub roses, or a flowering cherry can create a delightfill refuge below its arching canopy. Conversely, if we examine only one small part of a structure plantation such as a single plant in a woodland, it is the ornamental qualities that may well be the first to attract our attention.

Ornamental planting is an important part of the landscape, not only in parks and gardens but also in a wide range of developments such as streets, squares, car parks, recreation facilities, housing, health and educational campuses, industry, business and retail complexes, in short, anywhere that enjoyment and pleasure are not rigorously exduded.

The character and scale of ornamental planting varies from, for example, the extensive areas of mass shrub planting on a large campus to the most intensive and detailed borders in a communal garden for sheltered housing. Large scale public sites demand planting that is reliable, robust and easy to maintain as well as ornamental, but for protected sites with restricted access planting can be more intricate and include a proportion of choice species which demand skilled maintenance.

In Part 1 we examined the principles of visual composition which bind the elements of a scheme into an expressive whole; let us now turn to some detailed considerations of the selection and arrangement of species for ornamental beds and borders.

Beds and Borders

In ornamental parks, botanical gardens and private gardens there is a long tradition of bed and border planting including seasonal bedding, herbaceous and mixed borders, shrubberies and island beds. In the majority of public and institutional landscape the intensive horticulture demanded by the bedding of annuals and tender exotics, herbaceous borders and some styles of shrub planting would be too costly to justify, and so we shall concentrate on the design of beds and borders for urban areas in which a high priority is given to economy of maintenance as well as to aesthetic impact.

Layout of Beds and Borders

The size and shape of beds and borders are an important matter for aesthetic judgement. First we must pay attention to the relative proportions of planting and grass or planting and paved surface. Either grass or paving can provide an attractive foil to planting. Their simplicity and constancy of texture will complement and support the richness of diverse ornamental planting. Because of the visual softness of grass it can occupy comparatively greater areas than hard paving without appearing dreary or bleak. Of course, there are many locations such as streets and urban squares where large expanses of pavement are essential for functional reasons, and the amount of ground desired for planting may simply not be available. In these circumstances we may still be able to create an overall mass of vegetation which is in visual balance with the area of hard surface. What really matters is not the relative proportions of the areas of hard and soft on plan but the ratio of visible hard surface to visible foliage when seen from the normal viewing angles. The foliage mass and we can be increase by planting trees and large shrubs, and by using climbers and trailers to clothe vertical surfaces.

The second key question is what shape should a border or bed be? This may be dictated by the geometry of the patterns and forms of other elements in the space There should certainly be an integrity and some continuity of pattern between all landscape elements. In some cases, the shapes of the planting beds themselves could be used to create the dominant pattern form of the space, for example, the geometry of the circle expressed by a circular border to a central space can strong enough to draw other elements into its protective influence.

One aesthetic quality of planting which is in great demand is its ability to 'soften' the harsher outlines and materials of many urban structures. This is achieved by the varied colours and textures of vegetation and also by the rounded, sinuous and irregular outlines formed by shrubs and trees. These organic shapes are the natural product of plant growth, and so there is no need to introduce them into the shapes of planting beds in order to complement and soften geometric elements. Indeed, nothing looks more contrived than a wavy outline to an ornamental planting bed which is slavishly irregular. The edge to a planting bed is an artificial line and should not pretend to be otherwise. This is not to say that we cannot use informal curvilinear shapes but, if we do, they should be drawn with conviction and their scale must be large enough to remain visible after the planting has spread and broken up the line of the edge.

There are some technical implications for the layout of beds and borders which should be mentioned. In public areas planting is vulnerable to trampling by pedestrians and overrunning by vehicles. Beds can be given specific protection by raising them above ground level or by using a kerb, low wall or rail to deter access. But the correct location of the bed and its width are also effective means of deterring interference. A bed which adjoins pedestrian areas on both sides should generally be no less than 2 metres in width. This ensures that even if some damage is done at the edges a substantial area of planting should remain to grow and spread. A border which is backed by a wall along one side, however, is less vulnerable to trampling, and its width can be as little as 1 metre.

Plate 147 Ornamental shrubs may have a structural role within small spaces. This tree mallow (*Lavatera thuringiaca* 'Kew Rose') separates two seats in the precinct of Leicester Cathedral.

Plate 148 Woodland or scrub structure planting consisting mostly of native species may offer detailed decorative interest of flower, fruit and foliage as well as spatial definition and shelter.

Plate 149 The wiggles in the edge of this lawn are unnecessary because, in time, the natural spread of the trees and shrubs will provide a soft and varied outline to the planting. Furthermore, this edge is ugly because it is out of scale with the landform and the massing of tree and shrub species.

Plate 150 Established shrubs and herbaceous plants spill over the path edge at Knightshayes Court, Devon, to give a delightfully irregular natural outline. Note how the scale of the curves in the outline reflects the size of the plant groupings.

Plate 151 The edges of planting beds need protection in busy areas. These sloping walls of stone sets are both a logical extension of the paving and an attractive complement to the decorative qualities of the plant material.

Plate 152 Narrow planting beds do not provide adequate soil conditions and are vulnerable to trampling.

Plate 153 A traditional edging of stone to a herbaceous border has many advantages. Grass cutting is easier, plants can be allowed to spread over the edge, access and work to the border in wet weather will cause less damage to the edge of the lawn, and crispness of line is visually satisfying. (Photo: Owen Manning)

Plate 154 Corners of planting beds of 90 degrees or less are particularly vulnerable to trampling and should be avoided unless pedestrian traffic is minimal. The simplest answer to the problem is a 45 degree paved splay at the path junction. Even a tough ground cover plant like the *Cotoneaster dammeri* shown here cannot withstand more than occasional foot traffic.

Plate 155 The monoculture of juniper (*Juniperus horizontalis*) is out of place by this footpath where much more diversity could be appreciated. The bleakness of the space as a whole is exacerbated by the lack of enclosure. The scene is inhospitable and monotonous.

The manner of treatment of the edges of beds and borders affects the character and quality of design as a whole. Where the edge adjoins a lawn it is common to see the grass laboriously clipped and trimmed. This is done for the sake of neatness and ease of cultivation in the planted border, but it results in a rather stiff appearance and can cause the gradual reduction of the grass area through continuous trimming. The most covenient way to edge a lawn and planted border is with a strip of hard paving material such as brick or stone. This is a classic feature of many herbaceous borders which facilitates maintenance operations and allows plants to spread without risk of mowing damage. It also lends a crisp elegant line to the edge of the grass area and allows the designer more freedom in the shaping its layout. With a paved edge a lawn can more easily be laid out and maintained in angular and formal geometric patterns.

By far the most vulnerable parts of beds and borders are the corners. Frequent trampling of angular corners is inevitable and protection would be essential. The least intrusive way of reducing this problem is to give corners either gentle radii or generous splays in order to eliminate sharp, protruding sections of planting bed. But even these more gradual corners should only be planted with the toughest and most resilient species. Herbaceous plants or soft low shrubs would stand little chance of survival in corner locations.

The Planting of Beds and Borders

The sight of dreary shrub borders and monotonous expanses of ground cover is too common in the urban landscape. They consist of a very limited selection of utterly reliable shrubs, a high proportion of evergreens and usually very little to excite us by way of colour, form or seasonal change. Part of the explanation for this uninspiring character is the very real need to keep the costs of establishment and maintenance to a minimum. But these constraints can be overcome given sufficient plant knowledge and imagination on the part of the designer. We shall show how the maximum visual interest and a wide range of plants can be accommodated in public areas without sacrificing the dependability of the planting.

It is possible to introduce herbaceous plants which can add a softer and often more colourful note to shrub planting. Trees are also an important component of ornamental beds because they introduce height and volume of vegetation, and help to make the most of the available ground area. In Britain there is often a reluctance to plant even small, light foliage trees in confined spaces and close to buildings. But, provided that attention is paid to the locations of underground services and to the design of building foundation, there is no technical reason why many more opportunities should not be taken to enrich small spaces and complement the facades of buildings with suitable trees.

Trees, shrubs, climbers, ground cover, herbaceous plants and bulbs can all be combined to create rich and diverse ornamental borders in both public and private locations. The key to attractive ornamental beds and borders, just as to effective structure planting, is to fully exploit the available ground area by making use of the vertical arrangements of canopy layers and the seasonal rhythms of the growth. It is too easy to overlook these vertical and time dimensions when working on a two dimensional plan.

Canopy layers. In ornamental planting the main canopy layers are the tree layer, shrub layer and ground layer (we shall use the term 'ground layer' because this suggests the ground cover function of low shrubs and herbaceous plants.)

The tree layer should not be too dense. An open tree canopy will allow a greater diversity of species below, where the main focus of detailed ornamental planting is usually to be found. In addition, if ornamental beds are in small spaces or close to buildings a dense tree canopy may be too gloomy.

The shrub layer can include shade tolerant or light demanding species according to the conditions created by the tree canopy. The role of tall shrubs, ie. those above eye-level, in the canopy structure will depend on their form and habit. Some species such as *Choisya ternata, Pieris* spp. and *Viburnum tinus* have a dome like form and a dense evergreen habit which provides good weed suppression, at least until they reach an advanced stage of maturity. These tall ground cover shrubs therefore do not allow the establishment of a ground layer below their canopy. A similar role is played by thicket forming species such as *Symphoricarpos* spp. and *Cornus alba* cultivars. Many ornamental shrubs, however, exhibit a habit which does not provide effective ground cover; these include species with upright and arching forms such as *Rosa, Syringa* and *Weigela*, and especially those with a sparse open canopy such as *Tamarix, Abutilon* and *Genista aetnensis*. These more open habits provide the opportunity to establish a further layer of shade tolerant low shrubs or herbaceous plants below.

The ground layer will include low shrubs with a dense spreading habit such as *Cistus x corbariensis, Viburnum davidii* and *Hebe pinguifolia*, or prostrate layering shrubs such as *Hedera* spp., *Cotoneaster dammeri* and *Vinca* spp., or evergreen herbaceous species which form a vigorous spreading carpet such as *Lamium maculatum, Geranium macrorrhizum* and *Tiarella cordifolia*. Most really effective ground cover plants are evergreen, or at least partially evergreen: this is a matter of winter appearance as well as weed suppression. However, there are some shrubs which, although deciduous and less attractive in winter, come into leaf early in the growing season, and are so vigorous in their growth that they are equally as effective as many evergreens in their ability to suppress weeds. *Stephanandra incisa* 'Crispa', many of the shrubby *Potentilla* spp., and cultivars and herbaceous plants such as *Alchemilla mollis* and *Geranium endresii* are all good examples of deciduous ground covers.

Ground layer species may be restricted to areas where no taller shrubs or trees are planted or they may be extended underneath the canopies of taller shrubs and trees. Species must, of course, be carefully selected to ensure that they will thrive in the light conditions that will be found not only at time of planting, but also as the border matures and the trees and taller shrubs cast an increasing amount of shade.

It is particularly important when planning the ground layer to be sure that these low growing planted species will compete successfully with unwanted colonisers, that is, weeds. This is because, whereas some spontaneous growth under tall shrubs and trees can be visually acceptable and may not necessarily harm the planted species, low shrubs and herbs are easily overrun by weed, and its removal can be a much more laborious operation because of the inter-meshing of weed and planted foliage.

Good ground cover is therefore essential for ground layer planting. But once this is provided for, we can start to introduce additional low shrubs and herbaceous plants which, alone, would be difficult to establish and maintain weed free. These include two important groups of plants. The first is small deciduous shrubs or evergreens with a rather open habit such as *Caryopteris x clandonensis* and *Genista lydia*. The second is made up of perennials tall enough to grow up through and emerge above prostrate ground cover, for example *Hemerocallis, Iris, Hosta, Crocosmia* and many ornamental grasses. The upright habit of many of these plants is ideal both visually, because they contrast with a spreading canopy below, and culturally, because the ascending foliage does not cast too much shade on the ground cover plants. Spring bulbs such as *Narcissus, Galanthus* and *Crocus* can also be grown in

Plate 156 A mixed border of shrubs and herbaceous plants creates an unusually fresh and colourful decorative planting for an office development. Herbaceous plants in this scheme include *Bergenia, Iris, Astrantia major* and *Geranium* spp.

Plate 157 It is partly the close proximity between the small light foliaged tree and the building that makes this planting successful. Harmony of colour and complementary form and pattern make it a pleasing association of hard and soft materials. (Photo: Owen Manning)

Plate 158 This multiple layered ornamental planting includes a light tree canopy of *Betula jaquemontii*, a scattered shrub layer of azaleas (*Rhododendron* spp.) and a diverse low ground cover including *Tiarella cordifolia, Bergenia, Polygonum affine* and *Alchemilla mollis*.

Plate 159 *Tiarella cordifolia* and *Heuchera sanguinea* form a simple unifying carpet of ground cover below a selection of specimen fruiting shrubs including *Rhus typhina* and *Euonymus* 'Red Cascade', and taller herbaceous species including the evergreen *Iris foetidissima* in the foreground. This kind of planting association provides both decorative diversity and low maintenance requirements.

this way as an alternative to siting them in grass or bare soil. But we must be sure that the ground cover species will be low enough to allow the leaves and flowers of the bulb to easily extend above it. So the taller *Narcissus* could be planted amongst *Hedera helix* ground cover cultivars but *Crocus, Leucojum* and *Galanthus* would be more visible and persist longer in lower growing ground covers such as *Vinca minor* or *Ajuga reptans*. Herbaceous plants, including bulbs, which grow through low ground cover, could be called 'emergents' because their perenniating buds are below the ground cover, but they grow through this layer each season to emerge above it.

If we were to develop the vertical layering to its maximum potential we would plant, in a single area, a ground layer of prostrate shrubs or ground cover herbaceous plants with groups and drifts of emergent herbaceous perennials and bulbs. Above this layer we would include a variety of medium and tall shrubs which do not cast excessive shade. These would be in drifts or groups at moderate to wide spacing so that most of the ground layer below remained visible from the path at the edge. Some could be planted as individual specimens or as parts of small specimen groups made up of plants of various height. Finally, occasional trees would be included in groups or individually to add the top canopy layer and to punctuate the lower canopies with the vertical pillars of their trunks. This kind of spatial arrangement allows us to include considerable diversity without excessive complexity in any of the layers. It would be suitable for planting which we want to be rich and varied, such as the most intensive sections of large beds and in intricate borders in small spaces.

In many locations we may deliberately choose to simplify the layer structure for aesthetic reasons. For example, the bold simplicity of an extensive monoculture of shrub thicket or prostrate ground cover may be just what is needed to complement an intricate paving pattern or the fine facade of a building. We should also remember that multiple layer planting is comparatively expensive because it includes a large number of plants into a small area, and it relies extensively on low ground cover plants most of which require high planting densities. So a simpler layer structure may be a necessity because of cost. Medium and tall shrub thickets are a much cheaper method of covering the ground because far fewer plants are needed.

Successional growth. Another way in which we can make the fullest possible use of a given ground area is by choosing plants whose main growth periods occur at different times of the year. In natural associations we find pre-vernal societies of plants such as bluebell *(Endymion non-scriptus)* in oak woods which make use of the period before the tree canopy is in full leaf to make vegetative growth and flower. Bluebells and other spring bulbs could be used in a similar fashion beneath clumps of late leafing deciduous shrubs such as hazel *(Corylus* spp. and cultivars) and hardy hibiscus *(Hibiscus syriacus)*.

A succession of growth can also be achieved within the same canopy layer. For example, *Brunnera macrophylla* and *Hosta* spp. do not come into full leaf until late spring, often well into May, and this leaves a growth window in early to mid-Spring which can be exploited by plants such as bluebell, snowdrops *(Galanthus* spp.) and *Scilla*. By the time the leaves of the summer herbs have excluded the light the spring bulbs will have begun to die down and enter their natural period of dormancy.

Composition and Scale

For a detailed treatment of the aesthetic principles of planting the reader should refer to the previous chapters on the aesthetic characteristics of plants and principles of visual composition. The effect of variations in the scale of plant groupings, however, deserves further attention at the present stage.

It is sometimes said that if we look at a planting plan we should be able to deduce the essence of the composition simply from the pattern of plant groupings, that is, without reading the names of the species. This is because the scale of the drifts and clumps of each species, that is, the degree of diversity of an ornamental association, should closely reflect its role in composition.

On the ground the most intricate areas of planting will naturally catch our attention and attract closer scrutiny. Our eye will dwell on and enjoy these areas of detail after passing more quickly over stretches of more uniform or closely harmonious planting. This is true even if these larger drifts are more intensely coloured or of bolder texture. Because of this intricate associations are the highlights in a composition and should be reserved for carefully selected positions in the planting such as next to building entrances and garden pavillions, by the side of a flight of steps, at the pivot point of a path or in the foreground of the view from a seat. All these key locations have something in common, they are where we most naturally pause in our exploration of a space. Other sections of beds and borders should be comparatively simple, partly because of the faster speed of observation and partly because the change in scale will itself enhance both the bolder and the more intricate associations. In the simplest terms we could say that variety in scale is more important to composition than variety in species.

The relative scale of planting might well vary by a factor of ten or more. We would expect to see areas of plants in the simpler sections that are ten times the size of those in the more detailed areas. As part of a feature group, a single species might occupy only two or three square metres whereas alongside an approach path or at the side of a building a different species could cover 20 or 30 square metres. Between these extremes a transition can be made by intermediate scale groupings or, in some cases, we may want an abrupt contrast.

Accents

The highlights of an ornamental planting could be provided by a single, dramatic accent shrub or tree which has outstanding form. This role is well played by plants such as *Yucca gloriosa* with its sword-like leaves and imposing flower spikes or *Aralia elata* 'Variegata' with its handsome, variegated, pinnate foliage radiating from the tops of its sturdy stems. Striking colour can also provide an effective accent. If this is the colour of flowers or fruits it will of course be only temporary, however brilliant. But while in bloom shrubs such as *Embothrium coccineum* with its unique flame scarlet flowers, *Cornus kousa* with tabulate sprays of foliage clothed in creamy white bracts, and *Magnolia x soulangeana* with its white and purple goblets massed on the branches along with the emerging spring leaves are all unforgettable sights. The combination of fruit and autumn foliage colour can be just as striking. *Euonymus oxyphyllus* is clothed in early autumn with purple and red foliage just as its branches are strung with carmine and orange fruits. The feathery foliage of *Sorbus vilmorinii* turns a rich purple in vivid contrast to its white berries. Stem colour can be as effective as that of fruits and particularly when combined with autumn foliage display can provide an effective accent. *Acer griseum*, for example, combines peeling orange brown bark with the intense reds and oranges of its autumn leaves. The snake bark maples and some birches, especially *Betula ermanii, B. albo-sinensis septentrionalis* and *B. jaquemontii* all offer both ornamental bark and colourful autumn foliage. Form and colour highlights are combined in specimens such as *Cornus controversa* 'Variegata' with tabulate sprays of glistening silver variegated foliage, and *Acer japonicum* 'Aureum' with butter yellow, exquisitely shaped leaves spreading in horizontal tiers.

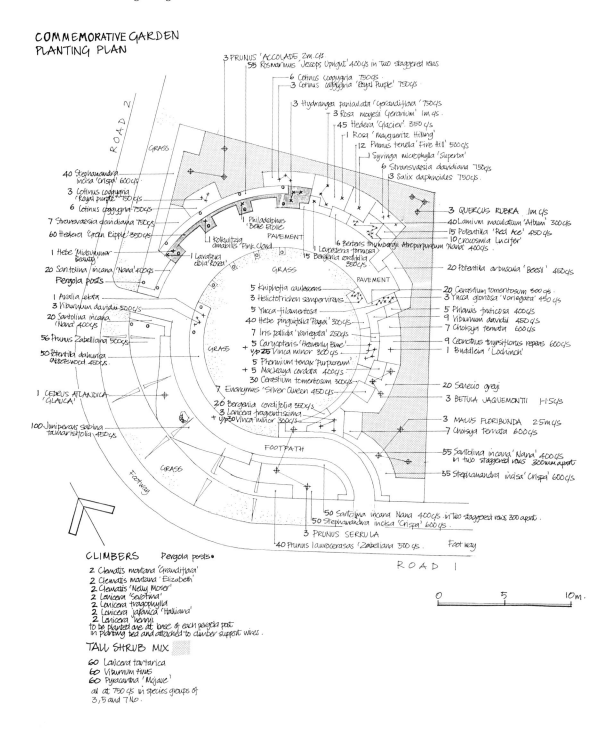

COMMEMORATIVE GARDEN
PLANTING PLAN

Figure 11.1 Planting for a public garden showing tall shrub mix enclosing the site on two sides, ornamental planting and climbers on pergola. Note the concentration of planting detail near seats and entrances. (Robinson Burrows, Landscape Architects)

Much of the effectiveness of an accent plant depends on its setting. The background should remain comparatively plain, and should contrast with the main characteristics of the specimen in front. *Yucca* foliage and flowers, for example, are most noticeable when their pale colours and bold texture are set against a dark, fine background such as *taxus baccata*, and the ascending lines of its leaves and flower spike are most dramatic when rising from prostrate form of *Juniperus horizontalis* or *Cotoneaster dammeri* or from the rounded dome of *Viburnum davidii* or *Cistus x corbariensis*. The rugged, dark green leaves of *Eriobotrya japonica* would provide a strong focus if contrasted with the feathery, glaucus foliage of *Elaeagnus angustifolia*. The exotic, luxurient green leaves of *Fatsia japonica* are particularly striking amongst the elegant, arching sprays of *Arundinaria nitida*.

Even plants which, in many combinations, are not visually dominant can become a striking accent as part of a carefully planned association. *Sambucus racemosa* 'Plumosa Aurea', for example, against a fine textured, deep green backcloth of *Buxus sempervivens* and with its leaves lit from behind by a low sun can be impressive.

Specimen Groups

The role of a visual accent can also be played by a group of, say, three or five species each with its own special merit, but which is designed to form a harmonious or specimen group. In such an association every aspect of form, colour and texture must be carefully employed to provide the right degree of tension between harmony and contrast to produce a dynamic visual focus.

Form is a good starting point for the composition of a specimen group because it is usually the most permanent of the aesthetic characteristics. Jakobsen (1977) emphasises form in his discussion of accent planting, and he describes relationships between two, three or four different forms which could together create an accent group. The simplest combination is the placing of a distinct bold visual dominant in a carpet or 'base plane' of ground cover. Three forms might comprise a sculptural tall shrub anchored by the domes of lower shrubs, but both rising above a prostrate ground cover. A further addition would give what Jakobsen calls 'A basic triad plant

Plate 160   The assertive forms of Adam's needle (*Yucca gloriosa*), in the foreground, and New Zealand flax (*Phormium tenax*), at the far end of the seat, make them among the most effective accent plants. Here their role is enhanced by contrast with the fine textures of the grass, hedge and stone.

Plate 161   These specimen groups mark the entrances to University of Strathclyde Residences. The bold foliage of devils walking stick (*Aralia elata*) help make a striking composition.

composition' set in a complementary ground cover carpet. The triad 'could consist of a sculptural, multistemmed *Aralia elata*, a dome shape or hummock of *Hebe rakaiensis* and a spikey linear form such as *Phonnium tenax*.

The textural and colour relationships of combinations must support the juxtaposition of forms. In the example given, the bold foliage of *Aralia* and *Phormium* is enhanced as well as calmed by the fine texture of the *Hebe*. A medium textured ground cover species such as *Pachysandra terminalis* or *Hedera* 'Green Ripple' would be an ideal bridge between the extremes of texture of the main triad. The *Aralia* and *Hebe* both have mid green foliage, that of the *Hebe is* rather fresher and more yellow in hue. This yellowish tint to the foliage could be picked out by choosing a *Phormium* with a cream variegation such as *P. cookianum* 'Cream Delight' or *P. tenax* 'Veitchii'. These bright warm greens and creams would stand out strongly from a dark green ground cover. *Pachysandra* would be a possible choice but a darker ivy such as *Hedera* 'Hibernica' or the typical form of *Hedera helix* which is less rampant. Alternatively the ground cover could contribute colour highlights in harmony with the main triad. *Hedera helix* 'Goldheart' has dark green leaves with a central splash of yellow, *Hypericum calycinum* combines a neat medium textured foliage carpet with a long display of abundant large yellow flowers.

Planting Patterns

Our discussion of canopy layers and specimen groups was concerned primarily with the vertical distribution of plants and the juxtaposition of their aesthetic characteristics in elevation, but must also consider their arrangement in the horizontal plane. Within each of the main canopy layers the different species could be arranged in a variety of different patterns. In our mind's eye we will have certain combinations and juxtapositions of plants, but we still need to decide exactly how to set these out on the ground.

Shrub and herb communities in nature typically consist of colonies of a species massed together, or small groups and individual plants intermixed with other species. Massing, grouping and mixing are also used in planted associations both in naturalistic associations and in the most exotic ornamental borders.

The planting patterns that we choose will depend on both aesthetic and technical factors. Some species are particularly gregarious and mingle well with others of similar stature to produce an attractive tapestry of foliage. Others are more self-contained and grow better and look more at home in groups of their own kind or as individual specimens. For example, large uniform expanses appear to suit the visual character of many spreading ground covers such as ivy species (*Hedera helix*, *H. canariensis* and *H. colchica*), green leaved ivy cultivars (*H.* 'Green Ripple' and *H.* 'Hibernica'), *Hypericum calycinum* and *Pachysandra terminalis*. These plants do not look their best in small patches or when part of a mixture. Taller shrubs which are especially effective in mass planting of special species include *Tamarix* spp., *Escallonia* spp., and *Elaeagnus x ebbingei*. These recommendations perhaps represent personal preferences, they certainly depend on subjective aesthetic judgements.

The commonest patterns that we see on planting plans are blocks of one species and occasionally of mixed species which are butted up together to fill the entire planting area. This is a well practiced technique, and has the advantage of providing a good bold mass of each plant which confidently displays its aesthetic qualities. It is also simple to draw and easily set out on the ground.

The shapes of the species blocks on plan have a great effect on the three dimensional appearance of the planting on the ground. Roundish or squarish areas will produce a patchwork quilt appearance from above. From eye level, however, the blocks will appear smaller in scale and self contained, even isolated, because their full depth is either foreshortened or hidden. The relationship between adjacent species in this kind of layout can appear rather rigid and formal, but if we allow the groups to interlock and interweave the relationships become more intimate and more varied and we can see new aspects of each species as they associate in different ways with their neighbours. One species can appear in front of, behind and within a block of another. In this way we can get the maximum value from a given number of species.

An effective method of associating blocks of species, particularly if the bed is narrower than it is long, is to stretch them along the direction of the bed to form linear drifts. These drifts can run in front of and behind their neighbours and bind the planting together into a richly woven tapestry. When viewed in elevation linear drift planting appears well grounded because the blocks of species are longer than they are tall. The spreading, horizontal outlines of plant masses can be punctuated by well placed vertical accents and anchored by the occasional solid dome shaped shrub or small group. Drift planting was used with great skill by Gertrude Jekyll in herbaceous and mixed borders. She was wise enough to be concerned not only with the visual composition when the plants were at their peak but also that they would not detract from the border as they faded:

> Many years ago I came to the conclusion that in all flower borders it is better to plant in long rather than block shaped patches. It not only has amore pictorial effect, but a thin long planting does not leave an unsightly empty space when the flowers are done and the leaves have perhaps died down. (Jekyll, 1908)

This advice is also applicable to shrub borders where there will usually be a succession of flowering or fruiting and, although we try to choose shrubs which look good for most of the year, it is inevitable that many will have a period when their foliage looks a little dowdy and the winter twigs of some deciduous species such as *Rosa rugosa* are far from attractive.

Another way of softening and enlivening blocks of single species is to introduce a degree of overlap and mixing at the edges. An intermediate strip between pine stands can be planted with a mixture of the two adjacent species. The width of the overlap can be whatever we wish, but something in the order of 10-20% of the width of the blocks would usually be a good proportion. The mix could be half and half, or the percentage of one species may be increased to compensate for the greater vigour of the other. This arrangement of overlapping groups is similar to some of the patterns of distribution we find in nature, and it will certainly give the association a spontaneous, informal appearance.

Overlapping will speed up the process of colonisation and competition which happens naturally in ornamental beds, unless constant effort is applied to maintaining the status quo at the time of planting. This dynamic development of ornamental planting should not be regarded as a problem. It is one of the excitements of design to watch the balance between species and the character of the composition develop. Landscape managers and gardeners sometimes regard it as their duty to impose a strict discipline, stifling change and rigidifying the appearance of planting. In most instances this is quite unnecessary. It is only if the planting no longer serves its function that we need to intervene to arrest this development.

On the other hand, designers should take the necessary care to choose species which are compatible in the growth rate and mode of spread. It takes a thorough knowledge and experience of planting for us to be sure that none of the species we

Plate 162   This delightful woodland wild garden at Wisley in Surrey consists of a mix of naturalised exotic herbaceous species including *Alstromeria, Campanula, Geranium, Astrantia major, Aconitum* and *Astilbe* mixed with natives such as *Digitalis purpurea* and *Hieracium*. The utmost sensitivity in management is required to establish and maintain this kind of planting.

Plate 163   Trees such as ash *(Fraxinus excelsior)* often colonise ground cover and shrub planting and are a benefit, provided they will not be likely to interfere with buildings or services as they grow to maturity.

Plate 164   Ferns and other small herbs have colonised these stone steps. They give an air of luxuriance and romantic decay and yet will not cause any significant damage to the structure.

include will have disappeared in four or five years time, having been overrun by stronger growing neighbours.

We can take the grouping and mixing of species just as far as we wish. In a similar manner to woodland planting we could cover a defined area with a mix of several different species provided their growth habits and requirements are compatible. The mix could be of ground layer or of taller species and can be specified as random or grouped. For example, *Cotoneaster simonsii, Pyracantha rogersiana* and *Cornus alba* 'Elegantissima' are shrubs that combine well in an intimate tall mix and *Vinca minor, Hosta lancifolia* and *Campanula porscharskyana* could be grouped to form a beautifully diverse ground cover in light shade.

Ecological Ornamental Planting

An ecological approach is not the preserve of native planting. The same principles of closely matching species to habitat and planning for dynamic plant associations can be applied to design with exotics including highly ornamental planting. It is also true that many exotic species with highly decorative qualities provide valuable food and shelter for wildlife. *Buddleja davidii is* well known as the butterfly bush, and many familiar garden plants such as lavender and *Skimmia japonica* attract great numbers of bees.

The use of ecological principles in ornamental planting was first advocated by William Robinson (1870) in a style which he called wild gardening.'... the term 'Wild Garden' ... is applied essentially to the placing of perfectly hardy exotic plants under conditions where they will thrive without further care.' Robinson was particularly interested in herbaceous plants, and thoroughly approved of the mixing of robust exotics such as Michaelmas daisy *(Aster novi-belgii)*, golden rod *(Solidago)* and evening primrose *(Oenothera missouriensis)* with attractive natives such as bluebell *(Endymion non-scriptus)*, foxglove *(Digitalis purpurea)* and lily of the valley *(Convallaria majalis)*. He also showed how hardy, vigorous shrubs such as *Spiraea* spp. and *Clematis montana* could co-exist happily with native plants. One of Robinson's objectives was to reduce the labour required to maintain plantings. Because we share this objective in the majority of landscape projects today, we find ourselves using many of the same exotic shrubs species, particularly in public and institutional landscape.

The principles of wild gardening with herbaceous plants have been taken up and developed by designers such as Richard Hansen (1987), who seeds and plants meadows and borders with exotic perennials carefully chosen to suit the habitat conditions. These plantings do not require conventional ongoing weed control, only the initial suppression of the most competitive colonisers in order to allow the introduced species to establish and naturalise.

The best British examples of wild gardens can be found in the woodlands of old established gardens such as Wisley in Surrey and Knightshayes Court in Devon. Here we can see perennials such as *Alstroemeria, Campanula lactiflora, Tradescantia, Astilbe, Astrantia major, Aconitum* and *Crocosmia x crocosmiiflora* spreading amongst showy natives like *Digitalis purpurea, Hieracium, Dachtyloriza* and *Geranium pratense,* and competing vigorously with other indigenous woodland field layer plants. The delight of this kind of association lies in the spontaneity and luxurience of its growth which gives us a sense of having discovered, almost by accident, some magical, exotic glade.

Even if we do not anticipate the dynamics of associations or stress the ecology of plant relationships at the design stage there will still be opportunities to benefit later from the natural opportunism of both native and exotic plants. A ground cover of *Hedera*, for example, is an ideal site for the establishment of tree seedlings. Most tree species have little difficulty in growing through this low canopy and, once above it, will benefit from the highlight levels but not suffer the intense root and foliage competition that would arise from vigorous weed growth. Trees such as oak and ash, which carry a substantial food store in their seed, are even capable of reaching the light above taller species such as *Lonicera pileata* and *Symphoricarpos x doorenbosii,* provided the cover is not too dense. Some ornamental shrubs such as *Buddleja davidii* and herbaceous plants such as *Alchemilla mollis* set seed prolifically, and their progeny can be found emerging in large numbers from patches of bare earth, gravel and the joints in paving and walls. We can allow selected seedlings to establish and form part of the association as long as they are not be likely to cause problems of shading or obstruction in the future. The result will be a charming spontaneity that could not be achieved by drawing board design alone.

Plant Spacing

Planting distances often cause some consternation to students attempting their first landscape planting schemes. This is because there are no hard and fast rules for what might seem as if it should be a straightforward aspect of horticultural technique. In addition, students may be familiar with the planting distances usually employed in traditional parks and private gardens. These are normally much wider than those appropriate to most landscape projects, and so the numbers of plants specified on landscape planting plans can seem to be inordinately large. There are both cultural, practical and aesthetic reasons for these differences.

In most planting schemes for public authorities or other organisations, and even in some private gardens, one of the foremost objectives will be to reduce the labour of maintenance to the lowest levels which is compatible with the character of the planting desired. If this is to be achieved we must design the planting such that it forms a weed suppressing canopy as soon as possible. Most landscape contracts include a two year aftercare and establishment period and the planting will stand the best chance of success after this period if substantial ground cover has already been achieved before the site is handed back to the client. The client is usually prepared to pay the capital cost of dense planting in order to keep the ongoing cost of maintenance as low as possible.

Ground cover also allows us to get the maximum visual interest in the given area. Bare earth is not as attractive as foliage and flowers, so why continue to pay for it, year after year?

The popular tradition of widely spaced plants in cultivated ground derives from the traditional methods of growing herbs and vegetables and flowers for cutting, and also from the Gardenesque school of design in Victorian England. The originator of this style was J.C. Loudon, who proposed that trees and shrubs be grown as specimens '... not pressed on during their growth by any other objects and allowed to throw out their branches equally on every side, uninjured by cattle or other animals; and, if touched by the hand of a gardener, only to be improved in their regularity and symmetry' (Loudon, 1838).

The gardenesque style has remained strongly represented in public amenity horticulture to this day, and has been reflected in public taste and many private gardens. A typical spacing for flowering shrubs such as the larger *Philadelphus* or *Rhododendron* in a traditional park would be 2 metres or more apart. This will allow each plant to develop a full, spreading canopy. However, if these were used in a landscape planting with the aim of achieving quick establishment and weed suppression their spacing would need to be of the order of 1 metre, that is, at least four times the density.

The high planting densities that are common in landscape work do sometimes cause problems as the scheme approaches maturity. Some species such as brooms (*Cytisus* spp.) and sea buckthorn (*Hippophae rhamnoides*) are apt to become drawn and leggy, and this is behaviour exacerbated by close thicket planting. In many cases, it can be overcome by hard pruning which will promote bushy growth from the base but some shrubs; *Cytisus* and *Lavandula*, for example, rarely recover from this treatment, and so for these we must either accept bare stems in the lower canopy or plant them more widely, with a carpet of ground cover below.

The precise spacing at which we set a particular species will depend on a large number of factors. These are its role in the association, the favourability or harshness of the soil and climatic conditions, and the level of establishment work and maintenance care that will be available. Let us try to establish some basic rules of thumb for ground cover spacings. The mature height of the species offers some guidance but, as we have seen from the variety of forms and habits that both shrubs and herbs display, there is no simple, direct relationship between height and spread, and the choice of spacing is further complicated by the relative rates of growth of different species. For example *Senecio* 'Sunshine' and *Spiraea thunbergii* both grow to 0.8-1 metre tall in cultivation, but *Senecio is* broader spreading and faster growing and so can be planted at approximately half the density of the *Spiraea*. The mode of spread as well as the vigour of prostrate shrubs will dramatically affect the time it takes them to form a closed canopy over a given area. *Rubus tricolor* and *Juniperus sabina tamariscifolia* are similar in height, but the speed of growth and the layering habit of *Rubus* enable it to cover large areas within two or three growing seasons. The juniper, on the other hand, spreads evenly but slowly, and to achieve cover in the same time must be planted at two or three times the density.

Because of such differences in habit and vigour good plant knowledge is necessary if we are to be sure of choosing the ideal spacing for any species in a particular location. However, it is possible to give ranges of density for plants in a number of difrerent categories, based on experience of their performance in a range of site conditions.

	Spacing Centres	Density
Vigorous alpines and compact herbaceous plants, eg. *Ajuga reptans*, *Festuca glauca*	200-300mm	25-1 l/m^2
Vigorous herbaceous plants and prostrate shrubs up to 300mm ht, eg. *Geranium macrorrhizum*, *Hebe pinguifolia*	300-450mm	11-5/m^2
Low upright or hummock shrubs 300-500mm height, eg. *Lavandula* 'Hidcote', *Sarcoccoca humilis*	350-500mm	8-4/m^2
Vigorous prostrate spreaders up to 500mm height, eg. *Hedera* 'Hibernica', *Cotoneaster salicifolius* 'Repens'	450-700mm	5-2/m^2
Medium shrubs 500mm-1.0m height. eg. *Senecio* 'Sunshine', *Viburnum davidii*	450-700mm	5-2/m^2
Medium shrubs 1.0m-1.5m height, eg. *Aucuba japonica*, *Hebe* 'Midsummer Beauty'	600mm-1m	3-1/m^2
Tall shrubs 1.5m-2.5m height eg. *Pyracantha coccinea*, *Berberis darwinii*	700mm-1.5m	2-0.5m^2
Vigorous high shrubs over 2.5m height eg. *Photinia davidiana*, *Cotoneaster x watereri*	1m-2m	1-0.25/m^2
Transplant trees and shrubs in mass plantation	1m-2m	1-0.25/m^2

Note that heights apply to the foliage canopy at early maturity and under average growth conditions. Within each category the least vigorous species should be spaced towards the dense end of the range and the most vigorous towards the least dense end of the range. In poor soil or high exposure, or if early aftercare work must be kept to an absolute minimum, spacing should be at the close end of the range; but if growth conditions are especially favourable and aftercare provision generous, we can widen the spacing and economise on planting stock.

For example, in average conditions *Senecio* 'Sunshine' can be planted at 600mm centres and be expected to form a more or less closed canopy after three years. If the growing season is long and moist two years will be sufficient. *Spiraea thunbergii* is rather slower spreading and would need an initial spacing of 450mm if it is to form ground cover after three seasons. In poor, dry soil it would be advisable to plant *Senecio* at 500mm apart and *Spiraea* at 350 or 400mm centres. In a deep, rich soil on a sheltered site we could plant *Senecio* at 800mm centres and *Spiraea* at 600mm centres.

The table above can be used as a guide, but the best way to judge planting centres is to observe other people's and our own planting schemes at various stages of development on the ground, and to assess the appropriateness of the spacings used for the conditions.

We should remember that it is really only when a species has been planted in order to provide ground cover that spacing is critical. If it is to form a specimen group with ground cover provided by a lower layer of planting, or if it is growing out of graves or rocks (inorganic ground cover), then its spacing is purely a matter of aesthetic judgement.

On planting plans it is best to indicate centres rather than density, because it is easier to achieve consistency by setting out at, say, 700mm centres than by marking 1 x 1 metre squares and trying to decide exactly where in the square the two plants should be located. When it comes to the effectiveness of the planting it is the distance between each plant measured on the ground that is important. However, in the case of very close spacings the specification of density is acceptable because at, say, 250mm centres the exact positioning of the 16 plants in each square metre matters little provided that they are evenly distributed.

When plant quantities are 'taken off' a drawing or we need to calculate a budget cost estimate we need to convert centres to densities in order to compute the numbers required. The table below gives approximate equivalents which are accurate enough for calculating plant numbers in most circumstances.

Centres (mm)	Density (No/m^2)
200	25
250	16
300	11
350	8
400	6
450	5
500	4
600	3
700	2
800	1.5
900	1.25
1000	1
1200	0.7
1500	0.45
2000	0.25

It should be noted that these densities are based on a square grid which can be staggered without affecting the numbers of plants. Much planting consists of even spacing but is not set out strictly in lines. This kind of arrangement should approximate to a staggered grid, and so the densities above will still apply. Because careful placing of individual plants is often needed at the corners and edges of a bed it is wise to allow a few extra plants for this, or at least to round up the numbers to the nearest five or ten.

Setting Out

The setting out of planting never requires as much precision as is needed for hard landscape. For most of the planting it is sufficient to draw the positions of species, groups or individual plants on the construction plan in such a way that they can be read with a scale rule by the landscaper. In some instances, however, the use of figured dimensions on the drawing is advisable. The exact positions of lines of plants in hedges or formal edging should normally be clearly dimensioned from the adjacent paving or fence. The positions of some specimen trees may be critical and so require figured dimensions from a building, wall or pavement edge. This is especially important in the case of formal avenues for which the visual effect is dependent on the regularity of the interval between trees. It may also be necessary to specify the distance of trees from the line of underground or overhead services to ensure that the risk of damage to both the services and the trees is kept to a minimum. Although most of these decisions can be made on the drawing board, we can often be more confident about the precise location of specimens or trees in relation to services if we are on site at the time of planting. It is quite acceptable to note on the planting plan that such and such a specimen or group is 'to be set out on site by the landscape architect.'

Much of the advice given so far is applicable to all kinds of ornamental planting, from a simple border at the foot of a building to a focal bed in a horticultural exhibition or garden festival. There are some settings, however, which have specific additional constaints and opportunities and we shall now discuss how the designer can take advantage of these.

Raised Beds and Containers

Raised beds and planted containers are common in streets, squares, courtyards, car parks and private gardens. They may be constructed for a number of reasons: if there is no topsoil at natural ground level and excavations cannot be made to provide it, if the planting needs protection from trampling and other abuse or if the designer wants planting to be combined with an instant barrier (provided by the structure of

Plate 165   If they are to promote luxuriant growth, planting containers must be of sufficient width and depth to provide adequate soil volume and avoid rapid drying out. (Photo: Prof. A.E. Weddle, Landscape Architect)

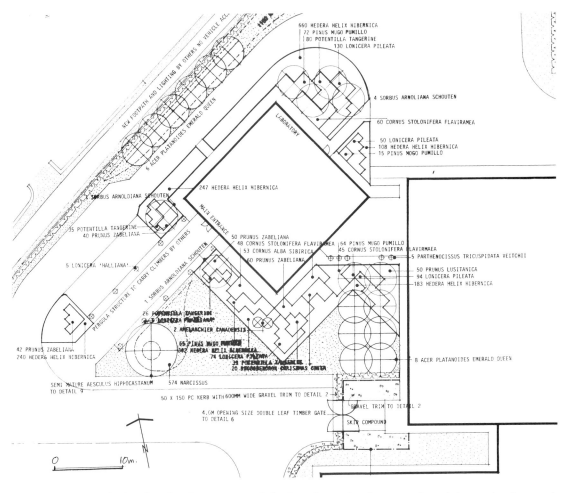

Figure 11.2 Part of a drawing showing ornamental shrub and tree planting around a unit in a technology park. (Ian White Associates, Landscape Architects)

the bed or container itself). Small containers, pots and hanging baskets are used to provide temporary and mobile flower and foliage displays for buildings, gardens and shows.

When we choose species for raised beds and containers we must bear in mind the inhospitable growth environment that they will experience. The soil will almost certainly have to be imported and may be composed of a mixture of mineral based, natural topsoil and manufactured composts, and so we must exercise care over its specification and quality control. We should ensure that, unless the planting is to be of undemanding ground cover species only, a minimum soil depth of 400mm is provided. 500mm would be preferable for small beds. Proper drainage must also be included to avoid waterlogging and, because they are vulnerable to drought, some raised beds and containers are provided with automatic irrigation, but in many cases the cost of this is not justified for the small quantity planting involved.

Unless they are irrigated, the plants in raised beds and containers will experience more frequent and more severe water stress than those in natural ground. This is

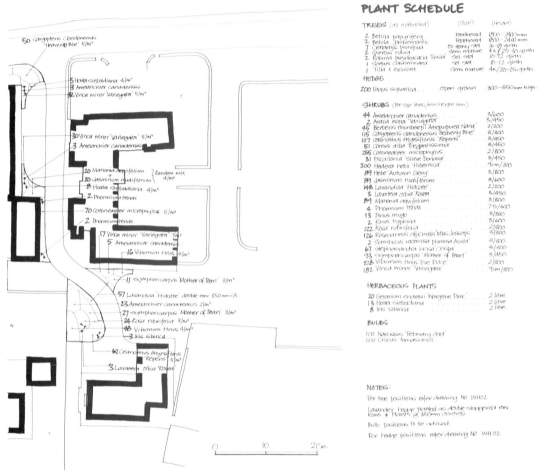

Figure 11.3   Part of a drawing showing planting for a residential development. Note the domestic character of the planting which includes familiar garden species such as lavender, rose, tree mallow and hosta. (Richard Sneesby, Landscape Architect)

because the surface area for water collection is usually smaller, the lateral move-ment of ground water is obstructed, and the soil in the bed is either disconnected from natural ground (thus preventing upwards movement of water from the natural water table), or it is at least raised further above the natural water table. Furthermore, if a volume of soil is raised above a layer of drainage aggregate its water holding capacity is partly dependent on its depth to width ratio. The narrower and higher the bed, the less water will be held against gravitational drainage by surface tension in the soil pores.

So we should avoid high, narrow beds and design raised planters which are as wide as possible (a width of less than 1 metre is likely to make establishment significantly more difficult). Having achieved this we will still need to choose drought resistant species, particularly if the bed is in a sunny position where soil evaporation and plant transpiration will be accelerated. Planting of large stock sizes in raised beds is not advisable, because the greater transplant shock and the often high proportion of shoot to root volume will make them particularly vulnerable.

Plate 166 A generous width is needed if raised planters are to include standard trees. The soil imported for the planters here rests on natural ground and this allows drainage and water uptake by the plants (standard *Sorbus intermedia* and *Hedera colchica* ground cover).

Standard trees in raised beds rarely establish and are often seen with severe die-back.

We will also want to make the best possible use of what will probably be a restricted area for planting. Tall shrubs will provide considerable bulk of foliage, and trailing plants can be located towards the edges of the bed to cascade down and clothe at least part of the sides. If trailing plants are not used the proportion of hard surface to planting will appear greater than if the bed were at ground level because the visible area of the wall of the bed will be added to the area of the surrounding pavement. Furthermore, because the sides are seen in elevation their apparent area will be proportionately greater than that of horizontal paving.

One asset of raised beds are that they allow small shrubs and herbaceous plants to be easily inspected at close quarters. Because of this raised beds can be used to make planting more accessible to people with disabilities, and they also provide the opportunity for highly intricate and small scale planting which can only be appreciated from close-to. The planters and troughs traditionally used for displaying choice alpines are examples of the scale of horticulture that can be accommodated in raised beds and containers. But note that this kind of planting is most successful if generic scale relationships are maintained by locating it in comparatively small scale spaces.

Walls, Pergolas, Trelliage and Living Fences

These elements all provide various degrees of spatial definition. They give enclosure, separation and shelter but they usually combine this structure role with an important decorative function, so we shall discuss their planting in the present chapter. The vertical surfaces of walls and the open frameworks of pergolas, trelliage and other plant supports provide prime opportunities to grow a range of ornamental plants which cannot be established in the open. In addition, the contrasts between hard and soft materials can heighten the aesthetic qualities of both.

Walls, whether free standing or part of a building, have a significant effect on the microclimate of their immediate vicinity. Walls which face between south-east and south-west experience a high proportion of direct sunlight in the northern hemisphere. They absorb and re-radiate the sun's warmth on a similar principle to electric storage heaters which contain purpose made bricks to store and slowly radiate heat. A south-west facing wall is ideal for plants which are not fully hardy. The mid-day and afternoon sun is absorbed and the warmth retained for a longer period after sunset than from walls which gain direct sunlight earlier in the day. Walls and fences also give shelter from wind and thus reduce both transpiration on hot days and wind chill in the winter. Even north facing walls offer a degree of shelter and create a more attractive growth environment for many shade-tolerant plants than open ground.

We should remember that east facing walls catch the early morning sun, and if this occurs after a frost the rapid warming of the plant tissues which results can damage the foliage or flowers of some species. So, for east facing walls we should avoid plants such as *Camellia* and some *Magnolia* spp. which come into leaf or flower early and are frost sensitive.

If there are walls which face south-east to south-west on the planting site we should not miss the opportunity to create beds at the foot where we can grow some of the species which are outstanding in their decorative qualities but may be unreliable without some protection. Species of *Ceanothus*, *Magnolia*, *Abutilon* and *Abelia*, for example, can be planted here with confidence that, given good soil, they will thrive and produce fine displays of flower.

West facing walls are good locations for plants such as *Solanum crispum*, *Camellia* spp. and *Itea illicifolia*, which benefit from protection from north and east winds, but do not like the hotter and dryer conditions of a southerly aspect.

A north facing wall, although it does not provide a site for growing tender specimens can be attractively clothed with shrubs which will flower and fruit despite the lack of direct sunlight. *Pyracantha*, *Mahonia* and *Hydrangea* spp. all enjoy the partial protection found against a north wall. Shade loving foliage plants such as *Fatsia japonica*, *Hosta* spp., and ferns find the conditions ideal, because shade is provided without the dry conditions often found beneath large trees.

Along with the advantages offered by wall culture we should also remember two common problems. The soil immediately adjacent to the bottom of a wall is likely to be dry because the masonry will absorb moisture. Furthermore, the lime in mortar and foundation rubble will often cause a more alkaline soil reaction and so calcifuges make poor wall shrubs. If a building wall is topped by eaves or an overhang without guttering the resulting drip can be more damaging to plants than that experienced beneath a tree canopy. Because of these constraints it is best to plant climbers and shrubs a little away from the wall and train them in towards it as they grow and to choose drip tolerant ground cover or low shrubs.

Pergolas, trelliage, fences and arbors also provide the opportunity to grow climbers. Indeed climbers are usually essential ingredients in the success of these structures. Climbers fall into two groups. There are those which, in the wild, rely on twining and scrambling over other trees and shrubs (eg. *Clematis* and *Lonicera* spp.), and those which attach themselves to tree trunks, rock faces and walls by means of aerial roots (eg. *Hedera* spp. and *Hydrangea petiolaris)* or small sucker pads (eg. *Parthenocissus* spp.) The first group are ideal for pergolas and trelliage where they can weave in and out of a lattice or other open framework or, if they are to be grown against a wall, need the support of wires or a trellis. The self-clinging climbers are less happy on an open framework, but need little encouragement to establish themselves on a wall or solid fence.

The selection of climbers for pergolas and trellis work will depend to some extent on aspect, but because the structure is permiable the variations in shelter and shade will be less dramatic than for wall planting. The more demanding climbers should be reserved for sheltered walls. Here we could try *Wisteria* spp., *Ytis* spp., *Akebia quintata*, *Aristolochia macrophylla* or even choice species like *Campsis grandiflora* and *Eccremocarpus scaber*. For free standing structures we should restrict ourselves to dependable but no less attractive climbers, such as clematis (especially *C. montana* cultivars, *C. alpina* and *C. macropetala)* honeysuckles (*Lonicera periclymenum*, *L. japonica* and *L. henryi)* and climbing roses (*Rosa* 'Albertine', *R.* 'Zephrine Drouhin' and other reliable cultivars). Although roses are amongst the most showy of climbers

Plate 167   A South West facing wall is an ideal location for growing tender climbers and shrubs such as *Camellia saluensis, Cytisus battandieri, Acacia dealbata, Abutilon* spp. and *Magnolia grandiflora.*

Plate 168   A well proportioned pergola well furnished with *Vitis vinifera, Wisteria* spp. and *Clematis.*

Plate 169   These steel and wire structures are specially designed to introduce vegetation into a busy confined space. The climber is *Wisteria.* (Photo: Owen Manning)

Plate 170   This pergola displays a relatively high proportion of structure to foliage, but the balance is successful because of the quality of the timberwork. (Photo: Owen Manning)

Plate 171   This decorative fence is designed with climbers in mind. *Hydrangea petiolaris* is able to scramble up the open timberwork with the aid of occasional tying to the laths. (Photo: Owen Manning)

Plate 172   *Vitis coignetiae* rambles through this double row of steel posts with the aid of wires strung between the posts and forms a sculptural combination of hard and soft elements at Broadwater Business Park, Denham.

we should remember that they do require considerably more pruning and training than the others, and for this reason may be unsuitable for many sites.

The object of most climber and wall shrub planting will not be to create a continuous mass of foliage which completely obscures the supporting structure. Rather, it will be to achieve a balance between the foliage area and the masonry facade or the pattern of the climbing framework. Because of this mass planting close spacing is not necessary, and most wall shrubs and climbers are treated as specimens or small groups, whilst ground cover for the planting bed is provided by a lower canopy layer. Thus, spacing at the base of a wall should be determined by the balance of surfaces desired and the positions of any windows and doors in the facade. Frameworks constructed specifically to support climbers can be more regularly and densely planted, but it is often best to retain a proportion of unclothed trelliage or lattice to provide an attractive contrast to the climbers foliage. This can be achieved by spacing most climbers between 1 and 3 metres apart, depending on their vigour.

Trellis or open framework fencing is sometimes combined with climbers where a dense barrier and screen is required in a short time in a narrow strip of ground. This kind of structure is akin to a narrow hedge and can be accommodated within a width of about 0.5 metre, provided that adequate ground preparation is made. Such a 'living fence' would be planted generously with the more vigorous climbers. Russian vine (*Fallopia baldschuanicum*) and traveller's joy (*Clematis vitalba*) are the fastest growing and need only be planted at 2 metre centres along the line of the fence. If the living fence is located close to shrub planting it may be necessary to carry out regular tying-in and cutting back to ensure that such rampant climbers do not smother nearby shrubs. Other suitable species are Japanese honeysuckle (*Lonicera japonica* 'Halliana') which, being evergreen, is excellent for winter cover, *Clematis Montana* and cultivars and the deciduous honeysuckles (especially *Lonicera periclymenum* and cultivars). These are a little less vigorous and should be planted at approximately 1 or 1.5 metre centres in order to achieve rapid cover.

Ornamental Planting for Specialised Habitats

We have discussed design techniques and selections of plants for beds and borders

Plate 173   Established trees and shrubs such as this fastigate yew *(Taxus baccata* 'Fastigiata') can provide natural support for the more vigorous rambling roses (shown here) and climbers such as mountain clematis *(Clematis montana)* and honeysuckles *(Lonicera* spp.)

Plate 174   Even the most stately of architectural elements such as this balustrade can be complimented and enhanced by climbers. The species shown is a cultivar of common honeysuckle *(Lonicera periclymenum).*

which may be located in sites with various aesthetic characters and a range of microclimate and soil conditions. Ornamental planting can also be found in more specialised habitats such as ponds, boggy ground, screes, rockeries and drystone walls. Here we need plants which are specifically adapted to the more demanding environmental conditions. In addition, the design objectives may be rather different. For example, complete vegetation cover is unnecessary in a scree garden or a pool because the stone and the water are intended to be part of the composition.

For discussion of the design of these specialised plantings and of suitable species the reader is referred to the gardening and landscape literature on these subjects. Especially recommended as an introduction are Gertrude Jekyll's *Wall and Water Gardens,* introduced and revised by Graham Stuart Thomas (1983), and Allan Hart's chapter 'Water Plants' in *Landscape Design with Plants* (1977).

Although choice of species and establishment techniques will be quite different for a pool margin as compared with a shrub border, the principles of composition and the process of choosing and arranging plants will be the same. The guidance offered in this chapter should be regarded as a basis for ornamental design in all locations, but under more specialised or difficult growing conditions horticultural expertise becomes increasingly important if we are to achieve a similar level of aesthetic success with the planting.

CHAPTER 12

Conclusion

With the help of planting design we can create a landscape which is both useful and beautiful. It gives us the opportunity to enrich peoples' everyday lives and to create special places of great beauty. To do this is no mean achievement, and this book's premise is that success depends on an understanding of how plants can be used to give meaningful form to space and how their aesthetic qualities can be used to enrich those spaces.

Planting is living sculpture. If we regard planting design as an art, then it is the art of drawing that is most meaningful to us from nature and of expressing that part of us which is most in tune with the natural world. With planting we can enhance the pleasures that nature offers to both the senses and the mind. Like any other art or craft, planting design communicates meaning; to any person who stops to notice, it will say something about the ideas and the intentions of the designer. It is hoped that this book has helped to establish a language of planting design which will enable the designer to speak more purposefully and more eloquently. Of course we will not always need to express personal or social purpose directly: on occasions we may wish nature to speak for itself. This is certainly possible even within some of the most intensely humanised environments, but because of the extent of human pressure and urbanisation on much of the world's habitable landscape, a conscious decision is now needed to make room for nature. As planting designers we are able to assert many of the benefits of this.

The technical and scientific aspects of planting have not been the focus of this book. However, we should not forget the importance of horticulture for the success of landscape design, nor the power of the natural sciences to argue the case for environmental protection and positive ecological action. Ecologists have shown us the complexity of vegetation and inspired a new enthusiasm for natural vegetation and nature-like planting as a habitat for wildlife and as a thing of beauty in its own right. Good planting design is a way to unite the technical skill of the horticulturalist and the scientific wisdom of the ecologist with the emotional and spiritual vision of the artist.

Another harmony of opposites is found in the mutual dependence of convergent and divergent thinking in the design process. Creativity is a gift which all people have and its true power arises from the ability to bring together and direct different human skills and points of view. It is hoped that this short exploration of one field of creativity will help to exite, inspire and motivate its readers to use their creativity to make meaningful and beautiful landscapes.

References

Appleton, J. H. (1975) *The Experience of Landscape*, London & New York: John Wiley & Sons.

Arnold, H. F. (1980) *Trees in Urban Design*, New York: Van Nostrand Reinhold.

Ashihara, Y. *(1970) Exterior Design in Architecture*, New York: Van Nostrand Reinhold.

Austin, R. L. (1982) *Designing with Plants*, New York: Van Nostrand Reinhold.

Bacon, E. N. (1974) *Design of Cities* (Revised edn) London: Thames and Hudson.

Baines, C. (1985) *How to Make a Wildlife Garden*, London: Elm Tree Books.

Baines, J. C. (1986) 'Design considerations at establishment', in Bradshaw, A.D., Goode, D. A. and Thorp, E. H. P. (eds.) *Ecology and Design in Landscape*, 24th Symposium of the British Ecological Society, Oxford: Blackwell Scientific Publications.

Beer, A. R. (1990) *Environmental Planning for Site Development*, London: Chapman and Hall.

Beckett, G. and Beckett, K. (1979) *Planting Native Trees and Shrubs*, Norwich: Jarrold.

Birren, F. (1978) *Colour and Human Response*, New York: Van Nostrand Reinhold.

Blackmore, S. and Tootill, E. (eds) (1984) *The Penguin Dictionary of Botany*, London: Allen Lane.

Booth, N. K. (1983) *Basic Elements of Landscape Architecture Design*, Amsterdam: Elsevier.

Caborn, J. M. (1975) *Shelterbelts and Microclimate*, Forestry Commission Bulletin 29, HMSO.

Caborn, J. M. (1965) *Shelterbelts and Windbreaks*, London: Faber.

Carpenter, P. L. and Walker, T. D. (1990) *Plants in the Landscape*, (2nd edn.) New York: W. H. Freeman.

Ching, F. D. K. (1979) *Architecture: Form, Space and Order*, New York: Van Nostrand Reinhold.

Clamp, H. (1989) *Landscape Professional Practice*, Aldershot: Gower.

Clouston, B. (ed) (1990) *Landscape Design with Plants* (revised edn), London: Heinemann.

Coombes, A. J. (1985) *Dictionary of Plant Names*, London: Hamlyn.

County Council of Essex (1973) *A Design Guide for Residential Areas*, Chelmsford: Essex C.C.

Crowe, S. (1972) *Forestry in the Landscape*, Third impression with amendments, London: HMSO.

de Sausmarez, M. (1964) *Basic Design, the Dynamics of Visual Fonn*, London: Studio Vista.

Dreyfus, H. (1959) *The Measure of Man: Human Factors in Design*, New York: Whitney Publications.

Evans, J. (1984) *Sylviculture of Broadleaved Woodlands*, Forestry Commission Bulletin No.62, HMSO, London.

French, J. S. (1983) *Urban Space* (2nd edn.) Dubugque, Iowa: Kendall Hunt.

Gilbert, O. L. (1989) *The Ecology of Urban Habitats*, London: Chapman and Hall.

Goethe, J. W. (1840) *Theory of Colours* (translated C.L. Eastlake) London: John Murray, and (1967) London: Frank Cass.

Greater London Council (1978) *An Introduction to Housing Layout*, London: Architectural Press.

Greenbie, B. B. (1981) *Spaces*, New Haven and London: Yale University Press.

Gustavsson, R. (1983) 'The analysis of vegetation structure' in Tregay, R. and Gustavsson, R *Oakwoods New Landscape*, Warrington: Sveriges Lantbruksuniversitet and Warrington and Runcorn Development Corporation.

Hart, A. (1977) 'Water Plants' in Clouston, B. (ed) *Landscape Design with Plants*, London: Heinemann.

Hansen, R. and Staln, F. (1987) *Die Stauden*, Stuttgart: Ulmer.

Haworth Booth, M. (1938) *The Flowering Shrub Garden*, London: Country Life Ltd.

Haworth Booth, M. (1961) *The Flowering Shrub Garden Today*, London: Country Life Ltd.

Higuchi, T. (1983) *The Visual and Spatial Structure of Landscape*, Cambridge, MA: MIT Press.

Hillier Nurseries (1991) *The Hillier Manual of Trees and Shrubs* (6th edn) Newton Abbot, Devon: David and Charles.

Hobhouse, P. (1985) *Colour in Your Garden*, London: Collins.

Jakobsen, P. (1977) 'Shrubs and Ground Cover' in Clouston, B. (ed) *Landscape Design with Plants*, London: Heinemann.

Jekyll, G. (1908) *Colour Schemes for the Flower Garden*, London: Country Life Ltd; reissued with revisions by G.S. Thomas, (1983). New Hampshire: Ayer.

Lancaster (1984) *Britain in View: Colour and the Landscape*, London: Quiller Press.

Lasceau, P (1989) *Graphic Thinking for Architects and Designers* (2nd edn), New York, Van Nostrand Reinhold.

Lisney, A. and Fieldhouse, K. (1990) *Landscape Design Guide, Volume 1, Soft Landscape*, PSA and Gower Publishing Co.

Loudon, J. C. (1838) *Arboretum et Fruiticetum Britannicum*, quoted in Turner, T.D.H., *London's Stylistic Development, Journal of Garden History*, vol 2, No 2.

Lynch, K. (1971) *Site Planning* (2nd edn), Cambridge, MA: MIT Press.

Lynch, K. and Hack, G. (1985) *Site Planning*, Cambridge MA: MIT Press.

Matthews, J. D. (1989) *Sylvicultural Systems*, Oxford: Clarendon Press.

Mitchell, A. (1974) A *Field Guide to the Trees of Britain and Northern Europe*, London: Collins.

Ministry of Agriculture, Fisheries and Food (1968) *Shelterbelts for Farmlands*, MAFF leaflet 15, HMSO.

Moore, C. W., Mitchell, W. J. and Turnbull, W. Jnr. (1988) *The Poetics of Gardens*, Cambridge, MA: MIT Press.

Nelson, W. R. (1985) *Planting Design: A Manual of Theory and Practice* (2nd edn), Stripes.

Newman, O. (1972) *Defensible Space*, London: Architectural Press.

Notcutts Nurseries Ltd., *Notcutts' Book of Plants*, published annually by Notcutts Nurseries Ltd., Woodbridge, Suffolk.

Papanek, V. (1974) *Design for the Real World, St* Albans: Granada

Pollard, E., Hooper, M. D., and Moore, N. W. (1975) *Hedges,* London: Collins.

Robinette, G. O. (1972) *Plants People Environmental Quality,* US Department of the Interior/ASLA.

Robinson, W. (1870) *The Wild Garden,* London: John Murray, reissued by Century Publishing, 1983.

Salisbury, E. J. (1918) *The Ecology of Scrub in Hertfordshire,* in Trans. Herts. Natural History Society, 17.

Scott, I. (trans.) (1970) *The Lüscher Colour Test,* London: Jonathan Cape Ltd.

Simonds, J. O. (1983) *Landscape Architecture* (2nd edn), New York: McGraw-Hill.

Stilgoe, J. R. (1984) 'Gardens in context' *Built Landscapes,* Battleboro Museum and Art Centre, Vermont, USA.

Sydes, C. and Grime, J. P. (1979) 'Effects of Tree Litter on Herbaceous Vegetation' *Journal of Ecology.*

Tanguy, F. and Tanguy, M. (1985) *Landscape Gardening and the Choice of Plants,* Sheridan (trans.) University Press of Virginia.

Tansley, A.G (1939) *The British Isles and their Vegetation,* Cambridge University Press.

Thomas, G. S. (1984) *The Art Of Planting,* London: J. M. Dent & Sons.

Thomas, G. S., *Colour In The Winter Garden London:* J. M. Dent & Sons.

Thomas, G. S. (1983) *Gertrude Jekyll's Wall and Water Gardens,* New Hampshtre: Ayer.

Thomas, G. S. (1985) *The Old Shrub Roses* (4th edn revised), London: J.M. Dent and Sons Ltd.

Thomas, G. S. *Perennials – A Modern Florelegum,* London: J.M. Dent and Sons Ltd

Tregay, R. and Gustavsson, R. (1983) *Oakwoods New Landscape,* Warrington: Sveriges Lantbruksuniversitet and Warrington New Town Development Corporation.

Tregay, R. (1985) *Design Revisited,* Sweden: Sveriges Lantbruksuniversitet .

Walker, T. D. (1988) *Planting Design,* Mesa, Arizona: PDA.

Ward, Richard (1989) 'Harmony in wild planting', *Landscape Design* No 186, Reigate, Surrey: Landscape Design Trust.

Index

accent planting, 106, 111
aesthetics, 8, 9, 113, 25–7, 82–3
Appleton, Jay, 43
Arnold, Henry, 17, 21
Ashihara, Y, 74
avenues,
    features, 230
    spacing, 232–4
    tree species, 230-2

balance,
    definition, 106
    and symmetry, 106
barriers, 45-50
beds and borders,
    accents, 245, 247
    canopy layers, 241–2, 244
    ecological approach, 250–1
    layout, 238, 241
    plant spacing, 252–5
    planting, 241–2, 244
    planting patterns, 248–51
    scale, 244–5
    seasonal growth, 244
    specimen groups, 247–8
    use of trees, 241
Brown, Lancelot (1715-1813), 123

canopy structures,
    single layer, 133, 135
    two layer, 130, 132–3
    three layer, 126–7, 130
    woodland, 193
Ching, FDK, 76, 113
clients,
    brief, 147
    contact, 146–7
clumps, 220–1
colour,
    effects, 101–2
    perception, 101
    themes, 117–18
    theory, 100

    tone, 100
    variation, 100–1
cone of vision, 115
construction drawings, 180–3
contrast, and harmony, 104–6
copses, 220–1

Dartington Hall, 72
de Sausmarez, Maurice, 50–1
Defects Liability Period, 186
design, see planting design

emphasis, 106, 111
enclosure, types, 45–50
entrance zones, space, 80–1

field layer, 196, 199
forestry, 4, 7
Fountain's Abbey, 65

gardenesque style, 252

harmony,
    and contrast, 104–6
    definition, 104
hawthorn, 222–3
hedgerows,
    definition, 221
    function, 221, 225–6
    spacing, 225–6
hedges,
    formal, 90, 92, 227–8
    function, 222
    informal, 228–30
    perimeter, 217–18
    role of trees, 229–30
rural,
    features, 222
    plant mixes, 224
    spacing, 224–5
    species, 222–4
urban,
    features, 226

plant mixes, 227–9
    spacing, 224
high scrub, 213
Higuchi, T, 45, 51

individualism, 123
inspiration, 122–3

Jakobsen, P, 247–8
Jekyll, Gertrude, 117, 249, 262

Kennedy memorial, 65

landscape,
    design, 13, 17, 145
    management, 187–8
Landscape Institute in Britain, 146
Loudon, John Claudius (1783-1843), 123,
        252
oak trees, 84
ornamental planting,
    beds and borders, 237–55
    canopy structure, 127, 130, 132
    construction plan, 183
    function, 237
    and pergolas, 259
    raised beds and containers, 255–8
    specialised habitats, 262
    and trellis, 259, 261
    and walls, 258–9
overstorey, 195, 199

Papanek, Victor, 25–6
pergolas, 259
plant associations, *see* plant communities
plant communities,
    canopy habit, 139–40
    description, 124–5
    design considerations, 126, 173
    development, 10
    growth factors, 136
    horticultural factors, 135–6
    life cycle, 140
    plant competition, 136–7, 202
    propagation, 137–9
planting design,
    and aesthetics, 8, 9, 13, 25–7, 82–3
    client brief, 147
    construction drawings, 180–3
    as a creative cycle, 188
    and ecology, 7–8
    establishment phase, 186–7
    and forestry, 4, 7
    and function, 3–4, 7, 25–7, 263
    implementation, 183, 185
    individuality, 122–3
    management, 187
    master plan, 116, 157, 164–5, 167, 171
    and natural vegetation, 7–8

and plant communities, 126
plant selection, 172–3
planting, 185–6
policies, 153–7
presentation of plans, 177, 180
purpose, 3
specifications, 183
successful, 8–9
survey, 147–8, 150, 152–3
themes, 116–22, 171
unity, 116
variety, 116
working methods, 145–88
plants,
    above eye-level planting, 33, 36
    arching form, 87–8
    ascending line, 92, 94
    canopy height, 28
    carpeting, 30, 84–5
    climbing, 259, 261
    colour effects, 100–2
    combination, 103
    and decoration, 23
    diagonal line, 94, 96
    effects of combining, 103
    form, 84–92
        arching, 87–8
        carpeting, 84–5, 87
        columnar, 88–9
        conical, 88
        dome, 85
        erect, 85, 87
        fastigiate, 88–9
        hummock, 85
        open irregular, 90
        oval upright, 88
        prostrate, 84
        tabulate, 89–90
        trained, 90, 92
    growth cycle, 12–13
    horizontal line, 94
    hue, 100
    knee to eye-level planting, 33
    and the landscape designer, 13, 17
    life cycle, 12
    line,
        ascending, 92, 94
        diagonal, 94, 96
        horizontal, 94
        pendulous, 94
        quality, 96
    as living materials, 10
    low planting, 30, 33
    medium height planting, 33
    pendulous line, 94
    quality of line, 96
    saturation, 100-1
    seasonal factors, 176–7
    selection, 24–5, 176

and space, 21
structural functions, 17, 21
subjective response to, 82–3
as symbols, 82–3
tall shrub planting, 33, 36
texture,
    coarse, 97–9
    effects, 96–7
    fine, 97
    medium, 99–100
uses, 13
viewing angles, 115–16
visual energy, 102–3
Pope, Alexander, 123
prospect-refuge theory of space, 43–5

raised beds, 255–8
Repton, Humphrey, 42
rhizomes, 138–9
Robinson, William, 251
rootstocks, 139
runners, 138

scale,
    appropriate, 113, 115
    generic, 113
    human, 113
scent, 118
sequence, 111–13
shelter belt, 8
sound, 118
space,
    abutting, 76–7
    as barrierm 45–50
    clustered organisation, 65, 70, 72
    contained organisation, 72
    elements, 45
    entrance zones, 80–1
    focus,
        asymmetric, 59, 61
        boundary, 61–2
        external, 62–3
        role, 57–8
        symmetric, 58–9
    height to width ratio, 55, 57
    hierarchy, 72, 74, 76
    human perception of, 43–4
    interlocking, 77, 79
    linear organisation, 64–5
    and movement, 50–1, 55
    public and private, 74, 76
    shape, 50, 51, 55
    and slope, 57
    theories about, 43–4

transitions, 76–7, 79–80
use, 44–5, 165
vertical proportion, 55, 57
stolons, 138
suckers, 139
symmetry, and balance, 106

themes,
    habitat, 120, 122
    seasonal, 118
    taxonomic, 120
thicket scrub, 212–13
topiary, 90–1
touch, 118
trees,
    in avenues, 230
    in beds and borders, 241
    in design proposals, 165–167
    function, 36, 42
    in hedges, 229–30
    nurse, 197
    oak, 84
    in raised beds, 258
    spatial use, 17, 21
    trained, 235–6
    in urban areas, 192

trellis, 259, 261

understorey, 195, 199

viewing angles, 115–16
visual composition, principles, 104
visual energy, 102–3

walls, 258–9
water gardens, 262
woodland,
    canopy structure, 193
    creation, 191–2, 193–5
    edges, 213–15, 217
    function, 192–3
    high canopy, 195–204
        mix proportions, 201–2
        planting mix, 198–202, 208–11
        spacing, 202–8
    low canopy, planting mix, 211

woodland belts,
    function, 218–20
    management problems, 219
    planting mix, 219–20
woodland scrub, 211–12